History of the Society of the Sacred Mission

ALISTAIR MASON

Foreword by
Adrian Hastings

The Canterbury Press
Norwich

To
D J M

© Alistair Mason 1993

First published 1993 by The Canterbury Press Norwich
(a publishing imprint of Hymns Ancient & Modern Limited,
a registered charity)
St Mary's Works, St Mary's Plain,
Norwich, Norfolk, NR3 3BH

British Library Cataloguing in Publication Data

A catalogue record for this book is available
from the British Library

ISBN 1-85311-079-5

Reprinted with corrections 1994

*Printed and bound in Great Britain by
St Edmundsbury Press Limited
Bury St Edmunds, Suffolk*

Contents

Foreword

Kelham in the early twentieth century was exciting because it was different. It was an Anglican theological college which catered for non-graduates and never sought to turn the working class into gentlemen. It was Anglo-Catholic and staffed by a religious community, yet also rather ecumenical. It followed much Roman Catholic example, but was definitely not papalist.

It was all this and more because of the man who founded the Society of the Sacred Mission and the theological college it served, H. H. Kelly. Everyone revered him. Unpompous, glad to laugh at himself, willing to go anywhere, Kelly was a long-lived prophet who founded institutions but than never quite knew how to relate to them. Many religious orders both reverence and are irritated by their founder. I suspect this was true of SSM. But, following his example, members of the Society took on a great variety of work in Korea, Australia, East and South Africa, Japan. They aspired, not without success, to serve an international Anglican Christianity but still found it hard to escape the limitations of Englishness.

The history of SSM across a hundred years is fascinating, diverse and often sad. It throws a great deal of light upon twentieth-century Anglicanism, both its glories and its failings. Dr Mason is just the right person to tell us about it, combining the detached analysis of an historian with the sensitivity of a real friend. His eye detects the weaknesses but we can detect the humorous twinkle of affection as he does so. His heart goes out to the high hopes of the endeavour while sympathising with the self-depreciation which has accompanied it. This centenary history would have pleased Father Kelly.

ADRIAN HASTINGS

ACKNOWLEDGEMENTS

My first acknowledgement must be to the Society of the Sacred Mission. Its Directors, Edmund Wheat and Tom Brown, and its members, have gone out of their way to help me in my work. From Paul Hume (professed in 1932), whom to know is to love, to Paul Phillips, the newest student in the Durham priory, who walked me to my car and asked if that earned him a place in the book, the Society has shown me consistent kindness and hospitality. Willen Priory is far more to me than the abode of the SSM archives. I also owe a debt to the priories in Australia, at Digger's Rest and Adelaide, for hospitality there, and to Laurence Eyers, who opened my eyes to Australian art. Dunstan McKee provided me with an excellent list of Australian contacts. Hilary Greenwood, so ill with the flu that he should have been in bed, made me welcome in Prague, as Douglas Brown did in Rome. In particular in connection with this book, I should mention Margaret Dewey, the Society archivist, who has had an answer for every question I brought to her. Hilary Greenwood, Douglas Brown and Ralph Martin read a draft of this work, and made very helpful suggestions. Steven Haws found some late slips. I cannot mention all the members of the Society who answered my questions and told me stories of the past.

I have been lucky to have Adrian Hastings as my colleague at Leeds, sometimes thunderously critical, sometimes gloriously enthusiastic, always a good model of how to write history. Among the friends and colleagues who urged me on, Haddon Willmer, Jacqui Stewart and Donald Mackay read parts of the manuscript and gave advice. John and Eileen McGuckin, who lent me their old portable photocopier, and Ingrid Lawrie, who consoled me again and again in my battles with LOCOScript 2, also deserve thanks.

David Hilliard not only put me up in Australia, but searched out documents for me, introduced me to likely contacts, and read my draft chapter. I am completely in his debt. I had useful conversations in Australia with Canon Gerry Reglar, Canon Keith Chittleborough, Keith Brice, Susan Straub, Evan Burge, Frank Engel, Ian Breward, Roger Sharr and Gerald Beaumont and others. I was a very hesitant researcher with a tape-recorder, and they were very patient. The social high point was tea in the Governor's residence with Davis McCaughey, Governor of Victoria.

George Every very kindly made available part of his unpublished autobiography. I have to thank Bengt Sundkler and others in Sweden, for their help in understanding Gabriel Hebert's relationship with the Swedish church.

Alan Wilkinson, working on his magisterial centenary history of CR, was always a friend and a helper. David Holmes, who was also working in the Willen archives until 1990, lent me notes, fed me, and was a model fellow-worker in the field. I have also had help from Brenda Hough, of the Church of England Record Office, and from a number of old friends of SSM and old students of Kelham who wrote to me with memories, such as Edgar Joyce of Bedminster. In Leeds, Clive Barrett and Francis House came up with suggestions and memories after hearing a paper I gave on SSM. There are others, too numerous to mention, who have helped me with this work. Its faults, alas, are still mine.

The Society of the Sacred Mission and the University of Leeds have both helped financially in making the publication of this work possible, and I am very grateful.

ALISTAIR MASON

Among the friends of SSM who made helpful comments I must specially mention Edna Mallett on Modderpoort.

AFM, October 1994

Chapter One

Anglican Brotherhoods

After the dissolution of the monasteries under Henry VIII, some English people, through the centuries, continued to feel drawn to life in communities and under vows. English Catholic religious houses were set up on the Continent; the Brigittines of Syon had direct continuity from before the dissolution. In the seventeenth century there were even nuns again at York. At any time in the seventeenth and well into the eighteenth century there would also be about three hundred Roman Catholic regular clergy (mostly Jesuits or Benedictines in roughly equal numbers) in England. Their life, itinerant or increasingly settled and parochial, was very un-Benedictine and not very Jesuit. The Protestant people of England took more notice when French religious orders came fleeing from the Revolution. Unobtrusively, but in greater numbers, the English religious houses moved back to England, so that by 1840 there was a considerable number of Roman Catholic religious communities of some size.

It could be argued that Anglican piety, with infrequent sacraments but a daily round of psalms and readings, was monastic in temper,[1] and good Anglicans, brought up on the Book of Common Prayer, were already committed to an ancient cycle of prayer. One might find, in the eighteenth century, that colleges and almshouses and cathedral congregations were, without vows, still regular. Fellows of the colleges at Oxford and Cambridge were forbidden to marry.

There was a strand of Anglicanism that was nearer to monasticism even than this. The 'Arminian nunnery' at Little Gidding between 1625 and 1647 not only had a regular religious office but some of its members took vows. Nevertheless the Church of England as a whole was much more a consciously Protestant church. Protestants felt that justification by faith alone ruled out anything that looked like a technique of putting God in our debt by doing extra things. Protestants felt that religious obedience was a threat to the freedom of a Christian, and that virginity was best seen as an appropriate precursor to a happy marriage. There were, especially in the nineteenth century, nastier refinements of these views, prurient imaginings of wickedness and cruelty behind convent walls.

With the Oxford Movement, notions which had seemed out of place in the Church of England became less so. In 1841 Miss Marian Rebecca Hughes, as a private lady, still doing her domestic duties, took religious vows, encouraged by Pusey and Newman. She died in 1912, Mother Foundress of an Anglican order of nuns, the Society of the Holy and Undivided Trinity. Anson, in *The Call of the Cloister*, a study of the revival of the religious life within Anglicanism, lists more than fifty orders of women founded in Britain alone between 1845 and 1900, of which two-thirds were still in existence when his book was published in 1956.[2] In 1986, with the general decline in such vocations, there were still 1085 nuns in 43 orders in England.[3]

The revival of women's orders was not entirely due to the Oxford Movement. Practical-minded Protestants admired the utterly practical work of Roman Catholic Sisters of Charity. This was from observation of the Continent; the first Roman Catholic order engaged exclusively in active work among the poor in Great Britain was founded in Ireland in 1828, and set up a house in England in 1838.[4] When Robert Southey, the Poet Laureate, wrote in the 1820s urging the foundation of similar sisterhoods, it was the Quaker Mrs Fry, remembered as a prison reformer, who set up a nursing sisterhood in Whitechapel. In the public eye nurses and nuns were almost indistinguishable.

When Southey died in 1843, Lord John Manners, leader of the Tory pressure group 'Young England' wrote to the *Morning Post*, 'the chief Church paper of the day', and, as he said, 'a few people met in my rooms in the Albany'[5] and decided to set up the first Anglican sisterhood in memory of Southey. As it happened, Dr Pusey was called in to devise the Rule, and hence the Sisterhood of the

Holy Cross was unobtrusively fashioned on Roman Catholic models. Perhaps one should say on two incompatible Roman Catholic models, as the Sisterhood asked too much of its members, combining two potent images of the religious life, the sleepless devotion of night stairs and 2 a.m. Matins,[6] and the daytime devotion of the holy sisters slum-visiting where the policemen walk in pairs. Pusey was prone to encourage ideas of sacrifice in women. He took his twelve-year-old daughter as a treat on a tour of convents in Ireland, to give her an idea of her future. (Poor Lucy died before she could become a nun). The Sisterhood of the Holy Cross, that first Anglican order, remembered Pusey's tours of inspection: 'These potatoes are too large, not according to holy poverty'.[7]

It is worth stressing that in Anglicanism the revival of the religious life has been predominantly a matter for women. The few orders for men have been less stable, and smaller, though some of them have been very well-known. Three were founded in the 1840s in England, if we count Newman's own foundation at Littlemore as a religious community,[8] and three in the United States. None of them survived as Anglican orders; three moved as communities into the Roman Catholic church. Between 1863 and 1870 there were another seven attempts, of which only the Society of St John the Evangelist (1866), the Cowley Fathers, at Oxford and elsewhere, remain. There was then a lull until 1889, when seven orders were founded in seven years. Three of these lived on, the Order of St Paul (1889), which settled at Alton Abbey in Hampshire, the Community of the Resurrection (1892), which settled at Mirfield in Yorkshire, and the Society of the Sacred Mission (1893), whose mother house was for a long time at Kelham, near Newark in Nottinghamshire.[9] There have been a few twentieth century foundations. The most influential of these have been direct copies of ancient models, the Anglican Benedictines until recently at Nashdom in Buckinghamshire (1914), and the Society of St Francis (1921), Franciscans whose mother house is at Cerne Abbas in Dorset. In 1986 there were 264 men living in the ten surviving male communities in England.[10] The larger orders remain international, so there are still, for example, Cowley Fathers in America, and CR in South Africa, and SSM and Anglican Franciscans in Australia.

With only 264 of them, it is obviously possible to know personally every Anglican monk or friar in England. There can never have been more than a thousand at any one time, even in the 1950s.[11] The small numbers involved might perhaps mislead. A great many Anglo-Catholics have had links with religious orders, and with individuals within them. The religious orders have a public and talismanic role: religious houses attract visitors, even in great numbers; many people seek out monks as experts in the spiritual life. But it is also clear that something of the glory is departed. The surviving religious with a great reputation, like Trevor Huddleston and Harry Williams of Mirfield, are old men. The public role of the religious orders, though still there, has considerably diminished in the last forty years.

Public expectations have consistently put great pressure on those who try to live the religious life. This is particularly true when there are very few doing so. Fr Ignatius (1837–1908) of Llanthony, trying to revive the Benedictine order in Wales, spent his life preaching missions and fund-raising, and was thus away from Llanthony for months on end.[12] He was too busy to practise Benedictine stability. But even if he was not stable, his community at Llanthony did last for 38 years. In a way, it is obvious that monks make monasteries, that the serious long-term commitment is a matter of an individual's choice, and that the people who actually live in a community, alongside each other month after month and year after year, form community. But somehow this commitment and living it through seems to make itself available when asked for. Individual anonymous people give their lives, in one sense to God, in another to the Father Founder. Rather ordinary people's lives were available to flesh out the imaginative schemes of somebody like Fr Ignatius, an unstable dreamer who scarcely deserved the sacrifice. The same thing happens with armies in wartime. Fr Kelly, founder of the Society of the Sacred Mission, whose imagination and whose schemes probably did deserve it, was very conscious of this military parallel.

> Now exceptional things are done only by exceptional men, but for obscure psychological reasons, which I cannot explain, as soon as you make a business of them most people can do them. If for some urgent cause, a man.. walked up a rifle range in the teeth of the firing, we should know he was a hero. We should write about him in the papers and give him a medal. He might not like it, but we cannot help that. Heroes are a valuable commodity, and we must do our best to keep up the supply. Yet we know that we can get almost any number of people to do these things at so many shillings a week without writing to the paper at all. We had quite a crowd of men on Spion Kop . . .[13]

Religious orders perhaps succeed when their members have made something of a business of the life; habits are formed, there is work to be done, and self-consciousness has gone. With small numbers and a highly public role, this proved hard.

Particularly with women's orders, it is very noticeable that they were shaped by the expectations of people other than their members. Dr Pusey once wrote 'I think that the plan of the Clergy "forming sisterhoods" is an amiable mistake',[14] but clergymen did it, light-heartedly. The 25-year-old Fr Stanton, just about to be appointed to his first living, at once laid plans to set up and run his own sisterhood.[15] Two of the largest and most successful of the women's orders look back to a Father Founder, the Community of St Mary the Virgin (CSMV, founded 1848) to Butler of Wantage, and the Community of St John the Baptist (1851) to Carter of Clewer. Anson writes, without apparent misgivings, of the Mother Superior of Wantage for 33 years

> It was her intense humility and lack of confidence in herself that proved to be her strength in after years. She relied far more on loyal obedience to Butler than on her personal initiative.

Was he making the same point when he wrote that she

'owed her success to leading her sisters to complete dependence on God'?[16] There was a dominant Father Founder at
Clewer, where a 'life-size alabaster effigy of Canon
T.T.Carter' has pride of place in the chapel.[17] Other orders
came to break free from their Founder. This could often be
done by moving away, geographically. There was a regular
pattern of communities founded for work in the slums,
first finding it useful to take away those who needed their
care (orphans, invalids or magdalens) from the slums, then
as a community shifting to the countryside to a more
contemplative way of life.[18]

There is a perfectly understandable search for self-fulfil-
ment that might lead to life in a religious community. Let
us look at what vows of poverty, chastity and obedience
might mean in Victorian England.

A vow of poverty has to be placed in context. We
should remember that poverty which included regular
meals, and quiet, and clean bedding and a Christian burial
could quite well seem affluent to many in England.[19]

It is easy to make sharp points against the rather stylised
sense of poverty of some middle-class Victorian religious.
At Littlemore 'a woman came in from the village to cook
the dinner, and her son cleaned the boots and knives'.[20]
Yet Fr Dominic the Passionist said 'I assure you I have
never seen any monastery so poor'.[21] It stuck in people's
memory that both Fr Kelly, of the Society of the Sacred
Mission, in their first house at Vassall Road in London,
and the Mother Foundress of the All Saints Community
underwent the public degradation of scrubbing their own
front door-step.[22] Even slightly self-conscious gestures have
their context. In a wealthy society, people felt the need for
self-sacrifice.

Let us turn to the vow of chastity. It might be useful to
have a comprehensible public, rather creditable, explanation
for not getting married, though in some ways the pressures
to marry were less in Victorian England, and a great many
people never did.[23] It is dangerous generalising about how
urgent the emotional commitment to celibacy was; it is
quite possible a late twentieth century writer might go
looking for sexual overtones that were just not there. The

well-known chapter in Geoffrey Faber's *Oxford Apostles* (1933) on 'Virginity and Friendship' can still cause hackles to rise. It may well be that a vow of chastity can be a way of coping with unacceptable sexual drives. Religious societies themselves nowadays have much more open discussion of these matters. A lot of people have been damaged by social and religious taboos on sexuality, but I doubt if this is a useful general clue to understanding the lives of Victorian monks and nuns. Not everyone was as tortured as Gerard Manley Hopkins. There were silly details of rules that suggest an unhealthy obsession with sex, but the problem lies in a taste for detail rather than in the field where the detail was applied.

There certainly seems to be evidence, when one turns from religious orders to their critics, that a vow of celibacy can arouse other people's deep anxieties. All-female or all-male communities, achieving some sort of collective happiness, exclude the viewer in some threatening way. Bishops were very resistant to the idea of people making vows for life. There might indeed be objections based on serious Protestant theology. God provides opportunities for self-sacrifice enough and to spare where we are. As even Keble wrote:

> The trivial round, the common task, Can furnish all we need to ask, Room to deny ourselves . . .

There is no need for public uncalled-for sacrifice, which is self-mutilation for its own sake. Neither God nor the human race need people who retreat from human relationships as if there was a short-cut to God avoiding human relationships. And so on. Nevertheless, some people serve God best in communities rather than married.

Finally there is the vow of obedience. Men with vision often had a dream of authority, of finding a disciplined group who would do what they were told. Here is obedience, people who had vowed to obey.[24] It does take discipline to be practically useful, and religious orders often ran institutions well. One might perhaps consider that the nineteenth century saw a growth in all sorts of institutions, and it may be that the customs and purposes of prisons and hospitals and boarding-schools and seminaries did more to shape nineteenth century religious communities than any memories of the middle ages.[25]

As the century progressed, it is easy to find bishops and church committees saying the church needed brotherhoods to work in the slums and the missionfield.[26] It is not at once clear whether this was seen as a cheap supplement to the ordained ministry or as specialist shock-troops selected from within the priesthood.

Consider the two possibilities in turn. Lay brotherhoods might be seen as a supplement to the clergy, something not very dissimilar to sisters of charity, only male. For practical day-to-day work it was possible to recruit lay workers. The difficulty was that being a 'brotherhood' they ran the risk of playing at being monks. The Victorians liked dressing up in medieval attire. By the 1880s it had become common for parishes to have choristers robed as medieval clerics.[27] Many Anglo-Catholic parishes had Guilds, Brotherhoods, and Confraternities, some of them with 'quasi-monastic rules involving the admission of "postulants" and the clothing of "novices"'.[28] To find a picture of the decorative, idle and self-dramatising young man who had notions about becoming a monk, one can perhaps best turn to novels.[29] Some of the shorter-lived orders were rather prone to this style of piety. The Anglican Congregation of the Primitive Observance of the Holy Rule of St Benedict (1896) on Caldey Island struck some observers as picturesque and scarcely real (there was much expense on oak-panelling and marble and even peacocks) though Lord Halifax, the leading Anglo-Catholic layman, saw it as the chief dream of his life realised. Here again we see the role of religious orders in fulfilling the dreams of the laity.[30]

'Brotherhood' also has overtones of the 'brotherhood of man'. It could well express the solidarity, the brotherly love, that the founder felt for the lay people he was trying to serve.

> Impulsive, warm-hearted, always a friend, undoubtedly the strongest impression was of Father William's immense affection for men. It was so genuine. He understood,

valued and saw all the good in the dock-labourers. And
they responded.[31]

This is a far cry from inward-looking brotherhoods for
dressing up and ecclesiastical chitchat. Another rather un-
clerical figure, Charles Hopkins, set up the Order of St
Paul (1889) 'For God and Our Sailors' in Calcutta, with a
very cheerful and distinctive style. Anson says it was more
like a Trade Union 'lodge' than a normal monastery. The
history of the order from then on was largely a struggle
between the Founder and the more conventionally monastic impulses of his brethren. They built a very quiet and
traditional abbey in rural Hampshire, and he went off to
lead marches of sailors on strike in a peaked cap, a blue
seaman's jersey, and a pectoral cross.[32] It is not necessarily
tragedy that an inspiring founder finds that his followers
have turned his dream into something more manageable.
Somehow ordinary recruits must have suitable targets. But
when one thinks what General Booth could do in the same
period with non-middleclass recruits, it does seem just
possible that useful brotherhoods could have arisen not
unlike Trade Union lodges. The Fabian Society itself developed out of an organisation called the Brotherhood of the
New Life, and its founder, Thomas Davidson, was deeply
indebted to the thought of Rosmini (1797-1855), the
founder of the Institute of Charity.[33]

This is one of the strands of late nineteenth century
religion that underlies SSM, the idea of a constructive,
down-to-earth lay piety for ordinary men, that will harness
the impulses for good so transparently there in working-
class adolescents.

The alternative understanding of brotherhood was to
have brotherhoods of specialist clergymen. There were
orders that were predominantly clerical, predominantly
Oxbridge graduates, like the intellectually powerful Community of the Resurrection. They had their own problems,
but they did not have to fight off pious noodles. The
Community of the Resurrection had a strong social conscience, and practical outward-looking ideas about how to
express brotherhood. Such ideas would lead it into political

comment, in England and South Africa, to work in the industrial north instead of Oxford, to opening a theological college for poor ordinands. All these were potential, not actual in the 1890s. Then it was merely one of a list:

> ... such communities as Canon Mason has gathered round him at All Hallows, Barking, and Mr Gore at Oxford, and Canon Bowers at Gloucester, and Bishop Yeatman for work in South London. (Fr Hall, SSJE, at the Church Congress, Birmingham, 1893)[34]

This way of understanding brotherhoods, as a way of using teams of priests usefully, instead of the inevitable parson in his parish with his freehold, was also to play a key part in the shaping of SSM.

In the last fifteen years or so of the nineteenth century the Church of England was more socially aware than before. Some of this came from an uneasy sense of failing in its own mission. There was a willingness to try new approaches. Opinion in the Church of England was turning towards social, rather than individual, answers to problems. This was the age of the Christian Socialist revival. Bishop Westcott was reigning in Durham; between 1889 and 1913, 16 of the 53 bishops appointed to English sees were paid-up members of the Christian Social Union.[35] Episcopal support may suggest that this was a moderate, non-party, sort of socialism. However, there is at least an emotional tie between nostalgia for medieval gilds, and nostalgia for religious orders. The shift to an incarnational theology, with the *Lux Mundi* school, went along with a concern with current social problems. This could impress non-religious people. It was George Bernard Shaw who wrote:

> Religion was alive again, coming back upon men, even upon clergymen, with such power that not the Church of England itself could keep it out.[36]

Whereas the political spirit of the Puseyite foundations had been Tory or utterly unworldly, 'to serve the Lord God apart from this most wicked age',[37] the religious orders founded in the 1890s tended to be politically committed. We have already mentioned the trade union activities of Fr Hopkins, of the Order of St Paul. Mirfield was self-consciously Christian Socialist, deliberately moving to industrial Yorkshire, with brothers who appeared on Labour platforms, and invited Keir Hardie to speak. The founder of the Society of the Divine Compassion (1894) was the Hon. and Revd James G. Adderley, like Charles Gore, founder of Mirfield, an aristocrat with a conscience, who wrote a Christian Socialist novel called *Stephen Remarx – the story of a venture in ethics.*[38]

It may well be that most Christian Socialism was a re-working of Tory paternalism, and still very remote from the poor. There is a telling contemporary assessment by C.F.G.Masterman of the differing approach of the various traditions of English Christianity to the working classes:

> We come from outside with our gospel, aliens with alien ideas.. The Anglican church represents the idea of the upper classes, of the universities, of a vigorous life in which bodily strength, an appearance of knowledge, a sense of humour, occupy prominent places. The large Nonconformist bodies represent the ideas of the middle classes, the strenuous self-help and energy which have stamped their ideas upon the whole of imperial Britain ... Each totally fails to apprehend a vision of life as reared in a mean street, and now confronting existence on a hazardous weekly wage, from a block dwelling ... Our movements and inexplicable energies are received with a mixture of tolerance and perplexity.[39]

There is a natural impulse to compete in claiming one's own tradition is more in tune with working people. The Anglican religious orders for men that arose in the 1890s, as part of their understanding of brotherhood, set themselves to break down barriers between classes. Reading Masterman, one is reminded how daunting a task that is in class-bound England.

'At this time there was a good deal of talk about brotherhoods out of which it will be remembered nothing came'. (Father Kelly, founder of the Society of the Sacred Mission, to whom we now turn).[40]

Chapter Two

Early Days

There is something suspect in beginning the history of a religious Society with the childhood of the founder. Relevance is projected back, and the one personality, already dominant, is given thirty years, or whatever, of pre-history that unbalances whatever the rest may bring. Herbert H. Kelly, the founder of the Society of the Sacred Mission, was quite sure that he was not memorable.

> Now herein is the wonder, not to ourselves perhaps, but certainly to others. Kelham is to them a very real power; from their way of thinking they assume it must be an individual power. But while I am (as its head) a conspicuous person, they are all as conscious as any of us that my own personal influence, whether as a writer, as a thinker, or as a man, outside our own circle, are just exactly nil.[1]

He exaggerated, as usual, but it would be unfair to him, as well as to the Society he founded, to canonise Kelly at the expense of SSM. Kelly had some wonderful ideas, but unlike most theological thinkers, he started a work that others could do, that does not seem work-a-day beside his theology. The Society deserves a history as well as the founder.

However, perhaps something can be made of Fr Kelly's own background. He came from the north of England, though there is no mention anywhere of a Lancashire accent. There was inherited money, from mill-owning and trade, on each side of the family, but his father went to Oxford and became a clergyman. Herbert was the third son, born in 1860, and his home experience was of Ashton-under-Lyne, a 'second-rate manufacturing town' just outside Manchester, where his father was vicar for 18 years from 1865. His parents were rather shy people, and the vicarage was not on the smart side of the town, so they had few friends of their own social class.[2]

One possible contrast between Kelham and Mirfield is that Fr Kelly was not tempted to romanticise the north.

His father was a non-quarrelsome Evangelical, and not interested in ideas. He taught part-time in the Bishop's School at Manchester, which trained men for ordination by study at home. His youngest son Alfred said he actually preferred non-graduate curates. Thus Fr Kelly had first-hand knowledge of how weaker candidates were trained. James Davenport Kelly became a Canon of Manchester, and so 'My father wanted me to come to Manchester, but I would not go where he was.. I did not think it was playing the game to use his influence'.[3]

The boys were educated at Manchester Grammar School, one of the great schools of England. It was however a day school, so Fr Kelly's enthusiasm for the disciplined community of boarding school life was not based on experience.

The eldest son had gone into the army, and in time became a brigadier-general. The clever second son died in his early twenties. Herbert Kelly went to Woolwich and trained as an army officer. He passed, though even then he was beginning to go deaf, a great handicap. Looking back he said

> ... my military ambitions were, from the first, ludicrously impossible. War, when you get it, is a matter of emergencies to be met instantly by that ready instinct which I never possessed.[4]

Again and again in the autobiographical writings, one comes across Fr Kelly's harsh perceptions of himself and his gifts. They are often phrased comically; there is always at least a grain of truth in them; and they do not disguise his real distinction.

While at Woolwich, he had had an Evangelical conversion, and so went up to Oxford in 1879, as the first step to becoming ordained. He read History at Queen's, as Greats and Theology were ruled out by his poor achievement at languages. He was a hard thinker, trying to find God in history.

Odd times I could do essays which (I believe) my tutor
thought distinctly good. If I make a guess, I fancy he put
me down as a probable third, with a possible second, if I
was in luck, would stick to my work, and leave theology
alone. My friends, (poor dears) thought I would get a first.
I said, 'I might, I should dearly love to. It would be
screamingly funny. The next funniest thing would be to
get a fourth. I bet on the fourth.' I had made a frantic rush
covering whole centuries in the last term, and I was tired. I
could do nothing but write generalities. I got a fourth. I
believe I trembled on the edge of a third.[5]

This is told humorously, but it describes real pain. There is
an oral tradition that they keep the Oxford fourth class for
flawed brilliance, and mere plodders get thirds, but 'I
trembled on the edge of a third'. He was already a deep
thinker, and we should consider, though he did not, that
an examination system that gave him a third would thereby
have been shown up. In later chapters we shall consider the
growth of his theology, and also the distinctive course of
study he instituted at Kelham. Here it is worth remembering that the Kelham course was very historical, and Kelly's
degree, almost useless as it was, was in History.

He never attended a theological college, but went
straight to a curacy, in a country parish in Kent. He
wanted to be near a man he had known at Oxford.

I ought to have gone to Cuddesdon, to learn the elements
of my business. I had never heard of the place, or of the
idea. If I had, I might have become a quite decent third-
rate curate. I might also have got to know somebody,
which is very useful (as will appear) . . .[6]

The reader would prefer, and one supposes is expected to
prefer, Fr Kelly as he is to a 'quite decent third-rate curate'.
In his curacy he read a lot, and was restless to find his life's
work.

So, like Dick Whittington, I went to London with a vague
idea of doing something. The Archbishop sent me to
Canon Mason, who was running a sort of brotherhood of
mission priests at Trinity Square. Mason looked me over,
and knew at once he could do nothing with such a half-

baked animal. I wasted a few months at Toynbee Hall. They also were not impressed.[7]

He was willing to serve in something more demanding than the ordinary parochial ministry. The places he tried first were not religious orders, and might seem on the face of it sensible suggestions. Canon Mason was the laudatory biographer of bishop Wilkinson of Truro (and later St Andrews), a bishop whose otherworldly unction sometimes seemed on the verge of false religiosity,[8] and Kelly was perhaps lucky not to be taken on. Toynbee Hall was a settlement in the East End of London where Oxford undergraduates lived among the poor, one of whom once said, 'I do so hate being lived among'. Some real good was done, especially to the undergraduates.

Kelly was then stranded looking for a proper curacy. He had the miserable experience of being offered a job, and then being asked to resign it, because a more promising man turned up.[9] He made something of failure:

> [I was] a 7th-rate curate, intellectually a 4th-in-history, with disabilities physical, as well as moral and intellectual . . . No ordinary Kelham man is expected to be so incapable as I was, or would be allowed to stop if he were.. My disabilities were an essential driving factor in all I learnt to do. 'When we think of vocation, we think naturally of what we can do. God may get you where he wants by means of what you cannot do'. This is the whole truth of my life.[10]

He exaggerated his incapacity, but it is part of the way of looking at things that he handed down to the Society he was to found. We should remember that he was surrounded in the Society by younger people, of a lower social class than himself, often prone to hero-worship, and his steady self-denigration might have helped rescue them from dependence.

Of course, compared with Charles Gore, who founded Mirfield, Fr Kelly was an unknown and a failure and desperately insecure. Gore had an aristocratic pedigree, went to a major public school, and, after a brilliant undergraduate career, became an Oxford don. The foundation of the Community of the Resurrection was merely one episode in the life of an eminent bishop and theologian. Even posthumously, he gives the impression of effortless superiority: if archbishop William Temple came to revere Fr Kelly, he also, perhaps more predictably, revered bishop Gore.[11]

In 1890, Kelly found his life's work. It did not, at first sight, look promising. We have Kelly's own account of the early days of the Society of the Sacred Mission in a pamphlet history he first wrote as early as 1898. This pleasant little book is the *History of a Religious Idea*. In 1908 he re-worked this as *An Idea in the Working*, which the Society has kept in print; the 1967 run is still available. The founder's own clever and perceptive picture has shaped the history, and it can be supplemented rather than challenged from the primary sources.

One primary source is a handwritten *Journal of the Corean Missionary Brotherhood* in the archives of the Society of the Sacred Mission. It looks like a school exercise book, in a large naive hand with red underlinings. The first section runs from Whitsuntide to Christmas 1890. On May 2nd 1890 was the first interview between Bishop Corfe, the missionary bishop of Corea (as they then spelt Korea) and Kelly. Bishop Corfe had a number of laymen who had filled in 'a little pink slip in the *Morning Calm*' (the diocesan magazine)[12] and he wanted them assessed and if possible trained for the mission. He did not want them to be trained as clergymen; he wanted only university men for ordination.[13] In practice Fr Kelly disregarded this requirement. The bishop had been a naval chaplain, and wanted discipline. Fr Kelly had similar views.

> Personally, ever since I was a cadet at Woolwich studying the art of war, I had been haunted by the dream of organised power . . . every part, large or small, grappling with its ever changing and different problems by its own independent intelligence and yet concentrating its determination under disciplined direction upon the attainment of one simple and common aim . . .[14]

Kelly, indeed, had earlier had ideas about training ordinands. He had approached Canon Scott Holland, his only influential friend, with an idea for a free theological college, so that no suitable man would be turned down for lack of money.[15] This Corean work seemed much narrower, and a second best. But Scott Holland advised him to take it.

Whatever the dream, in practice the work began as a missionary brotherhood training laymen for work in Corea, in the parish of St John the Divine, Kennington. This was not simply through the chance that its vicar was commissary in England for the bishop of Corea, and this was the Corean Missionary Brotherhood.

> Its vicar, the Rev. C.E.Brooke, was the son of a wealthy evangelical cloth manufacturer in Huddersfield and had been converted to Anglo-Catholicism at Oxford. He 'loved bricks and mortar', and while still a curate in 1871 he donated £10,000 to allow the nave of the new church to be included in its original construction ... By 1900 St John's was positively overweighted with organizations staffed by 10 curates, 25 district visitors, 150 Sunday school visitors, 170 other volunteer workers, 1 paid and 9 voluntary bell-ringers, 2 lay readers, 1 paid nurse, and 8 voluntary sisters.[16]

A parish like this could easily find a home for a small community of men. There is a printed handbill from Canon Brooke advertising a 'Home for Missionary Students in connection with the Mission to Korea'. It stresses the need to sacrifice *everything*, twice italicised.[17] Perhaps this is why most of the bishop's volunteers did not even reply to Kelly's letter.

> We laid down, therefore, three conditions:–
> (1) A man must be ready to work without pay, and
> (2) Therefore he must intend to live unmarried,
> (3) He must come simply to serve Christ, and be equally ready to take whatever place or work is assigned to him.[18]

Though this is tough, it is reminiscent of the UMCA (Universities Mission to Central Africa) which stipulated 'a common fund, no marriage, and a community mission'.[19] In the end one of the twelve volunteers agreed to come, another was found, and both came up from Cornwall, unknown to each other, to begin work on New Year's Day, 1891. (Kelly had lately been one of the team in an itinerant mission in the St Austell deanery).[20] A third man came within a week or two, and that was the first year's intake.

> I will describe our life at once, for it changed little for many years. We began with Matins and Prime at six, and, after a short interval – time enough to do our rooms – we went to the Celebration in Church at seven. Thence back to breakfast, which we managed ourselves. It was a plain bread and butter breakfast, with jam, I admit. Then began the house work. One man was responsible for accounts, one for washing up, and one swept the stairs. They changed round monthly. At 9 we had Terce, and then worked till dinner at 1.30 with Sext at 12. None was at 2, tea at 6 – bread and butter as before; Evensong in Church at 7, and Compline at 9.30. Silence was kept till Sext next day. It was years after – I forget how long – before we learnt to divide the Silence into a Greater, or absolute, Silence up to Terce, and a Lesser, from all talk other than about work, up to Sext. It was not a very well organised day, but we managed. Saturday was scrubbing day.[21]

The house on Vassall Road where they lived, 'very ugly but solidly built',[22] had enough room for two priests and eight students. When the Society expanded they bought the next house and knocked doors through. It was in grubby South London, and the Society in later years looked back on it with a strong sense of humble origins. It was in fact a four storey Georgian terrace house, with iron railings and steps and trees, of a style that most middle-class English people in the 1990s would recognise sadly as beyond their price-range.[23] Fr Alfred Kelly spoke of

> thousands of similar houses . . . in the Sahara of South London . . . the same venomous yellow-brown brick . . . in front, the same space (ten feet deep) with its two shrivelled trees and its rusty railings.[24]

In August 1891 the Journal reports that the Father Director wrote letters to the *Guardian* (a church paper) on the subject of Christian Brothers, and the editor not only published them, but wrote a leading article on them.[25] Canon Brooke also wrote to the *Guardian* on the same theme, and he had more weight than Kelly.[26] One associates Christian Brothers with rather harshly run boys schools, and Kelly was in fact thinking of a teaching order, but no adult teachers came forward. His thoughts then turned to recruiting boys.[27] In ways reminiscent of a boys school, the Corean Brotherhood had, as the Society was to retain, a strenuous eagerness at physical exercises. A student was hurt in an accident at the Gymnasium, and two days later the Director broke his arm there.[28]

There were always worries about more candidates, and the ones who turned up were often unsuitable. Many came and then left.

> As a matter of fact, in the next three years, we got six men for ordination, of whom three left (two broke down in health), and nine men for lay-work, of whom four left. Seven men in three years was not exhilarating.[29]

Setting aside their studies, which will be dealt with in a later chapter, it is clear that these young men were being challenged to live the life of a religious order. It is not necessarily clear that if, and only if, they could live like that, they would make good missionaries to Korea. Kelly was quite clear that this was not a way of life designed for religious *virtuosos*. With a stress like St Benedict's, he wanted a rule for ordinary people.

> No system can be sound which depends for success upon rare and special gifts, rather than upon the steady use of those more limited and commonplace powers which God ordinarily wills to bestow.[30]

The move to become a religious order had its own impetus. The Director's Report for 1891 speaks of the 'cells' in Vassall Road.[31] They were moving on from a missionary brotherhood to something further. From Michaelmas 1892 the journal was called the *Journal of the Society of the Sacred Mission*. Michaelmas is the angels' feast, and the sacred mission of the members is modelled on that of the angels.

'After the example and with the aid of the holy angels' they would work 'to the glory of God in His will'. This motto *Ad gloriam Dei in eius voluntate* was printed in red capitals in the Journal at the first. The young Society loved Latin. The journal reports the texts of the Father Director's sermons in Latin.[32] At St John's Kennington for the festival they sang the Missa de Angelis with the proper introit and gradual, and in the evening there was a sermon by Fr Page, mentioning the 'great advantage of public school or college life'.[33] Yet this was a society for young men who had no background in Latin or in public schools; in some ways the call to higher things was misdefined.

Kelly looked for advice on how to devise an appropriate Rule of life. For nearly a month in the autumn of 1890 he lived with the Cowley Fathers in Oxford, and was quite clear that their ways were not for him, though perhaps some of their rigour stayed with him.[34] He turned to Fr Baker of the Brethren of the Cross, a brotherhood so ephemeral that it escaped Anson's attention when he wrote *The Call of the Cloister.* Their (printed) rule said that:

> they shall look upon the lads they may gather together, as entrusted to them by God to train to heaven, and, while enforcing strict discipline, shall exercise towards them all patience and gentleness.[35]

Poor Fr Baker found in practice that his recruits were useless.

> The men who applied to me have either been broken down tradesmen or young men with a liking for the romantic side of the religious life.[36]

Kelly also turned to Fr Dale, chaplain of the convent of Benedictine nuns in Twickenham. Dale was on the Papalist side of Anglicanism; his father was a priest who had been imprisoned for ritualism, and Dale himself in 1893 was to go on to convert to Rome, to be followed twenty years later by that community of nuns, first founded by Ignatius of Llanthony, as a body.[37] One does have the feeling that Kelly did not have the best advice available. The resulting

Rule was perhaps too detailed. In October 1892 they sent it to the bishop, who promised to read it 'carefully and at once'. A fortnight later he was still promising.[38] In March he told them they should try it for a little before making it binding.[39] Fr Elwin of the Cowley Fathers wrote in 1896 agreeing with the bishop. The Society of St John the Evangelist, after all, had done without a *printed* constitution or rule for 16 or 18 years.[40] With hindsight, many years later, Fr Kelly thought in some other ways he had been too much influenced by Cowley.

> My fear is that the *system* is itself hopelessly wrong. (a) The insistence on obedience and responsible authority certainly has utterly obscured the insistence on the responsibility (initiative) of the individual. (b) We borrowed from Cowley a great deal too much conventional Religious life machinery (eg offices). And these two have conventional-ised men's minds past recognising anything. (If I had known of it, I would have followed the Oratory system).[41]

Like other Brotherhoods of the time, the Corean Mission-ary Brotherhood was somewhat isolated and somewhat inward-looking. They were, however, in London, in a large parish, and sometimes they were asked out. The publicity was worthwhile. 'November 14. Fr Kelly gives lecture at Epiphany Mission, Stockwell, on the Corean Mission, illustrated by Magic-lantern, and interposed with songs etc by members of the Brotherhood'.[42] At the consecration of a bishop of Nyasaland in St Paul's Cathe-dral, the whole community was 'provided with seats in the choir through the kindness of Canon Scott Holland'.[43] After consideration, they turned down Canon Brooke's offer of district visiting for the men, as they were not ready for it. Thus in practice began a long-standing Kelham renunciation.[44]

There is a group photograph of the young community taken in 1893. They are all posed looking in random directions away from the camera, and the effect is rather *outré*. It may be that the young shy Fr Kelly seldom caught a camera's eye, and the Brotherhood had taken its cue from him.[45] But one could also read it as emblematic of the problems of the early years.

The Society of the Sacred Mission, as such, was inaugurated on May 9th 1893, when Kelly, Badcock and Chilvers were professed as novices. The first distinctive mark of the order was a red girdle. There was the symbolism of the blood of sacrifice, and of girded loins, and being bound by wicked men.[46] It may also have had overtones of the red cord of honour tied by the enemy themselves round the wrist of military heroes in wars on the Indian Frontier.[47] The cowl, the crucifix on the girdle, and indeed the practical scapular, came later. The house on Vassall Road then had these three members and thirteen Associates.

From the early days, the Society placed function above rank. There were defined jobs, which rotated, and their holders, however junior, could within that sphere of work order Members to do things. The Journal has nearly a page of rules on the duties of the *ostiarius*, the door-keeper. This chore was allocated daily, a card being affixed each day in the room of the person responsible for opening the house-door. There are overtones of democratic rights, and the need to put down playful tricks: '(iv) . . . it may not be affixed in anyone's cell without his knowledge or leave'.[48]

The Festival at Michaelmas 1893 is reported in great liturgical detail, saying what everyone did; the hymns all have Latin names, and 'In the afternoon the Community play football in Brockwell Park'.[49] This is in character for the early days of the Society. It is difficult to assess how much is directly the young Fr Kelly, who obviously was the guiding spirit of the Society, and who would grow and change, and how much was shaped by the men themselves. There is an interesting letter from one of the novices in 1895 about the mood of the house.

> I noticed a growing feeling (simultaneous) among fellows of such different types as [four others] and myself, a feeling that things are in a rather bad way . . .
>
>> i the worldly tone which has possessed the house
>> ii the number of people not down to mattins
>> iii the absolute ignoring of the silence rule

iv the way people gad about

  v the way women and girls are talked about in a not so very proper way

  vi the way the work is scamped and neglected

  vii the wretched attendance at Mass and Evensong nearly all 'with permission'[50]

He blamed one of his fellows as the ringleader, followed by another, and had a string of practical suggestions: the villains should be chased down to mattins, the refectory locked at night, there should be a check-out book saying where people are going when they leave the house,

> . . .men should be made to sit in the men's part of the church, not in the aisle or under the tower where the sexes are mixed. . . they should wear their cassocks too. . . Mass and Evensong should be like an inspection parade, no absentees. . . a full muster of the corps.[51]

There were expulsions. As quite often happened, the most unsatisfactory student persisted with his chosen career and was later ordained in the Protestant Episcopal Church of the USA.[52] We might learn something from the anxieties of the troubled writer. He wanted military discipline, and girls were a problem, even in St John's, Kennington, where much of the seating was segregated.

In later years the Society had little nostalgia for the Vassall Road days. Life then was seen as quarrelsome, and the students as insubordinate and ambitious. Their villainies were not merely on the spiritual plane – some were common thieves. There was a 'V.R.' tone, used to explain later lapses. The men training for work in Central Africa were jealous of those for Korea,[53] and when the SSM itself was set up 'the immediate effect was perhaps rather to raise the spirit of resistance and suspicion'.[54]

Some people influential in the life of the young Society never actually joined it, such as the succession of early tutors. Mr Down introduced the habit of lecturing slowly by dictation, which the men loved, in 1892. Mr E.F.Smith, the next tutor in 1892, who came straight to Vassall Road from Oxford, would have joined the Society if his family had not stepped in. In practice he crossed Canon Brooke, was 'restless, insubordinate and captious',[55] and had a following among the men even after he had left. Important in a more constructive way was Miss Eva Jameson, who had been secretary of various Missionary Associations, and who took over the Society's fund-raising in 1897.

Victorians were very conscious of class, and often used it as a means of explaining behaviour. Kelly frequently generalised about the ways of his candidates, and of his Society, in class terms.

> He was not an effective student, being thoroughly British Working Man, and, while plodding, his mind was more on himself than on his subject.[56]

Modern historians are interested in class likewise, though sometimes from a different perspective. Kelly gives a list of the trades, more or less potentially useful on the mission field, that the students came with in 1898. They thought they could use the skills of the 3 carpenters, 1 printer, 1 stonemason, 1 blacksmith, 1 farmer, 1 architect, and 2 (pupil) teachers. They were less sure of the engineer, the foundryman, the factory worker, the domestic servant, the 2 signalmen, the 2 lay-readers (the Church of England was experimenting with paid lay-readers in the 1890s)[57], the 2 journalists, the 9 straight from school, the 7 shopmen, and the 16 clerks.[58] It is only partly due to the perceived needs of the mission field, and to the experience of teaching them, that educated Englishmen like Kelly normally found artisans easier to live with than clerks. And it was worthwhile catching them young.

> . . . it ran in our minds – as it runs today – that there were multitudes in that normal sunny youth of England, strong and capable, full of fun and games, who would willingly give up their own petty ambitions, suffer a great deal of hardship, labour gladly. . . provided only you did not ask them to stop enjoying it all and making fun of everything along the road. As things are, you can get a hundred English boys to be crucified if only they may laugh, for one who will do it solemnly. And being what they are, is it not much better that they should? It makes so much less self-importance.[59]

Part of Fr Kelly's drift is a happy acceptance of the boyishness of boys, which might well make for a good college, though for an order with life vows where people get old it is perhaps not as compelling. He himself said 'I was never anything more than a boy playing at being grown-up (I became a man, rather suddenly, after 1910, at the age of fifty)'.[60] But he had a divine purpose in view: boys can be trained to do God's will. He had discovered as a curate at Southlands that he had a way with adolescents. Kelham was unusual in taking teenagers, but not unusual in having no place for mature candidates. The Congregationalist Hackney college, in no way a particularly narrow institution, turned down a 27-year-old in 1880 because 'his mind and his opinions are too 'set''. [61]

This was not a matter of the Society, very occasionally, taking in a teenage novice. It was the Society's college taking in numbers of teenage students, with the boundary between college and society blurred. It was all the one House. The great college at Kelham came to dominate the public perception of the religious Society that ran it, yet in a way this was not a betrayal of the Founder's intention. He found himself with a job to do, training inchoate youngsters with a sense that they wanted to serve God somehow, and the Society of the Sacred Mission grew up as a means to further this and any other work that came to hand. Quite definitely, the work had priority, and in order to have a disciplined work-force, it seemed worthwhile to organise them as a religious order. The organisation was quite well considered, in Fr Kelly's own view, but it was always a means to an end.

> Let it, however, be regarded as the first aim to increase the number of those who give their lives to the divine service, especially by training those of whom at present use cannot be or is not made, whether through lack of means or of education or through other causes; and to deepen the wholeness of sacrifice in them, where the vocation exists, by building them into the organisation of the religious life.[62]

They got better men that way, than by recruiting to the 'religious life'.

> . . .our strength as a Society arose from the fact that we did not take men *for* the Religious Life but as workers for Christ. If we did ask for Religious we should get an altogether poorer stamp of men, and fewer.[63]

The Society had very little money. Fr Kelly had some private means, bringing in about £200 a year. His brother Alfred also became a member of the Society, and his sister Edith was a nun, and both gave their inheritance. In 1892 Fr Kelly gave £200 of his own money, there was £150 from Korea, £140 from the UMCA, and £50 from a special subscription for furnishings.[64] None of this amounted to wealth. The Society experienced real workmanlike poverty, through trying to run a theological college on a shoe-string. The students themselves, in rotation, ran the accounts.

> We lived in the utmost simplicity and frugality; and they too were equally interested in it. If a man's shoes wore out, he had to convince the Steward that they could not really be mended any more; and the Steward required a lot of convincing. When he gave way, he would pass the applicant on to the Storekeeper. The latter might have a second-hand pair drifted up from somewhere. . . When all resources failed, the Steward would issue an order for something. Done by the authorities, such stinginess of procedure.. easily creates ill-feeling. Done amongst the men themselves, it was an unfailing joke.[65]

They ran that college on less than £40, in a good year less than £35, per annum for each student. Typically, this was understood as not being poverty for the sake of asceticism: 'a system involving some specific separation from the normal life of the Church is no use at all. We cannot be ascetic.' [66] We cannot say that all the members of SSM consistently held this dismissive view of what others might see as the heart of the religious life, but it was a feature of Kelly's Society. It went with not taking themselves seriously.

There was to be discipline, but not for its own sake,

merely for its use. What is interesting is trying to see how Kelly used the values prevalent in Anglican public schools, 'bodily strength', 'a sense of humour', on students who were largely lower middle class. He had sharp things to say about the values learnt through being clerks. On the other hand, the SSM college succeeded triumphantly in having better priorities than trying to gentrify its students. There was also to be no 'appearance of knowledge'[67]; they must learn to think.

In 1897 the House moved from Vassall Road to Mildenhall in Suffolk. This was a beautiful country manor house, and in many ways the dream home of the Society. Away from the influences of London, everything worked. They were all young and happy and found keeping the rules almost a game. 'The House became in truth, what before it had only been in aim, a Religious House'.[68] Something of this Fr Kelly thought was due to Fr Woodward's notion of a Chapter of faults, obligatory for the novices. In 1898 he wrote about ' the acceptance of discipline, which from being a half-secret habit of a few became the ordinary, and all but universal custom'.[69]

Things moved forward at Mildenhall. They set up a printing-press. The boys had their own house, the 'Cottage'. Bishops recognised them in 1897 as a 'Theological and Missionary college', which enabled them to enter their men for the Central Entrance examination. They were less successful with other religious orders: Fr Kelly wrote reproachfully in 1897 that 'the steady determination of the Pusey House to debar us from their and Cowley preserves remained unbroken and successful'.[70] Some publicity was bad: Lady Wimborne attacked the House in the Times.[71] The Vicar of Mildenhall distrusted their high church practices. But otherwise Mildenhall was rural bliss. Unhappily they outgrew the house. They had an average of 15.6 in residence in 1896; 34.6 in 1900; and 66 in 1904.

In 1903, after a long search for something bigger, they found Kelham Hall, just outside Newark, convenient for access, sadly low-lying, but with plenty of room for games, and cheap. The noble family who had built this Victorian pile had gone bankrupt, so it was habitable but not finished. Fr Kelly did not choose it for its appearance.

> . . .it is Gilbert Scott insanity on the model – or rather a previous model – of S. Pancras Hotel – one endless waste of paint, gilding, granite columns, vaulted ceilings and the *vilest* gothic. Extravagant, tasteless, unfeeling. Every capital throughout the house carved elaborately and vilely – with the sole object of spending money.[72]

Growing numbers at the college outstripped a more steady growth in members of the Society. Even at Mildenhall the notion was there among the students that this was a theological college like any other. In 1902, recognising reality, the Society dropped the old conditions of acceptance, and asked simply for repayment once ordained of what the man's training had cost. Throughout its great history the students of Kelham college had fits of suspicion of being got at to be made monks, and wanting none of it. The Society in its turn was nervous.

> Feb.23 1911. He [HK] talked to the boys on Sunday night about VR [Vassall Road], which is as near as we can get to taboo subjects. . . to talk to boys as a group is tantamount to asking them to join.[73]

The surge in numbers, and the move to the more institutional Kelham, unsettled community life. In 1904 the Director's Report included a whole page of accounts of men being sacked, for reasons such as tempting the boys to smoke on the way to a football match in Lincoln, and going to public houses.[74] In 1906 'there were practically the first CE [Central Entrance (examination for Theological Colleges)] failures known in the House'.[75] All but one of those who failed was expelled. Dom Aelred Carlyle came to give a retreat and poached four men for his Benedictine house, then at Painsthorpe in Yorkshire. These were teething troubles; they settled down, and Kelham became Kelham.

Chapter Three

Who joined SSM?

Father Kelly was 34, and a graduate of Oxford already in orders, when he and Father Woodward became the first professed members of SSM in 1894. Herbert Woodward was then 44, and had been a missionary in Central Africa for nearly twenty years. He was not a graduate, and had been an architect's clerk for four years before he trained at St Stephen's House. He had been brought up in middle-class Congregationalism, though even as a young man he had felt something of 'the call of the cloister'. He went straight back to Zanzibar, and had no great influence on the future of the Society, though the Constitution officially came from both the founders. The cowl worn by the brethren was his idea.

These two had a different background from most of those later professed. The typical SSM profession was of a young man in his early twenties, with an elementary school education. The third profession, in 1895, was of Walter Russell, one of the lay volunteers for mission work, who had been sent out to be a printer for UMCA in 1893 working under Fr Woodward. He was later released incapacitated in 1904. So the third professed member, like the second, spent his career in religion in East Africa. The next three, professed in 1896 and 1897, Harold Firkins, Hugh Pearson, and Arthur Laws, were sent to Korea. When the work in Korea failed, Arthur Laws stayed there, and was released in 1900. Hugh Pearson had been to a public school, Ardingley, but was not very clever, and coming to SSM was a last resort in a vain endeavour to find some way of being ordained. Instead he became a lay brother, and spent his life, dying in 1957, as the indispensable handyman at Kelham. They said he was somewhat anti-clerical towards the end. Fr Firkins, from an orphan asylum in Wanstead, and then a shop clerk at Marshall and Snelgrove's, gave a lifetime to South Africa.

'Firks' . . . would go about Ladybrand location at 3.30am,
ringing a handbell to waken the faithful for the service at
4.00am[1]

Academically, he was a credit to Fr Kelly, because in South
Africa he kept up his patristics, and even wrote learned
articles for scholarly journals.

The other two professed in 1897 were Joseph White and
Henry Drake. White was a typical novice of the 1890s, a
23-year-old Londoner (though with some Scots blood in
him), with no academic credentials. He had tried to train as
a pupil teacher, but had failed an examination. Fr Kelly
found him ineducable – he failed the ordination examination – and he was sent out for lay work in Central Africa.
From then on he never looked back; Zanzibar arranged to
ordain him, and he spent the rest of his life founding
schools. He was Director of SSM from 1920 to 1925.
Those in SSM who had despised his intellectual capacities
despised them to the end, but they were willing to say he
was a saint.

Fr Drake might have seemed a much more likely future
Director, with behind him Lancing and Cambridge. But,
like Fr Woodward, he joined SSM and carried on his life
as a missionary. He was already a priest in the diocese of
Korea, and, after a short stay at the House, joined SSM
while on furlough. He was successively Provincial of Korea
and South Africa, but then went back on detached service
to Korea for most of the rest of his life.

In the next five years, from 1898 to 1902 inclusive, there
were fifteen professions. Three were already in priest's
orders, graduates of Oxford or Cambridge. There was a
mistaken impression that the Society did not receive priests,
or at least only for specific work as tutors.[2] The first of
these was Fr Norton, who was a missionary in South
Africa. There is a pen-portrait of him, unsigned, in a South
African file. It is evidence, at least, of how closely religious
observe each other.

. . . a dear old saint, with no discretion or judgement. A bit
of a poet, a beautiful linguist, and mad on plainsong, Percy
Dearmer, and any other fad. He aims at being a model

religious (off times) and won't say a word, because of
religious humility or something. Then tears you – or
anyhow me – in pieces as a reckless autocrat. Loses his head
if he's written to .. His letters.. give him all away. If he
could learn a little sense and stop being so self-conscious..
everything with him is a matter of *feeling* – very often
beautiful feelings . . . Then there's the music – Colin [Mill-
ington, SSM 1898–1907] says 'He has not a conscience
about Plain Song. It *is* his conscience.' Per contra, he is
very devout, patient with his people, always means right
. . . give him sympathy and a little deference and you can
lead him where you will ultimately. He has a wonderful
personal knowledge of his people, and I should think no
organising power at all . . .[3]

Fr Norton could write perceptively and movingly about
mission work. However, in 1917 he left the Society and
married, and that meant in those days that he was never
mentioned again.

The second graduate recruit in 1900 was Fr Alfred
Kelly, the founder's younger brother, then aged 28. Less
complicated than his brother, he was the sort of person
whom boys could hero-worship without harm. He was a
wonderful athlete, something of a comedian, had a very
logical mind, and his teaching was a model of briskness
and good order. As the young Provincial of South Africa
from 1903 to 1906, he crossed his province. Part of this was
his brother's fault. Fr Kelly made it quite plain that a
family appointment was merely a stopgap one, and wrote
to individuals in the province checking up if his brother
was doing all right. They responded by refusing to tell
tales, but somehow the idea that there were tales to tell was
enough. Alfred spent most of the last thirty years of his life
teaching at Kelham. He could get a good game of tennis if
he played alone against two others. He enjoyed making up
light verse about Kelham:

> Is this a Monastery I see before me
> This pompous, plutocratic, pagan pile. . .
> Boy novices are skipping on the stairs;
> Professed are whistling in the passages;
> Priests, smoking like the Dragon in the pit,

> With cards and novels fool away the night.[4]

He collected student howlers.'Q. Who said 'Would I had served my God as I had served my king'? A. Oliver Cromwell.' His natural mode of teaching was to discover and enjoy howlers. He was in fact a competent logician, submitting articles to *Mind*, and when he read books, whether William Temple or Karl Barth, what he saw were the defects in logic. In the internal battles of the Society he loyally supported his brother and teased the other side. He was a good after-dinner speaker, and a happy person.

> Nov.6 Dark Night of the Soul. Ran out of tabak; battery of torch periit. (Also tennis has practically ceased).[5]

These are the sorrows of the well-adjusted. Students were more likely to remember him with delight than his tetchy and incomprehensible brother. They died within months of each other.

The third of these graduate entrants was Fr David Jenks, second Director of the Society (1910–20). He had come from interesting work in the Middle East, with the Archbishop of Canterbury's Assyrian Mission, reviving the old Nestorian church.[6] He was a gentle approachable person, much more of a conventional Anglo-Catholic than Fr Kelly (he had had Roman fever in the 1890s[7]). He was spoken of as Fr David, or sometimes D.J., rather than Fr Jenks. He was the sort of monk who could set himself to teach spirituality. As Director he was not a great success.

> He was terribly conscious of his responsibility, and overanxious to win the support of his subordinates, which led him at times to be too diplomatic with men who had been trained under the downright methods of HK.[8]

As Director, his world crumbled around him with the 1914–18 War. He was disappointed when some of the men accepted his non-directive advice not to enlist. Most enlisted. The remnants of the college moved to Mirfield, and he found work in London as Secretary of the Archbishop's Group of Advisers for the 'Recruiting Campaign for Service in the Kingdom of God', and spent his time writing hundreds of letters, 'always containing personal matter affecting the individual, as well as general news',[9] to the men at the front. He then had some sort of breakdown, and it was obvious in 1920 that the Society needed to find a new Director.

From then on, he often visited Kelham and remained in SSM, but found work outside as a diocesan missioner. It was agreed that his health was not up to the Kelham regime. His background was wealthy (his nephew was Lord Mayor of London), and he took life more easily.

> Here was a monk who liked nothing better as a holiday than to get into plusfours, to fly to Paris or some other continental centre, and to go journeying on from there.[10]

Unusually for a monk, he joined the Freemasons. In the Tribe-Bedale era he became something of an anachronism, as indeed was Fr Kelly.

Graduate entrants remained untypical. The hope was that some of the professed brethren, once educated in the Society, would go on to take degrees and come back as tutors at the college. The first of the high-fliers was Gerald Murphy, one of Kelly's boys, professed in 1901. Before the 'Cottage' he had been educated privately, but the family background was rather rackety, and they had lost their money. All went according to plan: he graduated from Oxford and came back as a tutor, and was one of the contestants for the Directorship in 1920. But he went to pieces when he did not get it, blamed Fr Kelly for ruining his life, and left the Society in 1925. It was a tremendous blow to Fr Kelly, who had invested a lot of emotion in this the first and brightest of his boys. Fr Murphy spent the rest of his life as a rather embittered country clergyman.

There were others sent to university in this period, and none of them stayed in the Society. The Society parted angrily with John Pigg, professed 1902 and released 1908, who went to Oxford and never looked back. Harold Spackman (1905 to 1908) went on to Cambridge later, and remained friends. Some of the sterner brethren later raised questions about a photograph of Fr Kelly climbing a mountain with Mrs Spackman in Japan. George Branson, who was professed in 1904 and graduated from Oxford in

1907, was one of those released in 1915. This was the War: the brethren were recruited, and not all vocations could stand trench life. Three of the 1904 professions were released in 1915.

Two of those who left in 1915 were men who had come from Choir Schools, which is a step up from board schools. Fr Jenks had a low opinion of more socially presentable candidates, from Woodard schools and clergymen's sons, 'poorly educated and worse'.[11] The Society recruited men with regional accents, especially Cockneys. The original comments on Fr Arthur Amor, later Provincial of South Africa, whose background was Kensal Green and Walthamstow, were 'nice lad − rather too spikey and Londonish'.[12] Several came from local congregations in and around Nottingham. Some had more genteel backgrounds. There was sometimes genteel poverty: Fr Couldrey, professed in 1909, after graduating from Selwyn, the cheapest Cambridge college, could not afford an ordinary theological college, so came to Kelham. There was at least social aspiration in some of the names they were given at their baptism. The promising Fr Francis Wyllie, who was lost at sea in 1918, had been christened Robert Augustus Platch Wyllie. It is probably middle-class to be called by one's unusual second Christian name, as Fr (Joseph) Buxcy Neate was.

Fr Buxcy Neate, who was professed in 1901 and died in 1960, stands out in retrospect as the first of those who lived a life-time in the Society without finding a lifetime's occupation in one task. Yet he was always being offered jobs, like 'Rector of the Film-stars church at Hollywood, and Chaplain to the Actors' Christian Union'.[13] Some were indispensable in one particular work, like Bernard Bunce (professed 1910) who was 35 years in charge of the church office at St Patrick's, Bloemfontein, or Br James Berry, on whose Personal Record it says in his own hand 'Sacked from PO [Printing Office at Kelham] in 1974 after 49 years in PO', or Br Edgar Lintott, the secretary at Kelham (professed 1905, died 1946), who was the best-known member of the Society, as far as Newark was concerned. Without such a niche, the chances are a man would feel marginalised and leave the Society. When Fr Wilfrid Hambidge (professed 1909) was displaced as novice master by the new regime of the 1920s, his health broke down, and he spent the last twenty years of his life being waited on by nuns as the chaplain to a girls' school, though still a rather critical member of SSM.

Some were more fitted to close community life than others. Fr Frederick Rand (professed 1903) was happier on horseback in open spaces, and after years of begging for more remote postings, left in 1935. Fr Leonard Southam was happy enough, freezing alone in the Snowdon Ranger Priory, a former hotel given to the Society in the mountains of Wales. When he moved back to Kelham, he lived 'in a lodge at the front gate, with a lay brother to keep him company . . . he never found it easy to fit into the life of the house'.[14] The village of Kelham loved him.

In many ways it was a good life being a lay brother at Kelham. They were not merely cheap sanctified labour, but powers in the land. Everyone else was on rotas as their unskilled assistants. Br Edward Goodey came to Mildenhall in 1902, just before his fourteenth birthday. 'I think God wants me to work for him as a missionary'. (Incidentally, two of his sisters became nuns, one Anglican, the other in due course a Roman Catholic mother superior). He was a stern head-gardener, a 'pungent critic of indifferent work' and an inventor of gadgets.[15] William Hardwell, as a middle-aged man, heard they wanted a printer, and came. He was quite willing to join the Society, but he was there to do the work. He was professed in 1915 and died in 1953. He certainly exemplifies a different sense of a vocation to the religious life than, say, Fr Cyril Whitworth, from Radley and Cambridge, professed in 1917, who in 1931 transferred to SSJE at Cowley, wanting something more professionally 'religious'.

Three influential new professions between 1907 and 1909 were Edwin Cosgrove, George Carleton and Edmund Couldrey. Edwin Cosgrove became an authority on church music, not only raising the standard of the singing at Kelham, but becoming a visiting tutor to many other theological colleges (he trained Archbishop Michael

Ramsey to sing) and an adviser to the BBC on religious broadcasts.[16] George Carleton, who had been a tutor for several years before he was professed, went on to be a focus of an Anglo-Catholic forward movement in the Society, and nearly to break it in the 'Carleton affair' around 1920. Fr Couldrey is a perfect example of someone who dug himself in and became utterly indispensable. He taught the first two years of Church History from 1914 to 1951; he was Bursar from 1916 to 1952; and he was Sub-Prior of Kelham from 1922 to 1953. He was a master of all the details of the Society's Constitution.

Those who stay shape the collective memory. Fr Couldrey had an 'apparatchik''s good-humoured impatience with Fr Kelly's untidiness and spontaneity, and handed down stories like these:

> . . . in dealing with men he was very easily deceived while his deafness was a great handicap − . . .men have come, asked and received permission to stay in next morning, and after they have gone out HK turned to me and said 'what did he say' . . .
> . . .going to the Lakes, he took a hip bath with him, and the day turning out hotter than expected, at a station when changing and waiting for a train, had the bath put down on the open platform, knelt down by it and proceeded to unrobe and take off an unnecessary pullover . . .[17]

He honestly spoke of Fr Kelly as an inspiring lecturer, but the particular memories he handed down were of the mannerisms of a lecturer, someone who read Punch or sharpened old razor-blades while lecturing. In his turn, people told stories about 'Teddy' Couldrey. It was a world where heroes were jokily cut down to size. Thus, looking back on SSM's most famous scholar, Fr Gabriel Hebert, Peter Clark would say 'His notes were good; his books were excellent; but as a tutor he was awful'.[18] Fr Peter Clark, who first arrived at Kelham in 1914, but then enlisted, and came back to be professed in 1922, lived into his nineties, and Margaret Dewey's Chronicle has quite a number of his candid verdicts on those he had outlived. To the loving pen-portrait of Br Hugh Pearson he added cautionary asides: 'When there was a full moon, his temper was vile'.[19] Fr Ranford, briefly Warden and Prior in the 1940s, he found 'very difficult to live with',[20] and Fr Couldrey, for all his comic reminiscences, a dull lecturer; it is only fair to recall that Fr Peter Clark was in the same tradition. His own obituary says:

> How he would drone on in the Cedar Room at Kelham, ending with the well-worn phrase 'Another empire down the drain'! Nobody could say he was inimitable.[21]

It is possible for an oldest inhabitant to be quite delightful, flowing with reminiscence, and with a pungent turn of phrase, but also to have a limited perspective or an axe to grind. Fr Peter Clark's memories in the 1980s might need to be used with care, because he looked back with delight to a golden age of Kelham between the wars. That golden age was in some ways seriously flawed, and those who did not fit in should have been listened to more, starting with Fr Kelly himself.

The history of the Society between the wars will be told later. What should be stressed here is that of the 61 men who between 1892 and 1914 had been professed as members of SSM, only 28, less than half, were still within the Society by the end of 1920. It was a Society of young men: only four had died, three of them as the result of enemy action[22]. Many more had left the Society, or been put out.

As it were in exchange for the dead, the war brought some to join the Society. Immediately after it, a number of ex-soldiers came from the Knutsford Test College. Fr Sydney Holgate had vowed his life to God in 1916 in the water after his ship was torpedoed, and kept his promise.[23] Between 1919 and 1921 three men who were to be of great importance in SSM were professed, Reginald Tribe, Gabriel Hebert and Stephen Bedale. All three had been in Kelham before the war, so their professions could be seen as somewhat delayed. They were to be the dominant figures of a new era. All three were from a middle-class background, untypical of Kelham. Hebert and Bedale were from public school and Oxford; Tribe had been a consultant gynaecologist in London. From 1925 to 1943 Tribe was

director of SSM, when Bedale succeeded him. Bedale was
Warden of the college and Prior of Kelham for nearly all
that period. Hebert was over-shadowed within the Society,
but went on to have a far more considerable reputation outside.

Most of those who were professed between the wars had
come from grammar schools, though there were still a few
who had only been to primary schools. Every two or three
years there would be one who had been educated at public
school. Some of these public-school men, such as Felix
Macintosh (professed 1923) and Conrad Herold (professed
1926) found themselves at odds with the prevailing temper
of the Society, and after trying to appeal to Fr Kelly
against Fr Bedale, walked out. Others had less trouble, and
were given responsible positions: Richard Roseveare (professed 1928) was prior at Sheffield, Provincial in South
Africa, and then Bishop of Accra; Antony Snell (professed
1934) was a tutor at Kelham and then in Australia.

> This term we really have had an asset, in the shape of Snell,
> who is a first in Greats. He is very small in stature, but in
> all other respects a really great person. Unlike Carleton and
> others, he is taking Kelham theology quite seriously . . .
> not only great but useful. I shoved all my philosophy
> essays on to him.[24]

Br George Every, professed in 1933, was a lay church
historian, with a degree from Exeter. Kelham's own
home-grown Fr Victor Ranford, professed in 1927, was
sent to London for a degree, and came back as the first of
the new crop of Kelham's own tutors, after the disappointment when one after another of Fr Kelly's bright boys had
left the Society, culminating with Fr Murphy in 1925.

It was a disappointment that the Society was not recruiting in the areas where it worked in South or Central
Africa. Fr Bertram Lester, professed in South Africa in
1931, had been a missionary there, but was an Englishman.
Julien Durup, from the Seychelles, was professed in 1928,
the first non-white member of SSM, but found celibacy
hard, and was removed in 1938. Instead of recruits from
South Africa, the Society still found men in England to

staff that Province. If, as Fr Kelly said, only life-times count, then, for example, Fr Cecil Hemsley, professed in 1925, and buried at Modderpoort in 1986 after a lifetime's work there, should be counted.

We are now reaching a period when some of those who joined SSM are still alive. Fr Paul Hume, Director of the Society 1952–62, who was professed in 1932, is at the priory in Willen. His successor, Gregory Wilkins, Director 1962–72, who was professed in 1934 and died in 1980, was in a great SSM tradition,

> son of a cockney postman, conceived in the Old Kent Road and born in Ilford . . .

> . . . on the few occasions when he addressed gatherings or preached in public, he might leave an impression of being flippant or unorthodox. Although he was never uncharitable, he was merciless to folly and muddled thinking.

> 'I want putting on my tombstone: He never went to Taizé.'[25]

The working-class, often London, background, the light touch, and the lack of public weight, are all unsurprising in SSM.

The great change in the pattern of recruitment for SSM came after 1950, with Australian professions. More than 30 of the 93 professed since 1950 have been Australians. It is profitless being strictly precise, because English brethren have settled in Australia and vice versa. Another ten have come from other parts of the world, Japan and South Africa, and one Canadian, Fr Ralph Martin. He read Anson's *The Call of the Cloister*, with its pen-portraits of all the religious orders, and liked the sound of SSM. The Australian province, like the English one, was centred on a theological college, and any of its professed members who were capable of teaching in a college found themselves doing so. Several were academically very competent, such as Dunstan McKee, professed 1958 and Director 1972 – 1982, Douglas Brown, professed 1954, and Thomas Brown, professed 1963 and Director since 1989.

The Society has not lately recruited those with the

academic gifts needed to staff theological colleges. Of the 14 professed in the last twenty years, none had degrees, though several had successfully completed the training for the Anglican priesthood. A number of them had overcome poor school results to go on to this, and that achievement recaptures something of Fr Kelly's ambition. Of the 14 men professed in the last 20 years, only six are still in the Society, so we are generalising from small numbers. It would be possible, as in the early days, to give pen portraits of all the younger members.

Instead we turn to statistics. There is a graph of the numbers of professed, Table 1. In it we can see that the Society grew at a very steady rate until 1915 when there were 52 members. By 1921 and 1922 there were only 36, reflecting the losses in the War and the struggles over whether the Society should be more 'religious' (the Carleton affair). Then came the Tribe-Bedale era, doubling to 72 members in 1937, with a little falling off in the late 1930s, and then peaking at 74 in 1941. There was a slow steady decline to 62 in 1949, easily explained by the Second World War. New novices after the war could only work through to profession by 1950 – the first Australian professions were in 1950. Then there was 10 years growth, with 85 (the largest ever) professed members in 1961. One should remember that quite a number of these were above retiring age. There were still 79 ten years later, but since then there has been a steady, though not rapid, decline, reaching 60 in 1979, 50 in 1985, and 41 in 1991.

Another set of statistics, Table 2, gives the ages, to within 5 years, of the professed members of SSM. In 1898 all but the two founders were under 35, and two were under 24. In 1903 there were 10 over 30 and 15 under 30. It was a very young Society. In 1908, five years later, still more than half were under 30. In 1913, however, the dominant age-group was from 30 to 34, and in 1918 for the first time there was nobody under 24 (all on active service) and the largest group were aged 35 to 39. By 1928 the longest column is once again 25 to 29. Fr Woodward, the oldest, was by then over 70. By 1938, though there were 18 in the 25 to 29 column, there were 5 or 6 in every column from

Table 1   Numbers of Professed

1894	2	
5	...5	
7	8	
8	11	
9	13	
1900		
1	19	
2	22	
3	25	
4	29	
5	30	
6	31	
7	36	
8	38	
9	38	
1910		
1	46	
2	46	
3	49	
4	51	
5	52	
6	48	
7	46	
8	40	
9	39	
1920		
1	36	
2	36	
3	★..............................41	
4	45	
5	46	
6	45	
7	46	
8	.★...................................52	
9	53	
1930		
1	57	
2	61	
3	...★......................................62	
4	66	
5	67	
6	71	

7 72
8 ...★..70
9 69
1940
1 74
2 72
3 ....★...71
4 70
5 69
6 67
7 66
8 ....★...64
9 62
1950
1 63
2 66
3 ....★...69
4 72
5 71
6 74
7 77
8 ....★...78
9 79
1960
1 85
2 83
3 ....★..82
4 78
5 80
6 78
7 76
8 ....★...75
9 79
1970
1 79
2 75
3 ....★...74
4 70
5 69
6 67
7 64
8 ....★...62
9 60

1980
```
  1  .....................................................54
  2  ...................................................55
  3  .....................................................54
  4  ..................................................52
  5  .................................................50
  6  .................................................49
  7  ...............................................47
  8  ..........*..............................44
  9  .............................................43
```
1990
```
  1  ...........................................41
  2  ...........................................42
```

The *s at 5 yearly intervals mark the numbers aged 65 or over.

40 to 64, giving a good solid phalanx of middle-aged men. The Society was less eager to profess very young men, who had come up as boys at Kelham. None of the professed were under 24 in 1938, and never again would there be more than 2 as young as that. The generation who were 25 to 29 in 1938 were the last big intake, and continued as clearly the largest group, with twice as many as any other line, in 1943 and 1948 and 1953, when they were 40 to 44. There were only two under 30 in 1948, and 7 over 70. By 1953 there were 9 under 30, and in 1958 13, with another 13 under 34, actually outnumbering the 12 left of the big earlier intake. The dip in the 1940s shows in the pyramid, but the general picture is healthy. One feature of not keeping members to a life profession was that there were fewer pensioners to look after than might have been expected. There were only 5 aged over 70 in 1963. The largest columns in 1963 were men in their 30s. In ten years time, in 1973, there were still 9 under 30, though by then there were 19 over 60. The main bulk was still of men under 50. By 1978 numbers had dropped quite sharply: there were only 2 under 30, and the predominating age was between 40 and 55, men in their prime, but missing several of their own peers, who had dropped out, and with few young ones. In 1983 there was only one under 30,

Table 2   Ages of Professed at S.S.M: (founded 1893 – first professions 1894)

1898
```
80 +
75–79
70–74
65–69
60–64
55–59
50–54
45–49
40–44   *
35–39   *
30–34   **
25–29   **
To 24   **
```

1903
```
80 +
75–79
70–74
65–69
60–64
55–59
50–54
45–49   *
40–44
35–39   **
30–34   *****
25–29   *********
To 24   ******
```

1908
```
80 +
75–79
70–74
65–69
60–64
55–59
50–54   *
45–49   *
40–44   **
35–39   *****
30–34   ********
25–29   **************
To 24   ***
```

1913
```
80 +
75–79
70–74
65–69
60–64
55–59   *
50–54   *
45–49   **
40–44   *****
35–39   ********
30–34   ******************
25–29   ***********
To 24
```

1918
```
80 +
75–79
70–74
65–69
60–64   *
55–59   *
50–54   ***
45–49   **
40–44   *****
35–39   ************
30–34   ********
25–29   ****
To 24
```

1923
```
80 +
75–79
70–74
65–69   *
60–64
55–59   ***
50–54   **
45–49   ****
40–44   **********
35–39   ******
30–34   *******
25–29   *****
To 24   **
```

1928
```
80 +
75–79
70–74   *
65–69   *
60–64   ***
55–59   **
50–54   ****
45–49   *******
40–44   ******
35–39   ****
30–34   *********
25–29   **********
To 24   **.
```

1933
```
80 +
75–79
70–74   *
65–69   ***
60–64   **
55–59   ******
50–54   *******
45–49   ******
40–44   ******
35–39   ********
30–34   **********
25–29   *******
To 24   *****
```

1938
```
80 +
75–79   *
70–74   **
65–69
60–64   *****
55–59   ******
50–54   ******
45–49   ******
40–44   ******
35–39   *********
30–34   ******
25–29   ******************
To 24
```

1943
```
80 +   *
75–79   **
70–74   **
65–69   ******
60–64   ******
55–59   ******
50–54   ******
45–49   *****
40–44   ********
35–39   *******
30–34   ****************
25–29   *****
To 24   *
```

1948
```
80 +   **
75–79   **
70–74   ***
65–69   *****
60–64   *****
55–59   ****
50–54   *****
45–49   *******
40–44   *******
35–39   ***************
30–34   ****
25–29   **
To 24
```

1953
```
80 +   *
75–79   **
70–74   *****
65–69   ****
60–64   ***
55–59   *******
50–54   *******
45–49   *******
40–44   **************
35–39   *****
30–34   *****
25–29   *******
To 24   **
```

1958
```
80 +   *
75–79   ***
70–74   ****
65–69   ***
60–64   *****
55–59   *******
50–54   ******
45–49   *************
40–44   ****
35–39   ****
30–34   **************
25–29   *************
To 24   *
```

1963
```
80 +   *
75–79   **
70–74   **
65–69   ****
60–64
55–59   ******
50–54   ************
45–49   ******
40–44   ***
35–39   ****************
30–34   **************
25–29   *********
To 24   **
```

1968
```
80 +   *
75–79
70–74   ***
65–69   ******
60–64   ******
55–59   **********
50–54   ****
45–49   ***
40–44   ************
35–39   *************
30–34   *********
25–29   *******
To 24   *
```

1973
```
80 +
75–79   **
70–74   *****
65–69   *****
60–64   *******
55–59   **
50–54   **
45–49   ***********
40–44   **********
35–39   **********
30–34   ******
25–29   ********
To 24   *
```

1978
```
80 +   *
75–79   ***
70–74   ***
65–69   *******
60–64   **
55–59   **
50–54   ********
45–49   **********
40–44   **********
35–39   ****
30–34   *******
25–29   **
To 24
```

1983
```
80 +   ***
75–79   **.
70–74
65–69   **
60–64   **
55–59   *******
50–54   *********
45–49   *********
40–44   **
35–39   ******
30–34   * *
25–29   *
To 24
```

1988
```
80 +   *
75–79   ******
70–74   **
65–69   **
60–64   *******
55–59   ********
50–54   *******
45–49   *
40–44   *****
35–39   ***
30–34   *
25–29   *
To 24   *
```

N.B.
Table 2 includes
only those who
were present for
the whole year,
whereas Table 1
includes every-
one who was a
professed
member for part
of a year.

three over 80, and the predominating age was of men in their 50s. In 1988 there were 2 under 30, 4 in their 30s, 6 in their 40s, 13 in their 50s, 9 in their 60s, and 9 over 70. It goes without saying that some men in their 70s are filled with eager zest and worth two younger men, but the general pattern is one of decline.

What these tables of ages suggest, but do not make plain, is that the average length of time that men spent in SSM was well short of a lifetime. Men made a promise that sounds as if it might well be binding them for life. More than half, for one reason or another, did not keep it. There was a lot of guilt about this, both on the part of those who left, and on the part of those who wondered if they had driven them out. (Some were put out). It would be unreal to calculate the average length of time spent in the Society with 40 still living, with years of their life still to come in the Society. There was never a golden age, when most of those professed stayed for life, but there were sometimes clusters of near contemporaries who stayed in together.

It is difficult to do justice in any history to people who appear briefly, and have no conspicuous impact on the organisation. Some of the men who appear in these statistics looked on membership of SSM (and this may be a fair reading of it) as an opportunity to do a job, and when no job came, or the specific job was done, they left.[26] Others were unsettled, unready for work, caught up in some private quest or misery of their own. For a Society that prided itself on its skills in sifting men for God's work, SSM accepted rather many for novices, and even for profession, whom perhaps it should never have taken and perhaps too easily forgot.

> 'Now, let me give you a useful tip: always keep your eye on anybody who has been in a monastery and has come out again. He is sure to say that he chose to leave before taking his final vows, but the chances are strong that he was thrown out, and for excellent reasons, even if for nothing more than being a disruptive nuisance. There are more failed monks than you would imagine, and they can all bear watching.'

This is from Robertson Davies's novel *The Rebel Angels* (1981), and the character who is speaking, something of a psychological monster better to meet in a novel, describes his own experience in SSM, naming SSM and quoting the Principles. Apparently Robertson Davies found himself the literary executor of just such a person, and made a novel out of the life.[27] The monastic life does attract a variety of people. Most of the difficult ones, and perhaps some of the saints, leave quite quickly.

Those who stay make together a whole that is greater than the sum of its parts. There is no formula for a successful religious order, but SSM has done some things well that individuals could never have done. At the end of this chapter, it might be worth stressing that the Society has twice had surprising resurgences. Fr Kelly and Fr Jenks set up their college at Kelham, with new ideas about training, new ideas about ecumenism, and a healthy flood of novices. It all collapsed with the First World War. Fr Tribe and Fr Bedale started a golden age of Kelham, one of the great institutional expressions of Anglo-Catholicism, and again a healthy flood of novices. It had run out of momentum by the Second World War. In the 1950s the Society had a new lease of life, with buoyant numbers, and a large new Australian province. Since then, in common with many other religious orders, there has been decline. But the precedents of earlier resurgence are there.

From this account of the people involved, we turn back their work, and specifically to the way that theological students were taught at Kelham.

Chapter Four

How to Teach Theological Students

The Corean Missionary Brotherhood was set up to train missionaries. The Church of England had been training missionaries in some numbers for a century. Bishop Corfe himself had, when younger, set up and run a short-lived college in China. He wanted to try again in Korea, and had to be persuaded that men should first be trained in England. Even so, he was eager to carry off workers as soon as they were usable. Those preparing for ordination might take a little longer, but he took the printer within a year.[1] Another printer went to work with the UMCA in Central Africa. If lay workers had usable skills, they scarcely seemed to need training.

In its early days the college tried to learn Korean, but from the beginning Kelly and Canon Brooke had wider plans than Korea, and the Korean emphasis soon declined. A missionary already in Korea came back on furlough in 1895, was professed as a novice of SSM, and returned to Korea with the two senior students in January 1896. It was rather rushed, but there in Korea was the first overseas priory of the Society. This did not work: almost at once there was no community life. The diocese of Korea got two or three more missionaries, but not as professed members of the Society. Father Drake, who went out in 1898 as Provincial for Korea, continued in the Society, and, some years after the formal withdrawal of the SSM from Korea in 1904, went back to Korea 'on detached service' for many years.[2] All told, about seven or eight men went to Korea, some quite briefly.

Anglican missionaries in the nineteenth century were as likely as not to be non-graduates. Fr Trollope, the Korean missionary who joined SSM, was an Oxford graduate, but the other missionaries there were trained at Warminster and Dorchester and St Aidan's College.[3]

By 1900 this one very small diocese was training its nongraduate clergy at a different missionary college. The college, somewhat against the wishes of the diocese, shifted towards training for the parochial ministry of England.

One might naturally ask how different the work of any missionary college was from the ordinary training of Church of England clergymen. The answer was perhaps slightly embarrassing on both sides. The Church of England expected its clergy to be gentlemen, which normally meant a degree from an ancient university. This need not be in theology. There was a system of examining chaplains, and one could get up the basic minimum (Pearson on the Creeds etc) in a few weeks' reading. Fr Kelly himself was ordained on his degree in history without any further professional training. Theological colleges were optional, and largely served to reinforce party traditions within the Church. Missionaries were trained as if they were at theological college. There was almost nothing specifically aimed at the mission field. The real purpose was to try to gentrify the candidates, because in class-conscious England it was very clear that volunteers for the mission field tended to be 'not quite gentlemen'.[4] Perhaps because of embarrassment over this function, the colleges seem not to have been much in the public eye. There is one paragraph in the big three-volume history of the CMS about its missionary college.[5]

The course in missionary colleges, and in theological colleges for nongraduates, was a matter of basic books. This was also how Anglican clergy overseas were trained. Here, for example are the 'Subjects of Study' at Emmanuel College, Prince Albert, N.W.Canada where 'a regular course of Theology was provided for English and Canadian candidates for Holy Orders':

> Subjects of Study, – Divinity: Pearson on the Creed, Robertson's Church History, Browne on the 39 Articles, Proctor and Maclear on the Book of Common Prayer, Paley's Evidences, Butler's Analogy, Maclear on the Old and New

Testaments, Greek Testament. Classics: Caesar, Xenophon. Mathematics: Euclid, Algebra. English Literature: Stopford Brooke.[6]

Few colleges were as blunt in listing exactly the books required, but Church History, Prayer Book (or even Liturgiology) and Systematic Theology would often mean the study of one standard modern textbook. This was not greatly contrasted with the technical requirements in theology for graduate ordination in the Church of England. The diocese of Oxford under Samuel Wilberforce was considered strict in the 1860s because it sent a list of ten books to candidates for orders, on which they were examined on Thursday to Saturday with the ordination on the Sunday.[7]

Most men ordained in the Church of England had not studied much theology. There were considerable gaps in the degree scheme at Oxford or Cambridge.

> '... the persons least surprised at the Reverend Amos's deficiencies were his clerical brethren, who had gone through ["the Eleusinian mysteries of a university education"] themselves.'[8]

It was quite common for students from the theological colleges to beat the graduates of the ancient universities in the ordination examination,[9] but this was not taken to prove anything.

> '... taking the mere theological qualifications of the mass of literates and the mass of university men, we have little doubt that on the whole the literates are superior.'[10]

That phrase 'mere theological qualifications' tells us something about the status of theology in Anglicanism.

The Church of England ordained about thirty men a year from St Bee's college in Cumbria through most of the second half of the nineteenth century, but this was always seen as a regrettable necessity to staff the mountain parishes of Wales and the north of England, and individual bishops in the south quite often made a general ruling against ordaining nongraduates.[11]

There is a case to be considered here. Would it have been better, or would it have been possible, to give a university education to every young man with a calling to the ministry? Funds were set up to help deserving ordinands through university, but it was very expensive, the relevance of the subjects studied was not very obvious, and such an option could not help but be a target for worldly ambition. But otherwise only those with enough money to pay for an expensive education could hope to be ordained. The Society of the Sacred Mission came into the business of providing a non-university training for clergymen just when St Bee's was closed, and had to struggle against the same prejudice. It is worth comparing the style of the two colleges. Kelham had the advantage of being backed by the Anglo-Catholic wing of the church; St Bee's was middle-of-the-road. Kelham was rural, but deliberately on a good transport network; St Bee's, in a coastal village in Cumbria, was, to a southerner, utterly remote. Kelham was residential, and shaped its men by its corporate life; St Bee's men lived in licensed lodging houses in the village. Kelham was fiercely selective, and turned down most applicants; St Bee's would take almost anyone who could pay the fees. (There was never at Kelham a stream of 'harum-scarum Oxonians' who, having failed orthodox routes to ordination, fell back on this). Kelham had its own curriculum, and its own approach to theology; St Bee's existed to get men through examinations set, and marked, elsewhere. But both colleges served to provide a nongraduate ministry; and doubtless many of the St Bee's men were good and useful.

There were other theological colleges. Some of them recruited some carefully selected nongraduates. Father Kelly was almost certainly right in saying that they were 'very largely recruited from a rather thin stratum of the public schools which just falls short of the means normally required for a university'.[12] Means mattered: part of Kelham's publicity was comparative tables of how much a training cost at different institutions:

Table of Finance (from *The Church and the Ordination Question* 1907)

Institution Cost	Personal Expenses	Holidays	Course in Years	Residence Weeks	(Total)
Oxford and Cambridge					
£100	Inclusive	Exclusive	3	24	£500
Graduate Theological College					
£120	E★	E★	1	32	
New University					
£72	E★	E★	4	27	£400
Mirfield					
£65	Entire Maintenance (except clothes)		5	47	£325
Non-Graduate Theological College – Home Service					
£100–75	E★	E★	2	31	£250–200
Missionary					
£60–40	E★	E★	2	32	£170–130
Kelham					
£41	Entire Maintenance		6 (av)	42	£250

Nothing could be as cheap as a missionary college, but Kelham was undoubtedly a bargain for a complete training.

Among theological colleges, perhaps Birkenhead was somewhat less class-bound. That college, St Aidan's, Birkenhead, was, unlike St Bee's, residential. It foreshadowed twentieth century practice by laying the emphasis on pastoral training, with three hours on three days a week spent visiting:

> '. . . when he is going from house to house with these questions brought out into practical everyday life, it makes him understand the books much better.'[13]

It also foreshadowed later practice in recruiting mature students. A majority of its students were aged over 24.[14]

Kelham, under Father Kelly, did not believe in what was implied by 'practical' over against theoretical work.

> If we split life up into religious sections, moral sections, business sections, it is plain God does not; nor does he make that possible for most people . . .
> For just these reasons, we did not make any severance of

study and 'practical work', such as preaching or visiting. Indeed, it seemed to us wrong that a student should be set to teach others before he had learnt to understand himself.[15]

They felt strongly about this: '. . . visiting or preaching *for practice* . . . is detestable – an insult to the poor, and ruinous to the men.' [16] Here, as often happens, the reader might find Kelly's theology admirable and edifying, but realise that the decision that Kelly takes on what to do next contradicts much modern practice. Father Kelly persisted: he held the same ideas twenty years later.

> [It is] better and easier to learn to understand with books, which are very patient, rather than with the living souls for whom you are responsible . . .[17]

Only at the very end of the college's history were concessions made on this point.

Also contradictory of modern practice was the decision to recruit boys. From 1895 they took 16-year-olds, and indeed quite often 15-year-olds. At that age, in the social class Kelly was recruiting from, they had left school. If they were entering the Army, or government service, they would join then. Was hanging around for three years clerking in offices any advantage? They would then have three years missed education to catch up on. 'Every year after 16 is an irreparable loss.' [18] If what the church wanted was 'general culture', then the boys would get their Latin and Greek at Kelham.

> Secondly, which is far more important, we lose the freshness and whole-heartedness of a boy's first choice. There is a common idea that first choices, which are necessarily ignorant choices, are less true than second choices made after experience. On the side of theory, this looks obvious, but it is entirely opposed to experience. God, anyhow, has not made his world that way. The success of any choice depends far less upon its entire wisdom than on our entire devotion to it.[19]

It seemed to work; there were academic advantages in not having to re-start study; those who had come as boys were less likely to drop out, and were more likely to be the very best of the college's output, 'taking all characters together,

intellectual power, moral force and entire devotion'.[20]
One might have some questions what it did to a boy to fail
in that system. There was of course the precedent of
Roman Catholic junior seminaries, probably not an encouraging one to anxious parents. 'An indignant father' wrote
in 1899:

> If you and the rest of the confraternity of childstealers had
> their deserts ... your house would be burned to the
> ground.[21]

Also, when Kelham seems, in some details of its life,
reminiscent of a tougher boys boarding school, one should
remember that about half the intake were boys of 15 or 16.
For most of the history of Kelham, the boys were dressed
in shorts.[22]

Kelham, and even more Vassall Road and Mildenhall
before it, was a very youthful institution. The boys being
there did not merely affect the average age.

> ... the presence of boys has been a distinct gain to us. The
> simple enthusiasm and unquestioning delight with which
> they accepted the life have helped immeasurably to raise
> the whole tone of the house.[23] ... [it] adds an element of
> gentle brotherliness which is wanted in a house exclusively
> male.[24]

Apart from Kelly himself, the college only gradually found
a permanent teaching staff. It tended to be local curates, or
young men fresh from university. Kelly was very anxious
that it should not be a one-man-show, but very largely the
idea was his.

Unlike some other colleges, Kelham is not explained by
listing the examinations the students were prepared for.
However, there were external examinations to contend
with. From 1897 the boys were prepared for the 'Central
Entrance Examination for Theological Colleges'. This included the classical languages (a book of Caesar, a book of
Xenophon), logic, English history, Scripture, and a Greek
gospel.[25] With this as the official entrance requirement, it
is not surprising that St Bee's, and two other colleges, had
to close down. It was obviously designed to see that

candidates for the Anglican ministry at least had a grammar school education. The boys at Kelham did not begin courses in theology until they were nineteen. It took all their enthusiasm to see them through the preliminary course.

> Our own experience shows that in almost all cases that even the first stage, i.e. the Central Entrance year, is a very severe strain, a dead grind. Nothing is more striking than to see the change which comes over men when they are able to start their theology.[26]

At the end of the complete course, and not, as in some other colleges, piecemeal through it, the students sat the 'Universities' Preliminary Examination for Holy Orders'. The Kelham course was conspicuously not built round this 'drily linguistic and historical' examination, which non-graduates generally had little more than a 50% chance of passing.[27] The students passed it, and tended to be congratulated by the examiners on the serious thought they gave to the questions. It seems, none the less, to have been the sort of examination in which rote learning was likely to triumph.

Kelly was an entertaining and allusive teacher, with the sort of mind that in later years would delight archbishop William Temple. He would certainly have made a creditable professor of theology. What earns that sort of compliment however almost certainly was above the heads of most of his students. We shall deal later with Kelly's impact on theologians. Our concern here is how theology was taught to straightforward ordinands.

> Theological education has two main studies, dogmatics and history. The first of these is a science of abstract principles as they are in themselves. To the latter belongs the observation of the same as they are found commingled in actual life.. In principle the pure idea comes first; but in practice it is generally learnt first through facts.[28]

However understood, dogmatics and history have not played a large part in most Anglican courses training clergymen. Two-fifths of the Kelham course was spent studying Scripture; there is dogma and history in Scripture too.

> The English idea of theology in the 1890s was limited to Scriptural exegesis and some acquaintance with the controversies and councils of the early Church and the Christian fathers.[29]

Even scriptural exegesis can be more, or less, theological:

> What is known as criticism, geographical and Oriental illustration, take a somewhat secondary place as referring after all to details. The theological and philosophical, inner, or what is sometimes called mystical meaning is of first importance.[30]

But it would be hard to find a theological student elsewhere in England who had done four years of ecclesiastical history. This took them from Roman history to AD800 by the end of the second year, and to the Reformation by the end of the fourth year. There was no point of principle involved in getting no further than the Reformation. There was no specific teaching of English history:

> ... the ecclesiastical and intellectual movements of the Middle Ages are so entirely bred on the Continent that it is difficult to make their echo in this country even comprehensible to one who has no consecutive knowledge of what is passing elsewhere.[31]

One might mention that the Universities' Preliminary Examination covered church history only to AD350, apart from a section specifically on English church history.[32] These students at Kelham, taught all this material they would not be examined on, must have trusted their teachers.

Typically of a good teacher, he taught them not to do so.

> First, you will never learn anything till you have killed your memory; secondly, you should never believe a word I or anyone else say till you can see it for yourself.[33]

The effort was always to make them understand the issues at stake. The students had one class, on Greek or Latin, and one lecture a day, and the rest of the day they worked on the books.

> It is no use talking of ideals, admitting the importance of intellectual independence, individuality, and the like, if at the same time the student is required to attend and get up three or four lectures a day of assorted information, so that he has no time for reading anything but text-books. We are in fact making ourselves accomplices in the crime of setting his mind on the supposed requirements of an oncoming examination.[34]

The student should be able to guarantee five hours reading after the lecture, for it to be any use. An essay was due at the end of the week.

Kelly discovered at once that the Oxford style of lecturing, relying on the students taking notes of what was significant in the lecture, would not work. The preface to the duplicated Church History I gives a detailed history of the course. 'The earlier lectures were dictated, but from 1893 they were written, and copied by the class'. In time they became typed duplicated handouts, and there are shelves of them still. The last dated church history lecture was in September 1922. They were re-duplicated in 1928, with no serious re-writing, and an edition of 150 copies was retyped and re-duplicated 'without alteration' in the summer of 1951. There might be a question about a course where nothing was changed in thirty years, but in 1951 the old man was only dead a year, and the Church History course was seen as particularly his own creation.

These foolscap books of close typescript are not immediately enticing. The students were meant to go on from the set sections to find real books. Some of the lectures were actually published by Longmans, but basically they were simply for use in teaching. Summaries were given of each lecture; for example:

> *Lecture 10* Church Unity
> 1ff What makes a unit? 8ff Synods 9 Differences from modern formal procedure 10ff Primary object agreement: decisions secondary. Procedure legislative. 16ff Metropolitans[35]

This is characteristic of Kelly. He begins with wide philosophical questions, brings in modern comparisons, and
wants to find out what the people involved were trying to
do. Consider the philosophical questions, like 'What makes
a unit'?

> With the ordinary man the most obvious course seems to
> be to omit the advanced or philosophical part of the
> course ... Like a good many, or perhaps, most, obvious
> methods, it is radically wrong. The art of thinking is the
> one necessity a man needs to learn, certainly if he is to be a
> priest ... Furthermore, instead of being small the subject
> should be as large as possible. Main lines of meaning and
> effect interest him, and he can see their importance ... The
> greater, the more salient, the facts, the plainer, the more
> interesting, the meaning.[36]

Kelham naturally looked over his shoulder at the universities. There was a definite shift in its estimate of what it
saw. In the 1890s, when a lot of the teaching was being
done by young men fresh from the Oxford Schools, the
college was deferential. This was a cheap substitute for
slow learners. Even in 1901 they were proposing a 'small
hostel at Oxford or Cambridge' if someone would find
them 'another priest and £300 a year'.[37] Mirfield found
money to build a huge and magnificent student hostel at
Leeds, but nothing was forthcoming for SSM. Individual
bright students, who had completed the whole Kelham
course, like Gerald Murphy, went on to do degrees. Fr
Murphy, one of the first intake of boys, came back with a
degree in Moral Sciences from Cambridge to be a somewhat incomprehensible lecturer at Kelham. Others went
on to degrees, and did not come back, and the Society felt
aggrieved.

As the SSM, and its students, gained in confidence, the
comparison with Oxford and Cambridge grew sharper.
Most Kelham men had ordinary gifts, and they learnt
slowly. But the truth was that most graduates of Oxford
and Cambridge, apart from the high-fliers, were just the
same. The men who got pass degrees, or low grades of
honours, Thirds or Fourths, had middle-class accents and

more social skills than Kelham men, but they were no cleverer. Most of the ordinands from these universities fell into this category. The universities, to their shame, taught above the heads of these students, and then gave them degrees for memorising some basic books, and reproducing in examinations this half-remembered, scarcely-digested rehash. Kelly quoted with glee the don who said:

> There is no greater educational fraud palmed off on the British public than the pass degree.[38]

It is worth asking whether the English degree system, based on the transferability of the skills of narrow specialist work, is right for students of average attainment.[39]

It was not merely the academic side of college life at Oxford and Cambridge that was damagingly élitist, in Kelly's view. There is the natural thought that university life is not merely study. A rowing Blue is worth more than a degree in many circles. But there were élitisms there too. Colleges scarcely worked for many students. In a college, '30% would constitute the college . . . 40% [would belong] to sets of their own . . . 30% [would be] mere outsiders and belong to nothing'[40]. If Kelham, or Kelham-style, men were to go to such colleges, they would be lost. It would merely 'increase the percentage of the lower strata' because it is 'Public School boys [who] constitute the nucleus of a College. So far, we believe, Mirfield cordially agrees'.[41] Kelham, with its totally structured existence, did not have spectators on the fringe. Everything that could be done to break down the experience of 'them and us' was done.

Thus far Kelham had lost confidence in the practical results of a university degree for most students. There were, after all, practical results of the Kelham scheme, where ordinary students were doing work that matched good honours work at a university.

> Examiner: 'The system produces in quite ordinary men the kind of work we here (at Oxford) expect and get only from high honours men'.[42]

By 1908, Kelham no longer saw its position as one of contrasting practice. There was principle involved. Theol-

Fr Kelly with the Corean Missionary Brotherhood in 1892 and 1893.

The Young HHK.

Archdeacon Woodward with Br Russell and Br Moffatt in Zanzibar.

Mr Hebert's junior Greek class, 1920.

Swimming.

Kelham refectory – note the state of the walls.

Lay-brothers, *c.*1915 – if I said they were curates of Portsea, would you know

ogy, or perhaps better, theological studies, as taught at the English universities, was 'altogether a false method for the training of the clergy'.[43] The universities had their characteristic method of handling every subject. At a university

> ... the theological student deals with facts belonging to his own theological sphere, exactly as the students of politics, philosophy and natural science deal with theirs. [But] ... Theology is not the science of one group of facts, and it has no sphere which can in the sense of limitation be called its own. [It is] the science of life as a whole ... or the wholeness of life.[44]

Here is a typical Kelham theology. 'Christianity ... of which Theology is the science, does not proceed towards Unity; it begins with it.'[45] As we can see, Kelham (and Vassall Road and Mildenhall) had been working as an institution for some time, before its characteristic practice was defined as the true method of doing theology. It might look like a rationalisation of practice. On the other hand, one might well say that Barthian neo-orthodoxy, which makes a very similar theological statement, never carried it through to change the ways of divinity faculties. Kelly was perhaps right:

> How can an idea so new be really set before the Church ... If I publish my Dogmatics will that do? If we could gain the Professional [sic] Chairs of both Universities, will this avail? The mere mention shows the absurdity. Nothing will do it, except doing it.[46]

Theology as done in universities starts from the wrong place and employs the wrong method. Even [if]

> ... he has taken his 'Arts' degree in Theological subjects, it still remains that a study of theological subjects is not Theology.[47]

Theology is 'the science of life as a whole', so in your studies you start from the basic principle of the will of God, and everything works out from there. There are theologies reminiscent of this, but not systems of teaching theology. In practice, it worked very well with less gifted students, who could see that things were at stake in what they were discussing. Perhaps it made Kelham men cocky, because they had a key that unlocked every door. Perhaps theology does; we must now turn to investigate this theology.

Chapter Five

Kelham Theology

'So you're at Westcott House,' he said.
'Yes, Father.'
'I envy B.K.'
'Why, Father?'
'He's dead.'
There was a pause. I waited to see what he would say next.
'I can't forgive B.K. for turning out all those young men
who haven't got a gospel.'[1]

This is the 'old man', Father Kelly, on another great trainer
of clergymen. Theological college principals, like headmas-
ters, easily become the focus of a personality cult. Did they
really have such an influence on the students they taught?
Westcott House, under B.K.Cunningham, became, more
than any other theological college, a school for bishops.
Perhaps a good theological college principal can bring out
the gifts that win men promotion. Not that B.K.Cunning-
ham was trying to make bishops; he was remembered by
his students as holy and humble. He may well have been
humble: he never became a bishop himself, and successful
principals of Westcott House do. Some students hoped that
his niceness rubbed off on them. Now no-one ever considered Fr Kelly for an English bishopric. When the time

came to move on from running the college at Kelham, he found some lecturing in a theological college in Japan, which he loved, but it could scarcely count as promotion.

Kelly was somewhat shorter on niceness than B.K.Cunningham. He was often snappy. What sort of answer can anyone expect who wishes himself dead? Perhaps unanswerable sayings are in some way a deaf man's kindness. The listener is spared from shouting commonplaces. What about 'young men who haven't got a gospel'? It is the Evangelical party which traditionally makes 'gospel' the touchstone: a sermon with 'not enough gospel in it to save a tomtit'. Father Kelly had been principal of a theological college widely perceived as Anglo-Catholic, and aroused suspicion among Anglo-Catholics by fraternising in the liberal SCM (Student Christian Movement). There he raised Catholic questions for many Protestants, but here he is raising what is on the face of it a Protestant question.

It is easier said than done to combine the strengths of the different traditions found in Anglicanism. It is commonplace among bishops, and, it might be said, among the products of Westcott House, to try to, and to end in charming blandness. Westcott's formula was the naturalness of the English gentleman, avoiding any hint of clerical professionalism. Gentlemen are above party divides. In any case, quite frequently good people in one tradition have surprising elective affinities with good people in others. Patterns of wickedness also recur. Thus any liberal will notice at once the hard busy worldliness in common between some Roman Catholic bishops and television evangelists. There are also sins that include liberals as well as others, like cheerful intolerance. It is too easy and bland, especially of the uneasy and unbland Father Kelly, to say that he combined the best of three traditions in Anglicanism, Catholicism, Liberalism, and Evangelicalism.

There is a tension in the very notion of a theological tradition. A theology is a matter of thinking; a tradition manages quite well when it is unthinking. Quite properly and innocently, colleges which are called theological colleges largely serve to inculcate habits of response and practice within a tradition. Arguing about ideas seems somehow adolescent, and there are deeper things to do. There is a real difficulty here. When people have tacit house-rules that forbid argument, one's first thought is that they have closed minds, and are protecting an orthodox party line. There are orthodoxies, and people are protective, but there is something more positive than this. In every tradition something else is needed than a party line that is a simple set of answers that can be memorised. If it were merely a matter of getting the answers right, then the real expense of a theological college is not called for. But the notion of training clergy simply in a school of thought, by, for example, setting essays on a correspondence course, rouses deep and natural suspicion. It was not even an option at the beginning of the century. The shared life of a college, then and since, is very important. Now Father Kelly was an ideas man, and he wanted his students to think through their theology. There lies one pole of the tension. On the other hand, Kelham, and also the Australian SSM college, St Michael's House, was a life. Student after grateful student said that most of the lectures were not much use, but that living in a community had changed them. Kelham had all the marks of a 'total' community, and 'total' communities have very strong traditions.

In a petty sense, thus, it is very easy for a theological college to develop its own way of doing theology. Catch-phrases will be repeated, especially if there is someone like Father Kelly, with a pungent turn of phrase. The SSM has its *Principles*, a little pamphlet almost short enough to memorise, full of stern aphorisms, and Kelham men (and St Michael's House men) are likely to quote them. Consider *XIV Concerning Choice of Work*.

> You may not choose your work; indeed count not yourself worthy of any work.

> You may prefer, however, that which is most dangerous, least notable, least popular. There will generally be room for you here.

> Seek that which is lowest and most servile. This you can nearly always do safely.

Many read of washing the disciples' feet, who think themselves above cleaning another man's boots.

It is better to serve the least esteemed than the great . . .

If however, you should be called to high and spiritual
work, you may indeed fear and tremble, but you are not
permitted to refuse as though you doubted your own
powers, for you ought to be quite sure of your own
incapacity – and of God's strength.

How he undercuts self-confidence. We must come to a
sense of our own failure, recognise how much of human
life, of religious life, is 'bragging'. Things like this earned
him the label Augustinian. It is not a promising adjective,
as the great doctor of grace has become a patron for cynics
and pessimists. Probably the required self-forgetfulness,
insofar as it could be learnt, was learnt in the habits of
obedience of a wellrun institution, rather than in thinking
out the implications concerning choice of work. There are
kindred spiritualities elsewhere in Western Christianity.
They may make us want to raise questions, but, as a
prescription for happiness, they have their successes. Naturally, following this line of thought, those who look for
happiness do not get it.

For here is the paradox – the ostensible objects of the
player – runs, goals, or what not – are quite secondary
both to the joy and to the value of the game; nevertheless,
if the player does not keep his attention fixed on the lesser
matter of making runs and so forth, the resultant experience
is not likely to be soothing to his feelings, nor will it give
uplift to his character.[2]

This is an example of 'theological football'. Actually here it
is both cricket and football, but Kelham preferred football.
At Kelham they took games seriously, and theologised
about them. If you were losing matches that you should
have won, then this was evidence of a spiritual malaise.

'If your football has anything to do with the love of God,
it will rot it, for the better you play, the more you will be
pleased with yourself – therefore the less with God; but if

your love of God has anything to do with your football, it will buck it no end'.[3]

I am not yet clear how the reversal of 'anything to do' makes the difference, but something comes across. Everyone knows that a game is only a game, but then all human activities are, first, to be taken seriously, and second, not to be taken seriously. The paradox is typical of Father Kelly. Now the public schools of England in the late nineteenth century developed a cult of games. Sometimes one feels that Kelham, with its intake of fifteen-year-olds, and its compulsory games, is too near English public schools. Perhaps the difference is that Kelham also had a cult of pigs.

> 'Come, and I will show you my proofs of the existence of God.' (What I actually said was 'proofs of the Resurrection' . . .) . . . I love pigs. They are so delightfully ugly, and so blissfully self-satisfied over it. . . . Is there a God who understands that bundle of incompetence and commonplace, ugliness and self-satisfaction, which makes the most obvious 'experiences' of the sublime thing I call my personality? Can he make any use or sense of it, even if he smiles a bit over its funny absurdities as I like to think he did over the pigs?[4]

A cult of games as such finds beauty and mastery, which are there, in games well played. God is manifest in beauty and mastery. Father Kelly rubbed home the fact that unless God is concerned with the ugly and the humdrum, there is no hope for most of us. Perhaps any hesitancy we may feel here is simply more evidence of pride, but in some ways there is something unhappy about Kelly's line of thought here. One might like pigs without feeling oneself as roughly equivalent to pigswill. 'Incompetence and commonplace, ugliness and self-satisfaction': the Rule devised for the Society of the Sacred Mission is anything but evidence of incompetence; the nearest Fr Kelly's prose gets to the commonplace is its use of pungent slang for effect; his face, full of life and sensitivity and wisdom, is not ugly in any obvious way; and self-satisfaction scarcely describes the phrase we are looking at. Yet, on a dark day, phrases like these speak home to many of us, and it is good to think God loves us then.

Perhaps this low self-esteem is Anglican. 'There is no health in us', says the Prayer Book. There is far more self-distrust in Fr Benson, the founder of the Cowley Fathers, and Kelham enjoyed a sense of being cheerful and worldly compared with Cowley.

> I do not want even to seem to criticize religious societies such as Cowley . . . but it must be plain that for this which we set before us, this of which we are to be witnesses, a system of perfected devotion, a system involving some specific separation from the normal life of the Church is no use at all. We cannot be ascetics.[5]

It is not easy to compare the theological ethos of one community or college with that of another. More can be done with the theology actually taught. When the Society of the Sacred Mission in the 1890s began training ordinands, its candidates had to be put in for the University Preliminary examination for Holy Orders. Consider the faults of that examination in the eyes of Father Kelly. The general Church History paper stopped at the fourth century. The only church history to be examined afterwards was English church history. There was no general paper on liturgy, merely one on the Prayer Book. The nearest thing to dogmatic theology was the history of the Creeds and the 39 Articles. Kelham, from the first, wanted to go further. English history and English liturgy were incomprehensible apart from the wider context. This is a catholic insight (in the wide sense of world Christianity against simply English), yet Anglo-Catholic theological colleges, in their formal teaching, were all the same satisfied with teaching for the University Preliminary examination, the standard model for English theological colleges.

As so often in the world of education, the standard model was very reminiscent of a course that had worked for more senior and more gifted students. Thus one meets school-children being taken through the outline of what their teacher was taken through as an undergraduate. In this case, the University Preliminary examination, and the theological college courses, were deeply indebted to the Oxford honours school in theology. Many of the staff of theological colleges were Oxford graduates, and though they might be party churchmen, eager to train clergy in their own tradition, yet it was the ethos of the college, rather than the content of the course, that would do this. The world of examinations, often a world of coaching students half-heartedly through subjects experienced as drily incomprehensible and irrelevant, was not central to the real scheme of values of theological colleges. There was a high turnover in theological college staff, and most were young recent graduates, just the sort of people who re-use their undergraduate notes.

Fr Kelly had a simple belief that theology mattered. When he managed to persuade his students that it did, the rest of the world decided he was a brilliant teacher. They were not in practice, however, convinced that theology did matter. Here is B.K.Cunningham himself:

> . . . the only thing of the kind at present to be found in the Church of England is 'Kelham', but this is the wonderful creation of an educational genius, and no church can afford to sit still and wait for a succession of Father Kellys.[6]

The unspoken message there is that the Kelham course has nothing worth copying, because it only works in the hands of an educational genius. Kelly was quite convinced of his own utter ordinariness. Both were wrong.

Kelham theology did not issue fully-blown from Fr Kelly's head. Here, for example, is an early model. In 1901 in the Dogmatics course, they were using Aquinas for natural theology – the Divine Nature, Ethics, Creation, the nature of man – and Maurice for revealed theology – the Incarnation, at least partly, the Church and the Sacraments. There was, as there would have been at Oxford, a great deal of the Early Fathers of the church. Most of the students had read some Gibbon, whose non-supernatural explanation of the rise of Christianity makes Christians think, which Fr Kelly wanted. They all had used the Dictionary of Christian Biography, which was more than a handy reference work. There was also Bigg's standard book on the Christian Platonists of Alexandria. Fr Kelly was worried that they were not reading enough of the primary sources. To counteract this as they learnt the language in the Latin class they could be set chunks of the Latin fathers: Augustine's *De Fide et Symbolo* and the *Commonitorium* of Vincent of Lérins. What one might conclude from this is that the Oxford model still prevailed, except that it was followed with zest and fewer short-cuts than one might expect in a theological college for nongraduates. They were also reading the sub-Hegelian British theology of the time, the Cairds and Illingworth.[7] There were hints of Fr Kelly's own line. A Quarterly Report in any case might be expected to name-drop a little. It is so tempting to see Fr Kelly as always an elderly *enfant terrible*; in fact, as a principal of a college, he could be crisply competent and indeed very nearly bland. There is a real difference in mood between the self-doubt of the *Principles* and the cheerful success-story of the reports for public consumption.

However, 'I was expected to follow the customary system. I never dreamt of doing so . . .'[8] His students would do real theology. A type of theology prevalent at the time was a Liberal Protestant 'essence of Christianity', which was fashionable in England as well as in Germany. Kelly, without being too dismissive, can explain the temptations of Ritschl, and refuse them. Ritschl drew a sharp contrast between facts and values. For facts we look to scientists, but what makes us human is our capacity to give value to things, in particular, to give divine value to the man Jesus. For Fr Kelly, this throws us back in the end on our subjectivity, which is no use. We have to be able to know we are dealing with realities, with the living God.

Fr Kelly was himself a theologian. There are, of course, professional theologians, who are chartered to think. They publish books. Fr Kelly wrote a few books, contributions to collections, and learned journals. Some of his liveliest writing went into the *SSM Quarterly*. Naturally enough, several of the earlier books are explaining what the Society of the Sacred Mission stands for: *The History of a Religious*

Idea (1898), and *Aims and Methods of Theological Study*, and *An Idea in the Working* (1908). He tried publishing a history book, covering the first five centuries, *The History of the Church of Christ* in 1901–2, but it failed. His later unpublished church history notes were much more worthwhile. He wrote two little books, relevant in their day, *England and the Church* (1902), and *The Church and Religious Unity* (1913). Then he went to Japan, and came back a prematurely old man, to tremendous strife in the Society. In 1928, however, he published what was probably his best book, *The Gospel of God*, and *Catholicity* in 1932.[9]

It is worthwhile looking more closely at *the Gospel of God*. This book, first published in 1928, is a short work, of just over a hundred pages. The real scholarship is worn lightly: there are no footnotes, no index and no bibliography. Fr Kelly also tends to quote from memory, and hence in paraphrase. His style is rather slangy, lively and pungent. He is eager for us to understand, so he will go back again to philosophical first principles (the Many and the One), then try concrete illustrations, with a moral pointedness that brings things home to the reader's conscience.

'I am trying to write a book about God, and the place God has in our life' is the opening sentence. He says at once that God is distinct from religion. This is not just because he thinks his readers may be suspicious of religion. He himself distrusts religion because it is man-made. Well on in the book, after a review of man's search for meaning, indeed man's search for God, he says:

> The answer cannot be something which comes from, and thereby is the expression of, ourselves. It must be something which comes *to* us; a Gospel which is preached to us, and preached to all.[10]

Nevertheless, he starts from human experience. He is scathing, to the point of injustice, about a Christianity of religious experience, the 'self-centred, anti-cosmological religionism of Ritschl and Harnack'. [11] He distrusts a religion of private feeling which opts out of saying there is a God who rules the earth. If, in fact, much of the book talks about the human condition rather than directly about

God, it is about the desperateness of the human condition.
He was criticised for this, and in a prefatory note to the
second edition he quotes with approval the suggestion 'Do
tell people to read the last two chapters first'. These,
chapters Six and Seven, are on 'God and the Soul' and
'The Gospel', and bring the good news needed to those
who have found their lack.

He starts from how useless life is without a purpose. If we
go out to enjoy ourselves, we are bored.

> If you seek this enjoyment and fun in themselves, you will
> never get more than spoonsful. This is called 'enjoying
> oneself', and the self is not worth enjoying. So is life made
> that all real joy begins from forgetting the self for some-
> thing better worth going after.[12]

Our hope lies in self-forgetfulness. Only thus can we see
things in context.

> Man – and I am speaking here of the simplest and common-
> est human soul – is in himself a whole infinite, made for
> the infinite, yet by himself a small fragment, astray in a
> vast universe.

> Man, infinite in his ideals and purposes, is yet so petty in
> achievement. Infinite in our aspirations and possibilities, do
> we not know ourselves in the paltriness of our motives?[13]

The motives of all of us are under question. Fr Kelly
worried about ordinary people. What are the chances of
'the simplest and commonest human soul'? The phrase has
slight overtones of Victorian hierarchy. Though Fr Kelly
wrote 'the notion of any *radical* difference between rich
and poor.. filled me with horror' he can say, in the same
sentence, that 'it is a sheer fact to be faced that people differ
immensely in sensibility, as in capacity, for ideals'.[14] He
did not despise people, and tried very hard to speak honestly and relevantly to the condition of the simple and
common. Consider how to talk about the carpenter.

> He lounged over, took the axe out of my hand, worked
> the stone himself, and in five minutes put an edge on that
> axe, such as little amateurs are allowed to dream of on
> Sundays, if they've been good. I never asked that carpenter

what his ideals in life were. I doubt he would have known what I was talking about, and I do not think the answer would have been helpful in an ethical book, but he and I are friends, so to speak; also he is a very good carpenter.

I have more ideals than you need listen to just now. A really sharp axe is one of them, but I cannot sharpen an axe and he can.[15]

Kelly and the carpenter were friends. I suspect the carpenter would have died for Kelly. But when Kelly tries to write theology about him I feel the writing is embarrassed, and joking because it is embarrassed. It is reminiscent of Kipling, the humble little narrator entering private worlds, taking people at their own evaluation, being one of the boys, and yet we never quite forget that he is a distinguished novelist and they are merely grist to the mill. The realer the carpenter is, the more difficult to draw morals from him as if he were not there.

If, in the end, Fr Kelly is not patronising, this is because he undercuts all the achievements of the élite who have ideals, particularly religious ones. '. . . it is a very disastrous thing indeed if our Christian faith turns out to be a Gospel only to the rich – in ideals.'[16] The arguments he uses for undercutting idealism come from 'practical' people. The 'practical' are not the inarticulate, the carpenters of this world, whom we can live with, but the worldly-wise, who have views, and will share them with us.

That attitude rather annoys us, because it is so definitely opposed to our own. It seems to provide a shelter for the merely selfish conservatism of the well-satisfied. But many of these anti-idealists are extraordinarily good people with a very high sense of duty.[17]

He tries so hard to be fair, particularly to people whom he dislikes. The worldly-wise have a point: it is sadly true that there is a great deal of self-indulgence in idealism, and conflicting ideals seem to do more damage than simple worldliness.

What do we do when confronted with conflict, especially the conflict of ideals? As so often in his teaching, he goes

back to the very first principles of ancient Greek philosophy, 'unity and difference'. There is in the end a resolution
of the problem of the Many and the One. There is an
over-arching unity; it is we who see things wrong. We see
things wrong because in our way of seeing everything is
centred on us, what he calls 'the illusion of the horizon'.
'. . . the world appears as a circle drawn round you as its
centre'.[18] Observe that this is the way we are made; our
field of vision has a horizon. The horizon is not really
there, a line at the end of the world, any more than the end
of the rainbow is there on the ground in the next field but
one, but in that case 'The illusion of the horizon is the
illusion of personality'.[19]

These are challenging ideas. He is anxious that we should
argue them through. Fr Kelly trusts his readers to be able
to follow an argument honestly. The human reason can be
objective.

> . . . it is quite plain to us that this order of things is not
> intelligible just in itself, in the shape in which it presents
> itself.
> . . . It can be understood only by virtue of something
> beyond itself, which contains the perfection, the complete-
> ness, the actuality, of what in the existing world is plainly
> an incompleteness, a possibility – . . .
> This assumption, this 'faith', is to us a matter of life and
> death, intellectually and morally.. I call it a matter of
> 'faith', but it is also good solid reasoning.. for faith is the
> acceptance, the trust, the basing of action, upon what is
> reasonable, even if our reason is inadequate to its full com-
> prehension.[20]

'Grace perfects nature': Fr Kelly here has a confident
natural theology, basing action upon what is reasonable.
This modest self-reliance – 'inadequate to its full comprehension' – is in the Thomist tradition. It is built into a chapter
on religion in general, something, we remember, he distrusts. He talks about the religious experience of the
'forest-savage', and his authority is C.C.J.Webb:

> . . . as the hidden power is dislodged from totem, mountain,
> wizard, we discover that we have been seeking throughout

after nothing less than the Ultimate Reality. The attempt to identify God with the Absolute is religion.

'Man's search for the Absolute' is perhaps rather a philo-sophical phrasing for what is going on in religion. C.C.J.Webb (1865–1954), was the first Professor of the Philosophy of the Christian Religion at Oxford, steeped in the *philosophia perennis* (the perennial philosophy found in all religions). There is a useful tension in Kelly's book between quite a fully-developed philosophical natural theol-ogy and a 'Barthian' rejection of all man's search. 'The answer is not reached but given, and by quite another road.'[21]

God is 'Some-one actually existent',[22] a Reality. Fr Kelly has worries about the word 'reality', which is too abstract. And God actually does things.

> We worship God, seek after God, because we recognise that he is, that what he does is, much the biggest and most real factor in life.[23]

'Does God do anything?'[24] (a Kelly catch-phrase). '– the Ultimate Will has reality first of all as power'.[25] Something is real that can produce real results. He holds up for inspection and mockery theologies of a good-natured but inadequate God. But if God shows himself in power, then why is the world filled with wickedness? What has gone wrong?

Kelly will not settle for the solution of the problem of evil which opts out of the world of dire facts into the nicer world of eternal values, or the Kantian world of 'practical' reason, where our experience makes things true enough. There is something sane and brave in saying 'our estimates of good shall be held secondary to the question of fact and truth'.[26] Value judgements are useless until we know the facts; they do not have priority over facts. Not that we shall get the whole truth: 'The reality of truth and the reality of experience, therefore, stand apart . . .'[27] Living the Christian life is a matter of struggling with this, and 'trying to understand what God does and to bring our judgement into accordance with his'.[28]

Part of this involves confronting the problem of suffering.
This is partly what theodicy does. He has some sobering
ideas about how the world is, and must be.

> It rather sets me wondering whether there is any very solid
> meaning for an individual good. This is a 'good' tree and
> growing well, but is it evil that so few acorns ever get a
> chance? The pigs eat a good many. The swallow is a thing
> of beauty, and it eats a lot of flies. We have plenty to spare
> . . . If you do not drown your kittens, they will starve, and
> an over-stocked rabbit-warren is not a cheery sight. Nature
> works out a great whole order, by a method we call
> natural selection . . . birth involves death.[29]

This is a sombre realism, discovering the way things are on
the best Malthusian (or are they Darwinian?) principles.
Our own human self-importance is challenged. Are we
better than the animals? Looking at human history, and
looking at ourselves, there is something there that deserves
to be challenged.

> Brothers dear, where have we got to? . . . Are we so
> entirely lords of all things that it is up to us to grant God a
> place in his own universe if he can bring a good character?
> Is the Gospel message nothing more than this: that 'God is
> niceness, and in him is nothing nasty at all'? If so, are we
> not making God in our own image? . . . in what possible
> sense can we say that we believe in him? Surely it is for
> him to believe in us?[30]

And, like Augustine, he returns to the fact of human sin.
As usual, liberal healthy-mindedness is his chosen target.
People do say such cocky things: '. . . I may be able to
stand and look him in the face and say – I am a worthless
servant, I have not done much, but I have brought you a
character.' [31] Original sin is a fact of life, and it all boils
down to the self. The 'principle of sin' is the self: we
cannot but be self-centred. It is back to that idea of the
horizon again. 'The moment I grasp a purpose, it is my
purpose'.[32] 'The self is with you, dominating everything
you do, every step of the way' [33]. It is reminiscent of
Luther, and justification by faith alone. There is something
of gentle mockery too, of our irrepressible self-importance.

So, though there is a question, what are we to do, the other question, 'what God does with us, must be in the very nature of things, and is in fact, always final, and at each step decisive?' [34] This is a book about God, and the place God has in our lives. We had better believe and be baptised. These are straightforward things, not great accomplishments of human faithfulness, and all will not be made plain. The great matter is that God has found us.

The final chapter 'The Gospel' says something of what 'God has found us' means. 'What follows are mere orthodoxies, which I kept back till we were sure we wanted them'.[35] He starts with the Athanasian Creed, 'the most discredited of all orthodoxies': '. . . the first need is that he should hold fast the Catholic Faith' [36]. Salvation means wholeness, or health, 'a certain necessary rightness' and Catholic means 'the same for everybody' [37]. He then speaks of redemption, primarily 'a story of what happened'.

God 'hath in this last of days spoken unto us by his Son'.. 'Spoke' – this is not a Dialogue of the Soul with God'.[38] Kelly, typically, rules out our religiousness. And redemption deals with our limitation, our fragmentation, our inability to cope with the divine unity.

> In the crucifixion, every factor of life, every contradiction, opposition, dualism, can be found . . . Name what you like. Authority and freedom; democracy and autocracy; predestination and free-will; the things of God and the things of Caesar; socialism and individualism (any more)? . . . Everything is there; it is an at-one-ment of them all.[39]

How it atones them all is a matter of faith, and we do not understand it all at once. But faith insists the cross is relevant to these matters. Moreover, it is not only high matters such as these that God has a hand in, and not only in the cross. Kelly takes a passage of Chronicles, 'having', according to the commentary he quotes, 'a low degree of inspiration', of lists of unknown Israelites,

> ordinary unseeing people, like you and me. Probably they also had a low degree of inspiration, carrying on as they

> could while God prepared his time for . . . Jesus, who is
> called the Christ.
>
> Thus, while the Gospel is essentially an eternal Gospel, it is
> no less essentially the story of an incident in which that
> purpose was manifested . . .[40]

Thus history, including much ordinary history, like our
own, is what God has done. This is the Gospel of God.

No theologian, however productive, can teach and set
examinations solely on the contents of his own books. If
Kelly was to teach theology he had to find books, beyond
'Browne on the 39 Articles', indeed beyond Anglicanism.
What was available? Here, from the duplicated systematics
course De Deo [On God] 'Historical Theology' [41] is Fr
Kelly's account for his students of the books available.

> Of modern Anglican large scale Summas, Hall (U.S.A.) in
> 6 vols. is extraordinarily conventional, without any percep-
> tion that the theories have any real meaning. Possibly for
> that reason, he is quite useful as giving a short review of all
> the different theories, with the arguments for and against.

Kelly was in the habit of making sharp judgements on
books. Unless we know the books ourselves we cannot
really savour them. They are judgements that might appear
naughty to a more conventional mind. He continues:

> Bp Gore's 3 vols. are much coloured by his own peculiar
> Hegelianism derived through T.H.Green. Archbishop
> Temple's Mens Creatrix and Christus Veritas give a certain
> summary.
>
> Martenson's Dogmatics (Danish Lutheran) and Dorner's Prot-
> estant Theology (German Lutheran – mid 19C). There are
> highly modernist Summas by Brown (U.S.A.) and Saba-
> tier.
>
> In the late 19C there was a multitude of small books,
> beginning with Mason's Faith of the Gospel; Mortimer
> (Summary of Aquinas); D.Stone; T.B.Strong; Lacey; Spens
> Belief and Practice (very modernist in method and very
> 'Anglo-Catholic' in result). A little later, books of essays
> (by different writers) came in with the vogue of 'Short
> Stories'. The most influential was Lux Mundi under Gore.
> Contentio Veritatis was a non-Catholic Hegelianism (Rash-

dall). Then *Cambridge Essays* – under Swete – of the critical Westcott standard; *Foundations* and others under Streeter; finally *Essays Catholic and Critical*.

A list of names is at first opaque to readers. What evidence does it give us? In the list, he names, but with a dismissive aside about their Hegelianism or their modernism, the leading Anglo–Catholic theologians of his day, like Charles Gore and Darwell Stone and Will Spens. (If we do not recognise the names now, such is fame). He also sends the students, not merely to Harnack, but to other continental Protestant writers. There is evidence that this list was first drafted before the First World War, though some of the books are from later in the century. Those by Temple are from 1917 and 1924. 'Finally', and perhaps the 'finally' is significant, is *Essays Catholic and Critical* which came out in 1926. Later in Australia, Fr Snell put a question mark beside Fr Kelly's typical imaginative, rather flippant, connection between the taste for short stories and for volumes of collected theological essays.

Here it is worth making a point about the historical development of Kelham theology. Kelham students worked their way through duplicated type-written courses, like 'Doggies' (Dogmatics), of which the *De Deo* was a part, delivered as lectures. It is often worthwhile to turn through a student's copy, and read the record of Fr Kelly's *obiter dicta* that he has noted down on the blank page opposite. Normally on the first page of any edition of these notes there is a history of earlier editions. The continuity is greater than the change, and as we have already noticed the last Kelly edition, in the late 1920s, tended to become the canon. During the great days of Kelham, unlike other theological colleges, there was a set of Kelham notes, volumes of duplicated foolscap typescript, on all the subjects taught, which every former student had. Some had Latin titles, like *De Deo, De Homine, De Revelatione, de Trinitate*; some were rather slight, more marginal courses, like Fr Alfred Kelly's on *Hymns, History and Literature* with 17 pages; some of the preliminary courses had very little theology in them, like *Psychology and Logic*. But every

student could carry away a shelf-full of bound hand-outs.
That way lies the making of a Kelham theology. On the
face of it, this way lies a rigid Kelham orthodoxy. On the
other hand, in their content and their way of presenting
the material, these notes force the students to think for themselves.

> ... we are not merely asking – what did great thinkers
> intend by them, but what did they mean to common
> people like ourselves? It is not merely a question of theory
> – what ought people to think? It is a question of fact –
> what have they thought?[42]

The student is always sent back to ask questions. It may be
also that, because these are merely typescript notes, something of the risk of a canonised new authority line was
avoided.

Before the Society found Kelham, at the earlier colleges at
Vassall Road and Mildenhall, their students were using
non-Anglican set books, Aquinas and Harnack. The choice
of either of these was a matter of scandal to some Anglicans.
Could Anglicans use the official Roman Catholic systematics, or a liberal Lutheran history of dogma? Anglo-Catholics approved of the choice of Aquinas as a party gesture,
and the college grew as a party college. But Kelly chose
the books for use, and both were used. The possibility of
using both is perhaps a characteristically Anglican possibility, and the rationale for it Kelly found in F.D.Maurice.

It is easy to hold a *via media* Anglicanism, that says that
Catholics and Protestants are extremists, and the sensible
Anglicans are in the middle. Then one need only read
Anglican works. Thus 'our incomparable liturgy' is normally 'our uncompared liturgy'. A middle way appeals to
an Aristotelian mind. A Platonist mind knows that truth
lies in the extremes. What does this do to Anglicanism?
F.D.Maurice (1805–1872) was probably the greatest Anglican theologian of the Victorian age, and deeply indebted to
Plato. He came to see Platonism as essentially a matter of
uniting opposites: the *coincidentia oppositorum*. '.. there was a
way out of party opinions, which is not a compromise
between them, but which is implied in both, and of which

each is bearing witness.. Plato himself does not say it; he makes us feel it'.[43] There is something rather pleasantly reminiscent of this in Fr Kelly's expression of his debt to Maurice: 'I doubt if there is anything in my mind I did not get from him [Maurice], but, so to speak, unconsciously'.[44] It is a matter of one's perspective whether one finds either Aquinas or Harnack extreme; they are both very sane writers; but to read either, or better both, stretches Anglicans.

Maurice himself poses difficulties as a set book for students, and there is no strong evidence that many Kelham men read much of him. But Maurice was a digger – 'My business is to dig'[45] – and did try to get beyond verbal orthodoxies to the realities underneath. This can be done, perhaps, with a medieval thinker with medieval technical terms like Aquinas, in such a way that we can feel we are still loyal to his main thrust, while jettisoning the technicalities of his theology. But is this all that is happening when Maurice, who was eager for the reality of baptism, renounced any Roman idea of an *opus operatum* theory of baptism?

> . . . whenever any great spiritual principle has been strongly revealed to men, a material counterfeit of that principle has always appeared also . . .[46]

I suspect Harnack might agree with that. His slightly more kindly simile for Catholic concretions is that 'Like every living plant, religion only grows inside a bark'.[47] Maurice could wrestle with any theology, and get something good out of it. Sometimes one feels it is too much 'Jews and Greeks tutors unto Christ', and with Maurice everything finding its true fulfilment in Anglicanism, but certainly not with Anglican 'notions'. Fr Kelly said of Maurice:

> I learned from him, primarily, his faith in 'Realities', as distinct from what he called 'Notions' – the reality of God, and faith in God, as distinct from beliefs. I learnt from him that God is not the same as religion; that the Church and Sacraments were also realities, far greater than our theories about them; that the theories, even negative theories, were witnessing to positive realities.[48]

As soon as one looks at F.D.Maurice's writings, one can see that Fr Kelly is indebted to him. Here he is digging:

> The mere Conservative is indignant, because it [a 'digger's' line of thought] will not assume existing rules and opinions as an ultimate basis, but aims at discovering their meaning and their foundation.[49]

This is actually Maurice praising Coleridge's *The Friend*, and the realities that Coleridge discovered there were those that make society a living organism. Digging is a matter of discovering rather than inventing. In the great matter of God we must hope to discover rather than invent. But does the discovering eye hamper the doing hand? Consider what Ludlow, the active Christian Socialist, thought of Maurice's 'digging'.

> Surely the whole work of Christianity is building and not digging . . . it does seem to me that you are liable to be carried away by Platonistic dreams about an Order, and a Kingdom, and a Beauty, self-realised in their own eternity, and which so put to shame all earthly counterparts that it becomes labour lost to attempt anything like an earthly realisation of them, and all one has to do is to show them, were it only in glimpses, to others by tearing away the cobwebs of human systems that conceal them. I do not think this is Christianity.[50]

This is an admiring friend raising, rather sharply, a doubt about a theologian who still deserves to be remembered as a Christian Socialist. Maurice might have done more, but his work for working people was real and solid. The question will come up whether Kelham was insufficiently activist, and it may be that like Maurice, Fr Kelly was more interested in glimpses of divine 'givens' rather than our own gratifying achievements in building the Kingdom. Also, however, like Maurice, there were achievements by the way.

There is also to be found, a few lines on in the *Kingdom of Christ*, the reminder how what a man reads matters: 'a sense of the connexion between his own life and the books which he reads'. It would be difficult to say whether this sentence is from Kelly or from Maurice:

I have learnt in this way the preciousness of the simple
Creeds of antiquity; the inward witness which a gospel of
facts possesses, and which a gospel of notions must always
want; how the most awful and obscure truths, which
notions displace or obscure, are involved in facts, and
through facts may be entertained and embraced by those
who do not possess the faculty for comparing notions, and
have a blessed incapacity of resting in them.[51]

This is so like the theory of education in Fr Kelly, with his
well-founded confidence in what ordinary men are capable
of thinking through, if you give them time and deal with
real facts. As Coleridge says, though he is even less plausible
than Maurice as a teacher of working men,

> ... this highest truth [the doctrine of the Trinity], which
> he presents us as demanding the highest efforts of thought
> and abstraction, must belong to the very humblest man;
> ... must in some way or other be capable of being
> presented to him.[52]

As soon as Christianity turns to the Greeks, any high
doctrine of the Incarnation, like 'He was the original man,
the type of all creation ...',[53] is likely to use Platonic
language. There is a chapter in David Newsome's *Two
Classes of Men* on 'Plato and Incarnationalism', in which he
says:

> There was, then, in Cambridge during the nineteenth
> century a strong Platonic element, manifesting itself above
> all in an incarnational theology. Coleridge definitely influ-
> enced Julius Hare; both thinkers profoundly influenced
> F.D.Maurice. F.J.A.Hort acknowledged that he learnt
> much from Maurice; Westcott, according to his own testi-
> mony, learnt less because he did not wish to impair his
> own independent judgment. But his thought, which is
> Platonic through and through, belongs to the same *genre*.[54]

In an incarnationalist theology, the incarnate word, the
Logos, becomes assimilated to the Platonic 'ideas', which
are the eternal reality. Even when Maurice comes to explain
atonement, traditionally the other pole to incarnation in
nineteenth century thought, he says 'Become what you
are', because redemption is a matter of recognition, of

what 'the true order was and is, and ever will be'.[55]
Torben Christensen says:

> Maurice's polemic stand was ultimately founded upon an
> idea of revelation, which sought to unite the fundamentally
> ahistorical Platonic idea of reality with the Biblical concept
> of history. In the resulting fusion, however, Platonism
> became the decisive factor.[56]

This does not mean that Maurice had no sense of history.
Early in the *Kingdom of Christ*,[57] he speaks of learning
from Coleridge 'above all, to reverence the facts of history,
and to believe that the least perversion of them, for the
sake of getting a moral from them, is at once a folly and a
sin'. One thinks again how indispensable history is to the
Kelham scheme.

> The Gospel which is the beginning of Christianity is the
> beginning of a history in which the Power of God has
> been continuously shown. I do not say that it is necessary
> for everyone to study this history, but it is necessary for
> everyone to realise that it exists, and that this history
> constitutes the Holy Spirit's commentary or interpretation
> upon the meaning of the Gospel. And it is at least necessary
> that those who are to be teachers of the church should have
> studied history.[58]

Kelly tried harder with history than Maurice did. It may
well be that he achieved a constructive misreading of
Maurice. In this, one should say, he is followed by
H.G.Wood and archbishop A.M.Ramsey, who also stressed
the Biblical and historical rather than the Platonist and
ahistorical side of Maurice. In any case, even if we have to
admit incoherencies in Maurice's thought, there are in his
writings other depths than Platonist depths. Kelly used
Maurice unslavishly but well.

'What does God *do*? Does God do anything, or is God
only a name for our ideals?' These are typical questions
from Kelly. There is an article by Michael Ramsey, quoting
them, in the 1960 SSM Quarterly. The archbishop was one
of the rehabilitators of F.D.Maurice, and one might say
that there is a shared, almost official, Anglican way of
looking at things that includes Maurice and William

Temple (much influenced by Kelly) and Michael Ramsey. The evidence for Temple's debt to Kelly is in the chapter on the place of the SSM in the ecumenical movement. Dorothy Emmet, in the chapter on Temple the philosopher in Iremonger's *Life*,[59] speaks of 'that great teacher Father Herbert Kelly, S.S.M., to whom he often acknowledged his general indebtedness'. Consider the possibility that if Anglicanism cannot rest with Biblicism, or an agreed systematic, it may, at its best, have a sense of the living God who underlies orthodoxies.

Still, 'What does God do?' What God does is history. This is why there is so much history in the Kelham course, though historians seldom have a sense of God at work in history. This may be something wrong with the way we do history. One of Father Kelly's own ideas is that the first adult intellectual discipline we master masters us. This was his argument against the notion then prevalent of reading some other subject at university, and then coming to theology later at theological college. The first discipline remained the real and normative one. History as done in honours History Schools is fairly godless.

> We were studying God's view of human life – what God was doing on the Somme, and at Westminster, and at Tilbury Docks. In this, our vision of 'Theology' was part of our vision of the Church. I do not want to know what you can do with Christ in a church (building) half as much as I want to know what Christ is doing in the street. . .
>
> This Kelham Theology of the will of God in the world was a Kelham gospel to the world. I do not mean that only Kelham believes it. Every orthodox Christian admits (etc) . . . We had made it the basis of our education – in that, I think, we were alone.[60]

Consider the things that are nearly like this. Protestantism at the Reformation secularised Christianity, and found God's will in married lives instead of convents, in honest trades as well as being 'religious'. This is a commonplace of Protestantism, finding the will of God in the world. But the ordinary customs of a secular society, though innocent, are not, thought Kelly, immediately expressive of God's over-ruling power. Most of these things we experience as in our own control, as our own doing. We might, because it is unwise to boast about fields where we can be left to our own devices, slip in provisos. *Nisi Dominus frustra*. Nevertheless, where do we see the hand of God?

Orthodox Christianity can see the hand of God in whatever happens. One technical term for seeing this is predestination. 'It has always seemed to me that Predestination, the doctrine of Purpose and an over-ruling Power of God over all life, is the true central point, to which all Dogmatic Theology leads up, and from which all Ascetic (practical) Theology leads down.'[61] Here we have the Augustinian Fr Kelly again. He was not, quite fiercely not, a Calvinist: 'God's will is always primarily the universal will', rather than a matter of picking out individuals. But what does it mean to discover the purpose and power of God in the general course of history? This can very easily, in England before the First World War, sound as if the British Empire is part of a divine plan. It is less easy when he talks, as he does, about the Somme. God's will is a matter of nations.

> They have aimed at making converts *out of* all nations. They have forgotten that Christ commanded them to make the *nations* his disciples.[62]

Of course a Social Gospel sounds like this too, setting aside individualism and finding God's will for the nation. But Kelham did not have a politicised theology. Politicised theologies tend to be stronger on justice than on love. Fr Kelly had doubts about justice; he thought that the only real place where the moral law of justice reigns is hell, and 'Thou shalt by no means come out thence till thou hast paid the uttermost farthing'. . .[63] It is noticeable that the working-class college at Kelham was not full of left-wing politics. This is one of the contrasts with Mirfield, scarcely working-class, but definitely left-wing. Part of this is because of Kelly's sense that God's will can be picked out in the past, rather than in the present and future.

> We do not know what God is doing, and still less what He is going to do, for these things God keeps in his own hands. He does allow us to know what He has done. There is first the revelation of Himself in the Gospel, and then the revelation of His Power in history.[64]

So the Kelham course did history, not in tiny detail, but certainly trying to find, in the broad sweep, God's hand in power. 'Every age has its own special lessons, not to be learnt elsewhere.'[65] So the temptation to leap over the Dark Ages in a church history course should be resisted. A sense of history, after all, can too easily be a sense that times have changed so we can disregard the concerns of the past. Or a reigning orthodoxy can appropriate history for itself, and remake it in its own image. But to find the Spirit at work, not most conspicuously in our own lives (which is a natural piece of self-centredness), but in the great movements of history, is not a commonplace stance in twentieth century theology.

> At Swanwick he would prowl about, like Socrates, asking 'Does God *do* anything?' The unwary victim would reply, 'Of course; God does everything,' only to be met with the retort, 'Ye-es; but don't you see that if all you can say is that God does everything-in-general, that is much the same thing as to say that he does nothing in particular?' The Bible to him was . . . a record of what God has done – *the mystery of his will* . . .
> 'The will of God is manifested to us first as power,' he would say . . .[66]

It is common, when encountering theology well done, to point out its resemblance to the best continental models. So people said that Fr Kelly was Barthian, which pleased him, though he had never read any Barth.

> If you want a name, I am called a Barthian. N.B. I never read Barth – I am an F.D.Maurician. I have been preaching that for forty years or more, long before Barth.[67]

It might be more fruitful looking for English parallels with P.T.Forsyth (1848–1921), who also was a Barthian before Barth, and a (Congregational) principal of a theological college in England. But normally the Continentals win. To continue the list, one might say that a man who was 'no pious person', and instead was concerned with God's presence in the midst of the secular, was pure Bonhoeffer. There are those who find things in common between Kelly and Kierkegaard, as realities are existential, and Kierkegaard was the father of existentialism. There is something in all of this, but the prevailing strand in German Protestant theology of this century has disparaged history. Theologians find the Christ of Faith rather than the Jesus of History. So the stress on God's real power in history is Kelham's own. William Temple, who always owned his debts to Kelly, said 'The typical locus of revelation is not the mind of the seer but the historical event'.[68]

Historical events are seldom transparently a locus of revelation. Even with hindsight, can we see the power of God? Presumably this is what faith is about. To make the careful study of history our means of discovering the hand of God has great advantages, in some ways, over our own ordinary religious subjectivities. One can actually argue out what happened. One need not get bogged down with petty detail or special cases. If it can be done, it feels as if one is actually uncovering reality. Perhaps 'uncovering' makes too much of our mastery of what we are dealing with.

> To believe *in* anything is to recognise that its reality is independent of, and transcends, our notions of it, and judges them. . . In answer to the plaintive query, 'But how can we get at the truth?' he would answer, 'You can't; but the truth can get at you.'[69]

Of course, just like Barth, Fr Kelly, in talking about the living God, can sound dangerous. People who talk about power instead of love, about how the truth can get at us, people who undercut our own self-reliance, are threatening. Now a certain amount of threat, like strong liquor, can actually be a thrill. Some types of religious threat have done damage. There is probably a risk to the person using this line of talk to threaten others. On the other hand, when one thinks of the tone of voice, familiar to many of us, in which clergymen address a God who is manifestly not there, then it seems obvious enough that if there is a God, He is a threat. It is worth coming back to the fact that God's power is not shown in frightening the thoughtless, but in 'what God was doing on the Somme, and at Westminster, and at Tilbury Docks'.[70]

> Asked by someone, 'But how do we *know* what is God's will?' he replied, 'You don't; and that's the giddy joke.'[71]

This saying is one of the talismans of Kelham theology. It is a theology of seeking to do God's will, and not knowing what the will of God is. This is threatening, but it is unfair to the Kelham tradition to stress the threat without stressing the laughter. There is a comical jolt in any thought that we are the ones who are talking about God's will.

Without further apology I turn from threat to laughter. They are close together in the Kelham tradition. There was a lot of natural high spirits and laughter over the years in SSM and its colleges. There was also a certain amount of rather nervous and strained laughter. Kelham wanted to be seen to have a sense of humour. There have after all been strands of Christianity that took themselves very seriously. This is true of much in the nineteenth century revival of the religious life. Pusey proposed to ban smiling in his personal rule of life.[72] In fact, it is probably a grace from heaven not to take oneself seriously. To notice this, and to try to act upon it, takes harder work. Fr Kelly said:

> It was in Japan, I think, that I first really learnt the power of laughing and making people laugh with you. You must laugh at yourself first, it is a very good antiseptic for vanity.[73]

Why was there a revival in the popularity of St Francis around the turn of the century? Some of it is just cheerful optimism, the happy 'once-born' without a sense of sin, with an extrovert self-forgetfulness. (St Francis was not like this). But clowns are sad, and the clowning side of religion seems to open to us ways of saying the almost unspeakable. It does not always work, especially if we work at it.

He just stood there and said the fundamental things laugh-

> ing, but deeper than tears . . . He makes you silently laugh
> nearly all the time, and then tears you with the sense that
> you have been very irreligious to be so deadly solemn over
> yourself; and above all that you have never really realised
> what the fear of God means.[74]

Now this is the type of effect that Father Kelly had on
some of his hearers. By this time he was in his stride as a
sage in Japan. The wisdom of Japan includes the possibility
of jokes and paradox, though Father Kelly read no Zen
masters to find this out. One notices how drenched in
emotion Miss Wordsworth's assessment of Kelly is. What
is more, this is the sort of writing the Society published in
its *Newsletter*. This is evidence that there was, however
deserved, a personality cult. In fact, getting rid of a direct
appeal to subjectivity has a strong subjective appeal. Still, it
does matter, much less than who is talking or how well he
talks, whether he is talking about something real.

> I laughed at the fine language which attracted them so
> much; imitated it, made them see its absurdity, and brought
> them back to the plain issues of faith in the reality of
> God.[75]

If only things were plain. '[The Old Testament writers]
never say, "We must remember that God is real, and not an
abstraction". . . .'[76] There is almost a matter of taste or fashion
in preferring concrete to abstract ways of thought. It is like
remodelling one's prose to replace Latinate polysyllables
with curt Anglo-Saxon monosyllables. This is part of
the history of English usage. Kingsley was capable of
addressing his fellow-countrymen as 'Men of England.
Saxons!' In the world of theology, there has been a 20C
fashion for preferring the concreteness of Hebrew to the
abstraction of Greek thought. Gustav Aulén, whom Fr
Hebert of SSM translated, in his *Christus Victor* (1930
trans. 1931), dismisses 'theories' of the atonement in favour
of a dramatic idea. 'We shall hear again the old realistic
message of the conflict of God with the dark hostile forces
of evil . . .'[77]. So to talk about a stress on objectivity or
realism might simply be to place Kelly in a familiar episode
in cultural history. But when we consider what is meant

by a stress on reality, Kelham was in some ways less self-consciously objective than some modern objective theologies. As one thinks of Kierkegaard's cheerful image of the professor dangling from his wonderful 'objective' scheme, this is perhaps as well. When they taught the history of doctrine at Kelham, the touchstone in some sense was the reality to the men themselves.

> This is said to be correct, and that incorrect, but I do not care about these words. I would rather ask, why is this doctrine vital, and that fatal, to a man's soul and capacity to live? Someone said it was, and he ought to know. Very well, we must go to him, and find out why he found it so; then each man must look into his own soul, find in his own life its questions and difficulties, its perplexities and diversities.[78]

There is something here of an appeal to subjectivity as well. This might well remind us of how Schleiermacher, the great Berlin theologian, father of liberal protestantism, came to put the doctrine of the trinity in an appendix to his big systematic book *The Christian Faith* in 1821, because he could not see how it related to direct religious experience. Father Kelly, on the other hand, loved the Athanasian Creed, with its trinitarian incomprehensibilities, the stumbling-block to English liberal thinkers, and claimed it was central to Christian teaching. Probably, as with some of the ideas of his master Maurice, there was a certain willed perversity in this.

Kelham theology can be measured against, not just other theological colleges, but the Honours school of theology at any English university in this period. The Kelham course was better devised, and covered more, than any other course available. Also, the students thought harder than ordinary students elsewhere. To compare places of study is not so much a matter of listing creative writers. There have been some dim Regius Professors over the years. It is a matter of how Kelham students actually worked on theology, not just in quantity, but as a framework for looking at the world. Here is what F.D.Maurice wanted, and notions like this drew Kelly to him.

> An original man is not one who invents . . . But he is one
> who does not take words and phrases at second hand; who
> asks what they signify . . . The original man is fighting for
> his life; he must know whether he has any ground to stand
> upon; he must ask God to tell him, because man cannot.
> All men are capable of this originality.[79]

In this sense of originality, there was originality at Kelham.
There was a great achievement here. Here is some evidence.
The bishop of Ely, in whose diocese the college at Mildenhall was, sent Dean Armitage Robinson to inspect. Armitage Robinson was an appropriate choice, as training men
for ordination examinations was part of his own life. Some
of the very best graduate Anglican ordinands did not
attend any theological college but read for orders under the
supervision of a leading clergyman. The most famous
group of these were Dean Vaughan's 'doves', but Dean
Armitage Robinson, first at Westminster, then at Wells,
filled his deanery with hand-picked leaders of the future.
Among those trained by him were 'Tubby' Clayton and
Bishop Gore. Here is part of his report, and he knew what
he was talking about.

> . . . the papers generally were far more interesting than
> most papers usually are. There was a sense of the reality of
> the problems dealt with, and an endeavour to get to the
> heart of them, which was in striking contrast to the ordi-
> nary examination style. It was as though the men were not
> accustomed to write answers to get marks, but took the
> questions as matters to be thought about very seriously.
> There was very little guesswork . . . never mere attempts
> to cover up ignorance.
>
> A far greater knowledge of Theology in the stricter sense
> was shewn and a much deeper interest in it than our
> Candidates usually display. The men clearly are led to
> think. . .[80]

Anyone with any ideals left in the teaching profession
should be stirred by this achievement. It reminds me of
A.L.Smith saying that 'out of a bundle of W.E.A. essays
taken haphazard 25 per cent. reached a standard of a First
Class in the Modern History School at Oxford'.[81] It does
not mean that Dean Armitage Robinson thought that

Great Chapter 1920. The priests on the front row are
Fr Murphy, HHK, Fr White, Fr Carleton, Fr Alfred Kelly.
Behind, first left is Fr Tribe, and third is Fr Couldrey.

The Old Man.

Fr Alfred Kelly ready for tennis.

Br James Berry in his
printing press.

Fr Stephen Bedale –
for once not backed
by hundreds in an
annual group
photograph.

these eager students were as interesting as himself or some
of his own students. There are hierarchies of achievement,
and possibilities of patronising people. One has a faint sense
that people who take 'the questions as matters to be
thought about very seriously' are innocents. To be seen
to be thinking hard in a way is to put oneself at a
vulnerable disadvantage to the spectator, who can be presumed to be in a more secure position. Fr Kelly very
often made sharp remarks – these are the sort of obiter
dicta one finds he made in the Church History lecture
course – about how the way to rise in the church is
never to think.

So it is not simply a matter of comparing lists of
publications by the members of staff. Some other early
members of the Society of the Sacred Mission, such as
H.H.Kelly's brother, Alfred Kelly, who published *the
Rational Necessity of Theism* in 1909, and David Jenks, also
were authors. But compared with Mirfield, there is not
much. A modern publisher might feel 'Perhaps we should
re-issue L.S.Thornton, or Dom Gregory Dix' (to choose
names from other Anglican religious orders); one might
even think of re-issuing Bishop Gore, who is so easily
available second-hand; but before Hebert, and apart from
Fr Kelly, the Society of the Sacred Mission published
nothing that has lasted. David Jenks, the second Director
(1910–1920), published in 1914 *In the Face of Jesus Christ*.
This course of meditations for every day of the Christian
year was still in print in 1949. It was based on the outline
meditations provided each week for the students at Kelham.
In tiny print, one side of a page to each week, there is a
theme, considered under three headings, each divided into
three sub-headings. There are Roman Catholic precedents
for manuals set out like this. Let us consider Vocation, on
the tenth Thursday after Trinity. I chose it because it
seemed relevant to ordinands and to members of a religious
Society.

> Ye have not chosen me, but I have chosen you.
> S.John xv.16.
> I. – The truth of vocation guards the divine Omnipotence.

(a) Almighty God might conceivably accomplish his purposes without man's co-operation . . .

(b) He chooses to accomplish his will through man . . .

(c) . . . he is not dependent on the offer of service . . . It is spiritually higher to be guided in such matters than to insist upon one's own judgement.

II. – It teaches the true end of man's being.

(a) . . . Man's true aim in life is to fulfil that for which he is purposed by God . . . generally determined . . . through natural circumstances . . .

(b) To realize and to follow vocation demands the surrender of the will to God. Irrational life fulfils its vocation necessarily; rational life can only fulfil it voluntarily. It is not that most Christians have not got vocations, but that they do not perceive vocations.

(c) How great is the privilege . . . that God should choose one for anything! . . . the road to saintship as well with the scullerymaid as with the missionary.

III. – The moral value of vocation.

(a) It removes the impertinence or diffidence of special vocations . . .

(b) . . . great humility: not my fitness but his will . . .

(c) . . . He who volunteers may well fear his capacity; but . . . 'When I am weak then am I strong.'

This is the characteristic spirituality of Kelham, whether written by Fr Jenks or by Fr Kelly. Consider the cold logic of II (b), where we have quoted the whole little section, all thought through, and pared to the bone. There is a slight unfairness that if books are there to help people meditate, they are shelved as devotional, which is on a slightly lower intellectual plane than works of scholarship, which have footnotes, and, perhaps hence, intellectual rigour. It is clear that Kelham, when meditating, thought hard.

Kelly's happiest days as a teacher were in Japan. The Japanese students gave him confidence, first to be more comic, and secondly to be more wilfully obscure, what Margaret Dewey called 'an increasingly elliptical and paradoxical style'[82]. Whatever Kelly's style became, there is a theological achievement at Kelham. It is utterly bound up with H.H.Kelly, but goes beyond him.

They still used his courses. Consider that they shipped

out *De Deo* to Australia, with Father Hebert. The systematics course there, in the 1950s, like many other courses at Crafers in the early years, consisted in going through duplicated copies of Fr Kelly's notes. A different teacher, half a century later, with a different perspective, even if using Fr Kelly's text, might be doing a different type of Kelham theology. Something happens when the teacher is no longer expounding his own text. In Japan in 1960 they were still going through Fr Kelly's lectures, given when he was Apologetics professor at Ikebukuro during the First World War.[83] The intention, certainly, was more for continuity than change.

For example, one of the Australian copies of the *De Deo* had been the one from which Fr Antony Snell taught the course at Crafers. What was 'modern' at the turn of the century might be scarcely so in the 1950s. However, Fr Snell puts sharp question marks beside the 'old man''s dismissive judgement of Hall's dry systematics. He also writes the names of other authors in the margin. One of them is C.B.Moss, and it is not clear whether he replaces Hall as an example of arid correctness, or simply as a book to recommend. I suspect the latter, though to my mind he fits the former. C.B.Moss was a conservative hard-liner who lived in a world of pugnacious certainties. Somehow the certainties of F.D.Maurice, and of Fr Kelly, perhaps because they were arrived at through a struggle for comprehension, were less 'take-it-or-leave-it'.

Things hardened a little, but the long SSM course, as planned by Father Kelly, was a great achievement. Very ordinary students probably did more and better theology there than at any other institution in the history of Anglicanism.

> What he taught was theology. When he said theology, he meant something very distinctive and not quite the same as what a lot of other people have meant when they use the word. . . (Archbishop Michael Ramsey, at a meeting in Manchester in 1960, the centenary of Kelly's birth).[84]

To say what he did mean by theology, we turn to another archbishop:

The other side of the training he wished to mention was its emphasis on the importance of theology. Its conception of theology was an attempt to understand God and the world He has made. It was not detached or academic. Much theology was simply thinking about what other men had thought about God; made theology into history; destroyed it as a living science; was departmental – whereas theology should be a study of all the mind's activities. This last principle was firmly grasped in the Kelham system of training ... The men at Kelham have a real grasp of the Christian view of the world. (William Temple, then Canon of Westminster, in 1919)[85]

In the next chapter we shall turn to the part played by Kelly and his students, carrying this theology, in the largely student ecumenical movement.

Chapter 6

Kelham and Ecumenism

From 1908 Kelly took a group of students every year to the S.C.M. conference at Swanwick. As is well known, the ecumenical movement very largely grew out of the Student Christian Movement. Much hangs on this.

First consider the numbers involved. In Britain, before the First World War, even with a number of newly-founded universities, there were never more than 50,000 students all told. This included students at training colleges for teachers and at theological colleges like Kelham. In 1914 S.C.M. had 10,000 members. Some were the old guard who stayed members for life, and some were nominal, but even so, it is a high proportion. In any one year, by about 1911, some 1200 students came to the S.C.M. conferences at Swanwick. Three conferences were run in consecutive weeks, to cope with the numbers. [1] Kelham sent staff and students to each week, a hand-picked two or three at a time.

Living in tents, mixing with large numbers in a charged atmosphere, even travelling somewhere strange, were all more unusual and memorable to pre-war students than such things would be later. (For the girls from single-sex training colleges there was actually the chance of meeting men).[2] It was definitely British Christianity's answer to a successful pilgrimage.

The S.C.M. has since gone on to be identified in student circles with theological liberalism. This was not its background. The British College Christian Union, which became in 1905 the Student Christian Movement, was made up of Christian Unions, as was the S.C.M.. Later, strictly evangelical Christian Union groups would go on to secede, and later still largely drive the S.C.M. from the field in the British universities. As some sort of fore-runner of this, the Cambridge Inter-Collegiate Christian Union,

C.I.C.C.U., dis-affiliated from the S.C.M. in 1910. The issues at the time were not clear-cut; in some ways C.I.C.C.U. wanted to be a purely Anglican society.

The student movement in the 1890s was the true forerunner of both the later S.C.M. and the later Christian Unions. Both, looking back, are likely to be tempted to embarrassment and the re-writing of history. These students were idealistic and very missionary-minded: behind the S.C.M. had been a Student Volunteer movement, recruiting for the missionfield. The 'Sacred Mission' had resonance in a period when the obvious way to give your life to God was to become a missionary. Every member of the Student Volunteer Missionary Union, set up in Great Britain in 1892, formally declared 'It is my purpose, if God permit, to become a foreign missionary'. [3] Its national meetings were held as fringe meetings of the Keswick convention, and they (B.C.C.U. and S.V.M.U.) had a tiny office in the Y.M.C.A. building. Keswick was best known as the focus of emotional undenominational 'holiness' evangelicalism. The change in style, at the time imperceptible, from Keswick to Swanwick is significant.

There are conflicting images of religion in the 1890s. On the one hand there is a cheerful optimism, 'the evangelisation of the world in this generation' (the Watchword of the S.V.M.U.), without any hint of a siege mentality. The great Social Gospel theologian in America, Walter Rauschenbusch, brought out in 1890 the official German-language edition of Sankey's *Sacred Songs and Solos*. The favourite speaker at evangelical student rallies in Britain was Professor Henry Drummond, of *Natural Law in the Spiritual World*, who combined modern science, Darwinism, with evangelical piety. Evangelicals a generation later would fight shy of Social Gospel and evolution. Though the B.C.C.U. (housed by the Y.M.C.A. etc) was under evangelical auspices, it was never partisan. They merely found it, in most cases, difficult to book non-evangelical speakers.

What is the place of this work among students in breeding ecumenism? In the nineteenth century the characteristic way of crossing denominational boundaries was the Y.M.C.A., which did it easily, because it was a lay movement. The S.C.M. was similarly lay. Some went on to be ordained, but even among the international leaders of the ecumenical movement there were laymen, and indeed lay women. It is worthwhile spending a little time comparing the Y.M.C.A. and the S.C.M., both of which shed some light on social groups from which the Society of the Sacred Mission grew, and the context within which it worked.

Our image of the Y.M.C.A. is influenced by its later developments. Where it flourished, in North America, England and Germany, it was already shifting towards providing sports facilities and cheap lodgings by the 1890s. Elsewhere, as in mainland Europe, it was a youth movement of the Protestant churches, eagerly trying to convert Catholics. Many Y.M.C.A.s insisted on evidence of conversion, and quarrelled with 'latitudinarian' clergymen. So its interdenominationalism had limits.

The S.C.M., working among students, would serve to shape a professional élite of the country. The Y.M.C.A., at least in Great Britain, was aimed at the lower-middle-class. They were perhaps the élite of that class. Here, with strong praise, is the Archdeacon of London in 1894:

> ... the very cream, I should venture to say, of honest English Christian manhood – content with its lot in life, satisfied to make the best of its surroundings, thinking more of others than of self, ready for everything that is good and useful, the backbone of its class, the example to other classes, a rising hope for England.[4]

This is a conservative and class-conscious tribute. It is from young men of the same class that Fr Kelly wanted to recruit his ordinands for Kelham:

> ... that normal sunny youth of England, strong and capable, full of fun and games, who would willingly give up their own petty ambitions, suffer a great deal of hardship, labour gladly, die uncomplaining and unrewarded, for the love of God and the good of men, provided only you did not ask them to stop enjoying it all and making fun of everything along the road.[5]

Sixteen of the fifty-one recruited to the SSM college by 1897 were clerks, seven were shop-assistants. It is the same pool as the Y.M.C.A. There is a difference in the fact that SSM quite quickly came to recruit boys before they had become set in their ways as bank-clerks or whatever. The Y.M.C.A. made good bank-clerks better by keeping young men off the streets and away from loose women.

The world of clerks (the Y.M.C.A. and largely Kelham) and the world of students (S.C.M.) were very different in 1900. It takes an imaginative leap to enter the ethos of student life then. One sees group photographs of young people looking and dressing older than their years. The standard history of the SCM has many such photographs. Here is a guileless compliment to John R. Mott from 1903:

> He is an orderly man, and always knows the right thing to do ... and, incidentally, the right clothes to wear ... When the graduates and undergraduates of the Melbourne University were to be addressed, it was an accomplished scholar in irreproachable evening dress who spoke as a student to students.[6]

The students at Kelham were proud of being scruffy, scruffy in cassocks of course. There does seem to be there a different dress-code than students generally had, even in democratic Australia. This visual point, that Kelham students stood out in cassocks, and not thereby immediately as formal against informal, as they would now, is part of their contribution to make Swanwick ecumenical.

Clothes are perhaps a small matter. Students defined themselves as real students by codes of slang. Kelham had a contrived code of its own : 'Medders' and 'Doggies' and 'squish'. At Swanwick codes must have been mutually incomprehensible. There was the somewhat factitious shared heritage of the 'Student Song Book'. This came from Scotland. The Scottish universities, from old tradition, recruited students from a wider social range. In class-conscious Britain, many Scottish students, like the fewer bright working-class boys who had made it through grammar schools in England, were eager to assume the protective markings of the authentic student tribe. Students encountering students were discreetly snobbish. It was a pleasant surprise to Scots and Welsh Presbyterians and English Freechurchmen, meeting the students from Kelham, not to be patronised by Anglicans. The apostolic succession is a small thing compared to the middle-class English assumption of superiority. (It was striking how well Fr Kelly got on with Williams of Aberystwyth and Phillips of Bala, not to mention Professor Cairns of Aberdeen).

The young, even in Edwardian England, are often more high-spirited than in posed photographs. Kelly said of Swanwick 'The main meetings are awful; but the ragging is divine.'[7] David Paton said that the practical joking of those days was much diminished later. Tense formal societies are more likely to make a meal of reversals of order; more relaxed groups find sudden reversals less thrilling. They had games with sacks on a greasy pole, reminiscent rather of pillow-fights in the dorm.

> Pillow fighting on the pole for the world's championship, an international potato race, . . . and Father Kelly well to the fore, were features of the occasion.[8]

It is historically significant that students from what was perceived as an Anglo-Catholic theological college went to Swanwick. In 1894, when the S.V.M.U. tried to gain access to Anglican theological colleges, the principals of the high church colleges refused to allow the travelling secretary to meet their students. Faced with this rebuff, the student movement tended to assume that theological colleges were unspiritual. Even so, at least a third of the members of the S.V.M.U. were theological students.

In 1898 there had been a national conference specifically for theological students. Most Protestant theological colleges were represented, but only six of the twenty-three Anglican ones, and these six were all Evangelical. At the conference there was a split on churchmanship lines: should they or should they not join in reciting the Nicene creed? Baptists and Congregationalists, unlike Presbyterians and Methodists, felt that reciting creeds, however orthodox, was not in their tradition. The creed was not recited. It is one of the real achievements of later ecumenism, that

Anglicans might not notice, that the United Reformed
Church was a union that bridged this divide.

The proportion of six to twenty-three exaggerates Anglican exclusiveness. When the student leaders that year approached the bishop of London, Mandell Creighton, not a
party man, he was in favour of Anglican theological students joining in. The Broad Church bishop of Ripon,
Boyd Carpenter, when the annual S.V.M.U. conference
was in Ripon in 1898, asked for an invitation to preach to
it, and '[t]he sermon was followed by a Celebration of
Holy Communion to which the whole conference was
invited to remain'.[9] This practice of an open invitation to
communion in the local Anglican church, so natural to
ecumenism involving only Evangelicals, had to stop when
Anglo-Catholics became involved. The decision was formally made by the B.C.C.U. in 1898 in order to 'draw in
the different elements in the Church of England'. 'We
could not be undenominational; we must be interdenominational'.[10]

The particular initiative that brought Anglo-Catholics
into the Student Christian movement came from Neville
Talbot, newly graduated from Oxford and due to start his
training at Cuddesdon. He was the first Anglo-Catholic on
the executive of the S.C.M. theological college department.
His approach to Fr Kelly was cheerful and almost cheeky:
'. . .all very well, but you've got to come just the same'.
They obviously got on well. (The schoolboy Talbot had
been a near neighbour when the college was at Vassall
Road). Neville Talbot was high-spirited, going on seven
foot tall, and very much part of the English establishment.
His father had been Warden of Keble, Bishop of Rochester,
first bishop of Southwark and would later go to Winchester. One of his brothers was Superior of Mirfield from
1922 to 1940. The other, who was killed in the war, had
'Toc H' named after him. We need not start on his cousins.
As David Paton said, in *No Pious Person*, [11] 'Neville Talbot
gave the S.C.M. what may be crudely termed some entré
into ecclesiastical high society'. It is interesting to see a
move by a section of the Anglo-Catholic establishment
into relationships with other churches. Perhaps Kelham

tried harder and persisted longer than Mirfield in sending students, but the Talbot network was more important than Kelham in making this form of ecumenism acceptable. Kelham had no such social cachet; if anything, it stood to profit from any activity that made its name known.

That said, Kelly and Kelham were very successful at Swanwick over the years. As was mentioned before, there is very largely a class boundary between Anglicans and other British churches, and the Kelham men were refreshingly non-upperclass. Also, though Kelly made a lot of fun of the half-baked notions of the idealistic young, some of the other British theological traditions (particularly but not only the Scots) took theology seriously, as Kelham did, and there was something in common there.

Here is William Paton, a Presbyterian, secretary of the International Missionary Council, and editor of the *International Review of Missions*, on Fr Kelly at Swanwick.

> Such men as Father Kelly of the S.S.M. did two things for crowds of the members of the Student Movement whom he met at the summer camps. One was that he incarnated a life of Christian devotion to which the obedience, fellowship and cultus of the Church were essential. The second was that in mastering this fact they found also that the Church was divided, deeply divided, and that the earnest camaraderie of their own evangelistic and missionary fellowship had no automatic remedy for this state of division.[12]

Thus in a way the Kelham presence was an irritant in a world of 'earnest camaraderie' where denominational boundaries did not matter. But it could only be so because they had no possibility of saying that he was not a real Christian. Real Christians get on easily and disregard denominational boundaries, or do they?

In 1912 Kelly wrote at the request of the archbishop of Canterbury, no less, an account of the connection of SSM with S.C.M . . .

> All my life I have been trying to get Church Protestant Evangelicals − who were my brothers − to understand us.[13]

To do this he concluded 'the way to Church unity lay
through Dissent'. [14] Hence his ecumenism. In 1909 he had
produced a little Tract on Unity wrapped in brown paper,
'the Khaki Dragon', addressed to the Executive S.C.M. In
it were his familiar arguments against subjectivism in piety.
'If I can thus [by meditation] of myself create a Divine
Presence for what purpose was there ever an objective
Incarnation?' [15] The Free Churches were interested. One
of them found Kelly's high doctrine of God 'the finest
Calvinism he had ever heard preached'. Kelly commented

> Of course it was Calvinism, though we call it predestinarian-
> ism at Kelham. Those old rascals did believe in God, if
> they believed in nothing else.[16]

The notes exist of 'The Grounds' of the Free Church
Fellowship set up at Swanwick, where Father Kelly re-
drafted it for them, taking out all the 'We are determined
to . . .'s. He was always on the lookout for activist moralis-
ing Ritschlian liberalism.

> The really primary . . question is whether the Name of
> God stands for anything at all; whether we need Him or
> whether in fact God is not wholly dependent upon us, i.e.
> it's all a question of Pelagianism.[17]

They seem to have enjoyed his intransigence. Fr Frere, of
Mirfield, at Baslow in 1908, had been temporising: 'modern
Churchmen could not make the same claims for Episcopacy
as they used to do'. [18] Kelly claimed that 'Englishmen love
having the thick end of the wedge put in first' [19] so on
purpose, even though the word did not come naturally to
him, he talked about the Mass. We must not, however,
overstress the intransigence. There is a document for
Kelham students going to S.C.M. conferences, called *Swanwick Tips* (1912).

> There are people who have an idea that the Catholic walks
> about imagining himself a penny-in-the-slot machine, full
> of correct answers to all the problems. It is a pleasant
> surprise to find he is an intelligent person who is trying to
> think things out.[20]

There were several good practical tips:

> All quarrels begin when you try to tell him what he thinks
> . . . never call anything a heresy . . . You are always safe as
> long as you are asking questions. When you get talking
> you are only safe when you are answering the other man's
> questions, and not always then.[21]

We must remember that these are Kelham students confronted with university undergraduates, and holding their
own. They may have listened a lot, but they put across the
Catholic line too. In 1911 the very competent theologian,
Professor John Oman, chairing a meeting, rather ungra-
ciously used his summing-up to answer Maillard, one of
the Kelham boys.

Kelham was the first high church college to be affiliated
to the S.C.M. In 1910 the conference of principals of
Church of England Theological Colleges followed, though
they became 'associated' rather than 'affiliated'.

> Father Kelly of Kelham was a great help and most amusing.
> He took up a superior attitude on being appealed to once or
> twice, taking care to explain to the principals that he was
> not in the same box as most of them since he and his
> college were part of the Movement. He was not a man in
> doubt![22]

Thus Kelham took the lead, though the endorsement of
more influential principals, like Canon Johnston of Cuddesdon, was needed to move the meeting as a whole.
We should notice that it was necessary to work down
from the principals, and that there had been a serious
change since the 1890s. Some of this was the flowering,
perhaps the last flowering, of Nonconformist influence,
under the last Liberal government of 1906. Important
Anglicans were prepared to get to know important Free
Church men.

The students were not likely to be consulted much in
Anglican theological colleges about joining S.C.M.; it was
up to the principals. If it was a one year course, as many
colleges had, there was little scope for summer schools and
conferences during the course. In any case students could

not be relied on to be ecumenically minded. In 1902 we find that

> [t]he one hope was to interest them in the Movement and keep it dark that they were going to meet theological students of other denominations.[23]

When the consciously high church students came to Baslow and later Swanwick, they worried the others. Thus in 1908

> [o]ne of the Welsh Nonconformist members brought to the notice of the Executive the fact 'that a student from a High Church college had tried to exert undue influence over a Welsh delegate . . .' The men from the High Church colleges were very self-conscious about their churchmanship and many of them nervously anxious to expound their position to all and sundry. They wanted to discuss the whole question of reunion. Happily the day came very quickly when they had their way . . .[24]

Kelly, some of whose students were very pertinacious in getting into arguments at Swanwick, was also skilful at peace-making. It was one evidence of the calibre of Kelham students that they coped easily and fearlessly with theological students on degree courses whom they met at Swanwick. The 'Old Man' was justifiably proud of them. Kelly became friends with Martyn Trafford, the Baptist travelling secretary of the Movement. 'No-one was more welcome at Kelham than Trafford'.[25] Things like friendship take time; conferences heighten relationships, and speed them up, but still it took a few years for the Evangelicals and Free Church men who went to the Swanwick conferences to see in Father Kelly someone after their own heart, 'a true evangelical'.

Fr Kelly's involvement with ecumenism was not limited to Swanwick. He was on one of the drafting committees for the 1910 missionary conference at Edinburgh. The actual work of the committee was boring, with a chairman who was self-important and empty, and it might be difficult to prove that the material presented to the conference served to change much. None the less, the Faith and Order

Committee in 1915, writing about the move from controversy to conference, wrote

> It is well that we should remember how much we owe to
> the few who in preliminary conversations plotted the
> issues, and in particular to two whose deafness demanded
> that they should follow the other man's argument with the
> closest attention, lest a link escape them . . . . It can hardly
> be a pure coincidence that two deaf men have done so
> much for the quality of theological conversation,
> H.H.Kelly and J.H.Oldham.[26]

It was a key step forward, seen as such at the time, that
there were there at Edinburgh 1910 clear-cut high Anglicans, such as Kelly. In his own account of what happened
he speaks of 'protestant bodies', who are the rest, for
whom union is a possibility, and 'the Church', represented
by the Anglicans.' . . . the impression left on my mind was
that they realized that it was a position which would have
to be accepted ultimately as the only final solution'.[27] So
Kelly's contribution was largely a cheerful, and humble,
intransigence. But the Anglo-Catholics were there, which
was the step forward.

> Any one who has enjoyed the luxury of sulking knows
> how pleasant it is to maintain one's own dignity behind a
> strict reserve, and knows also how annoyingly unconscious
> other people can be of one's absence.[28]

They were strongly criticised by the Church Times. The
S.P.G., the high-church missionary society, sent a delega-
tion only at the last minute, after a petition with 900
signatures against its participation. There were people there
from Mirfield, like Frere, better-known than Kelly. Kelly
always enjoyed the fringe life of a conference, rather than
the formal debates, but he gave one little speech, on his
own theme of what to teach students.

> Is the thing that we are teaching in our universities, the
> thing on which we are examining boys . . .- are they the
> knowledge of Christianity?. . . .[29] Supposing a bank manager
> asks us who are teachers of theology, what has Christian
> doctrine ever done for or what has it got to do with my

bank? Will anything in your teaching help me to understand my work better or do it with more energy or more
purpose? What has all your teaching to do with the life
men lead? Is it bringing home those facts, the virgin birth,
the resurrection, the cross, throwing light upon the actual
life, not that we parsons and ministers are leading, but that
the layman is leading with his lay interests and in his work
today? This is the view of Christianity that we want for
the mission field, that the missionaries ask from us . . . .
they hardly seem to imagine how entirely new a thing
they are asking . . . If we want to teach this Christianity
and this knowledge of it, we want enormously more
intellectual freedom in our colleges than we have got –
perhaps less criticism – more meaning, more thought, and
above all more independence. A man can only think what
he thinks himself . . .[30]

This is characteristic Kelly, trying to bring his theology to
bear on ordinary life, and to make his students think for
themselves. It went down well, but speeches at a conference, however good, do not change much. Acquaintances
made, and the setting up of the Continuation Committee,
were what really mattered.

It was because Fr Kelly crossed boundaries that he and
Neville Talbot were sent in 1912 by John R. Mott on a
tour of the United States and Canada. He had not met
Mott before 1910, but several Americans of Mott's circle
(eg Eddy and Gilkey) had been very impressed by Kelly at
the Swanwick conference of 1910, and had 'urged on Mott
the importance of Episcopalian cooperation in America'.[31]
Talbot and Kelly symbolised (Anglo-) Catholics who were
prepared to work in a general Christian youth movement.
Mott hoped to persuade American Episcopalians to work
with the Y.M.C.A. in the American universities. He had a
much wider goal than this, to set up youth movements in
the countries of Orthodox eastern Europe, where Episcopa-
lianism might open doors where a simply Protestant
Y.M.C.A. had no chance. It was not simply a matter of
finding Episcopalian stalking-horses: Mott did think that
Protestantism had something to learn from the Catholic
teaching on church and sacraments. However, the trip was

no great success, as American Episcopalian theological colleges had a very clear, perhaps class-based, sense of the difference between themselves and the Y.M.C.A.[32].

Fr Kelly was dismayed by the happy man-centred faith of American liberal protestantism.

> The old Protestantism began with faith in God. There were works to be done, but what they did was so dominated by this trust in God that they hardly thought of it as their own . . .
>
> The theological and quasi-credal basis of this faith has dropped out (I should say because of the absence of any effective and permanent presentation of it in religious worship, i.e. sacraments) . . . The faith still maintained itself, but it began to be recognised as a feeling – a 'feeling of assurance' . . . This confusion has in fact led men to substitute faith-in-feelings-about-God for faith in God himself. Then the door is opened to faith in activities, and God drops out much more obviously.[33]

The American Y.M.C.A., as its activism grew, and its undenominational theology became more shadowy, was particularly open to this line of attack. It was not simply a matter of worldly cuckoos in the nest taking over the Association.

> At one university I find a whole mixed committee (churchmen and all) full of the sweetest earnestness and prayerfulness, humble and contrite Christians, visibly resting all that they do on God, yet when they got talking of their Y.M.C.A. work, you would not imagine that they had ever heard of a God in heaven or on earth. They were just full of their own activities: they would set God's world straight for Him. It would have such an excellent effect on their own character, and doing it made you feel ever so good.
>
> . . . I believe it to be the great defect of this pietism that it has no idea how entirely it depends on a certain religious emotionalism. What could that touching sweetness mean to the ordinary student . . .?[34]

This gets something of the character of student piety in this era. John R. Mott accepted Kelly's analysis, even to the sacramentalism; he was no longer a student, and he was

working to put some backbone into liberal Protestants, and
that not simply by retreating to traditional Evangelicalism,
the rock from which they were hewn.

Kelly obviously finds these young people delightful in
their 'touching sweetness'. The delight was mutual. Liberals
are perhaps prone to passing enthusiasms, sparked off by
other people's certainties. Kelly was satirical about the
changing fashions at Swanwick.

> [in 1908] the camp wanted an answer, and decided that our
> religions were all a matter of 'temperament' . . . Next year,
> we had forgotten our temperaments, but most years before
> the war we had a new word. Occasionally we talked of
> mysticism. I remember one year when everything was
> Feeling, and another when it was Experience; another
> (1912) it was Personality, especially the personality of Jesus,
> with a wonder whether He was conscious of being God.[35]

But he loved their enthusiasms, and played with ideas himself.

A World War, which disrupted all higher education,
and the natural difficulty of keeping up external links with
students on short-term courses, meant that much of the
work had to be started again. Algy Robertson became one
of the S.C.M. executive in January 1924. He was an
Anglo-Catholic, and had to re-do the business of winning
back the Anglican theological colleges (but not of course
loyal Kelham) to the S.C.M. When they held a conference specifically for theological college students at Swanwick, April 12th to 17th 1926, it was the first for twenty
years. 240 theological students from all over Britain
heard, among other things, a powerful address from
Father Kelly on 'The Reality of God and His Purpose
for the World'.[36]

For Kelly, one of the great attractions of Swanwick was
William Temple, recruited for S.C.M. in 1907. On the face
of it, the friendship was rather unlikely. Temple, before the
First World War, was already an establishment figure, the
son of an archbishop, confident, cleverly donnish, with
some question over his orthodoxy. (Bishop Paget of
Oxford had refused to ordain him: he was, for example,
merely 'inclined, very tentatively, to accept the doctrine of

the Virgin Birth'[37].) Kelly was older, an outsider, and in his
own way fiercely orthodox.

> He used to come every year with a contingent from
> Kelham, and I remember on two occasions ... William
> Temple was also present, and it was a matter of amusement
> to all the members of the conference how William Temple
> flew to Fr Kelly, just like a bee does to a honeypot. The
> two of them, immediately on arrival, would seek out one
> another, and they would be closeted in a room where it
> was assumed that deep theological discussion ensued; but
> laughter – and William Temple's laughter reached a long
> distance – coming from that room indicated that there was
> more than theology in the air. It also indicated a thing that
> we remember about Fr Kelly – his delightful sense of
> humour.[38]

Temple was a generous-spirited man, always willing to
find praise, so the good things he said about Fr Kelly and
his books can be matched by good things he said of other
people. 'The doctrine of the Incarnation, permanently
present in its true purity to Browning, is hopelessly mauled
by nearly every clergyman who touches it'.[39] Was Robert
Browning really such a religious genius that he could be
listed in a trinity of prophets with Hosea and Luther? The
man 'from whom I have learnt more than from any other
now living of the spirit of Christianity'[40] was Charles
Gore. Was bishop Gore, a prickly and dogmatic saint, such
an example of the spirit of Christianity?

Temple said 'All over the world there are now people
who owe much of their understanding of faith and of
religion to Fr Kelly.'[41] He spoke of Kelly as 'one of the
few really great teachers now living', and of *The Gospel of
God* as a 'really great little book'. In a very attractive review
of it, he wrote:

> You won't always agree with Fr Kelly; but you will always
> find it worth while to discover why you disagree, when
> you do. And if your experience is like mine has been for
> some twenty years, you will fail to find a good reason for
> disagreeing, and find, with some vexation, that you have
> got to agree after all.[42]

This is not a compliment from a very clever man, prone to underestimate his own sanctity, to a professionally saintly man. This is one clever philosophical theologian recognising another. When he was archbishop of York, from 1929 to 1942, with many journeys to London, Temple often called in at Kelham en route to visit Father Kelly. Years before, Kelly wrote in 1916 to Father Jenks, his successor as Director of SSM.

> You labour on for twenty years – and nothing comes; one day you get one man, and in him you make history. It may be that my influence on Willie Temple may mean [more] to the C. of E. than anything I've ever done.[43]

What can we find as evidence of influence? Anyone who remembers Fr Kelly's pigs might call in evidence Temple's cat.

> 'How, in the face of that,' he once asked a friend with whom he was walking, as he stopped in the street and pointed to a cat washing its face, 'can they deny the existence of natural theology?'[44]

'They' are the Barthians, and we should remember that Kelly, in his own way, and working independently, was a Barthian. Temple himself said that Kelly 'set forth with vivid insight that element in the life of religion, to a renewed emphasis on which the theological school of Barth and Brunner owes its tremendous influence on the Continent of Europe. This element is the priority and initiative of God.'[45] As is well known, Temple felt towards the end of his life that his own theology had been too world-affirming and positive, what might be called insufficiently Barthian, for the darkening times. It is too crude to cite this as one more case of Fr Kelly having been right after all.

There was dialogue rather than steady agreement between Temple and Kelly. Thus, for example, in *The Gospel of God*, Kelly says '. . . our philosophical friends gave us a suggestion – 'Reality is value.' It is not for us to argue with philosophers.'[46] But he does, and concludes 'Values do not make things'. Temple, in *Christus Veritas*, published two years before, had written 'Value is, in the order of being, prior to existence'.[47] Kelly is obviously taking issue with Temple, and Temple loved him for it.

Here I quote at some length from Dorothy Emmet's chapter 'The Philosopher' in Iremonger's *William Temple*.

> That Temple was never really clear about what he under-
> stood by natural theology is to be regretted the more in
> that he himself expresses a most valuable view of the
> nature of 'revealed theology'. He holds that the fatal mis-
> take in much of Christian history has been to look on
> 'revelation' as though it were given in the form of proposi-
> tions, to be held as 'revealed truths' ... Revelation, he
> says, is to be found in the coincidence of divinely guided
> events with divinely guided appreciation. The propositions
> in which minds then seek to express and interpret their
> belief in the significance of such events are never themselves
> the matter of revelation. They are attempts to point to the
> underlying events ... There are, of course, still difficulties
> in this view. How is 'revelation' to be distinguished, if at
> all, from the prophetic consciousness? ... If the vehicle of
> revelation is events, how do we relate their doctrinal
> interpretation to empirical attempts to determine what the
> actual historical events were? ... [Temple] has put the
> view of 'revelation in events' with a clarity which has
> caused it to make its mark in contemporary theology. But
> if questioned, he would no doubt have been the first to say
> that he owed this way of looking at it to that great teacher
> Father Herbert Kelly, S.S.M., to whom he often acknowl-
> edged his general indebtedness. Father Kelly once put (in a
> letter to myself) the allied point concerning the difference
> between faith in propositions and faith in that to which
> they refer in his own characteristic way:

> > The holy Bradshaw teaches (p80) that 'the first train for
> > Sebastopol starts from Newport (Mon.) at 4.55'. If I go to
> > catch it, that is, so far, faith in Bradshaw, but that is
> > secondary. My basic faith is in in the train and the railway
> > system to which I surrender myself that these (not Brad-
> > shaw) will carry me there. This is sound theology.

> But when asked whether the criticism of 'revelation in
> propositions' was not part of his influence on Temple,
> Father Kelly says he gives the credit 'to the greater portion

of Christian history'. He holds that the tendency to look on the sacred book as strings of authoritative statements only came in with the growth of legalistic interests in the Western Church. On this question I can only defer to the Church historian.[48]

This is a careful assessment of a key part of Temple's theology, and the debt to Kelly is acknowledged. Temple came from the philosophical background of English quasi-Hegelian idealism. This meant that when young he had trouble with the particularities of the Redemption story. 'The key throughout is his firm belief in the Divine Purpose for Good, as realised in the relations of persons with the Absolute Person and with one another'.[49] This Divine Purpose is reminiscent of Kelly's sense of the mystery of God's Will. ('But how do we know what is God's will?')

Temple, as a great public figure, had different opportunities than Kelly, but in his practical concerns he was working out as Kelly was the same Christianity for a world and not for a private ghetto. This was the archbishop who said

I am putting this very crudely, but I believe that our Lord is much more interested in raising the school-leaving age to sixteen than in acquiring an agreed Religious Syllabus.[50]

Once again propositions, an agreed syllabus, yield place to concrete events, children at desks.

Are these just commonplaces of liberalism? There is a question how far the more liberal wing of the Free Churches, which jibbed at set forms of creed during the early history of the student movement, were making the same sort of point as Temple. It was tempting at the time, but mistaken, to co-opt Temple for left-wing politics. He said that the Labour Party, of which he was a member for seven years from 1919, 'often want us to give up being specifically a Church, i.e. the Household of our Lord, and become a political party'.[51] Both he and Father Kelly undercut simple activism.

The young people of Liberal Protestantism were a natural audience for Kelly's Catholicism and sacramentalism. The Free Churches were re-discovering the sacraments.

'Preach the Lord's Supper more often, and the tea-meeting less, as the Church's social centre and family hearth', wrote P. T. Forsyth in *Church, Ministry and Sacraments* (1916). Forsyth was the English Free Churches' Barthian before Barth, and principal (1901–21) of a Congregationalist theological college. In other moods, he would polarise Christianity between churches of the Word and those of the Sacraments, and he was a preacher of the Word. Even so, he wrote

> Does the word of our preachers produce as much spiritual effect as the Sacrament does on high altars?. . . Do we go from it with the Romanist's sense, as he retires from Mass, that something has been done which has affected the unseen, penetrated to the spiritual world . . .?[52]

Fr Kelly heard of this:

> . . . a student of some London Congregationalist hole, who talked sacraments very intelligently and said that his Principal, Forsyth, was a tremendous admirer of 'High Church' – wants enquiring into.[53]

There was a sense in the Protestant churches of depths of the Christian heritage that they had missed. Looking at the sermons and publications of leading Protestant clergymen of early this century one sometimes suspects that their congregations were more informed on Francis and Bernard and Dante than the average Roman Catholic congregation of the day. When we look at historical schemes in stained glass windows in Protestant churches, showing the company of the saints going back through the centuries, we normally comment on the modern period – saints like Oliver Cromwell, John Wesley, Lord Shaftesbury. But the early and medieval periods have interest too. With care, and sometimes imagination, the Protestant churches were trying to reclaim their Catholic past. They were ready for real monks, in scapulars with knotted girdles. In the reign of Pius X there were no Roman Catholic monks available for fraternising with friendly curious Protestants, and few of the existing Anglican monks were interested either.

Liberalism was at its best prone to self-questioning. With the perspective of history, the theologians who radically

questioned the shallow optimism of liberal theology seem
to draw on liberalism more, to speak to the liberal condition more. Even Barth will go in the same chapter as
Bultmann and Bonhoeffer and Tillich as part of a single
great German tradition. Thus Forsyth, for example, would
say 'An event is a miracle not by its relations to law but to
grace. The Incarnation would be equally a miracle however
Jesus entered the world.'[54] This resembles Kierkegaard
claiming that it is enough to be able to say that the Son of
God has lived among us. This is clearly a theologian aware
of the gracious act of God in salvation. But does it mean
that God is not bound to use a Virgin Birth? Is the door
open for a liberal saying like Schleiermacher 'Miracle is
simply the religious name for event'.[55] Thus are miracles
explained away.

It is worth setting some of P. T. Forsyth's ideas alongside
Father Kelly's.

> It is our revelation we have to preach, and not our reli-
> gion.
> The positivity of the Gospel means the effectual primacy
> of the given.
> Preach character more than has been done, but do it
> through a Gospel that takes the making of character out of
> your hands.
> The divine thing in the soul is not a mystic subjectivity,
> but objective truth acting upon us at closest quarters.
> A Church needs a religion carried upon final and creative
> truths, not crackling with brisk modernity and steaming
> with amiable haze.

That happy phrase 'steaming with amiable haze' could just
as well have come from Father Kelly. There is a real sense
in both of them of turning away from our subjectivities to
what God has done. Forsyth is more a theologian of the
cross, as a single event in the past: 'The most ever done for
us was done behind our backs'. But he continues, and this
is rather like Kelly: 'only it was we who had turned our
backs'. 'We are in a world which has been redeemed; and
not in one which is being redeemed at a pace varying with
the world's thought and progress.'[56]

There is a difference between their prose styles, though people found both difficult. Forsyth's style was 'antithetical, paradoxical, sententious, aphoristic . . . something like walking on cobbles'.[57] Much the same could be said of Father Kelly, but Forsyth is less slangy, if sometimes less reserved. Auden has a phrase about 'The preacher's loose immodest tone'. Very occasionally this fits Forsyth.

Forsyth would say 'The Spirit of God is a Spirit of History'[58] and 'History is commerce, and even conflict, with the transcendent'.[59] Out of context, he, or Kelly, might sound Hegelian. Hegelians were more at ease with history. Both of them, on the other hand, have a sense of divine realities that put other concerns, even historico–political concerns, into perspective.

> Do not take my arm and lead me away to the dwellings of the pound-a-weeks and the nothing-a-weeks and tell me if I want realities to consider these. Long ago I was there, and worked there, and considered there, and have been considering ever since. The squalors and miseries of life are not its realities. They are its actualities. They would break every feeling heart that is not stayed upon life's realities from elsewhere. And they would submerge every society that cares nothing for the reality it touches in God and His Gospel alone.[60]

It is thus quite possible to find parallels between Kelly and Forsyth, and to place them both within, and reacting against, the progressive liberalism of the English-speaking Christianity of the period. There is less use in trying to place either of them in conservative traditions, Catholic or Protestant, who even when they come to the same conclusions, have different assumptions and questions and methods. We may see this spelt out when we consider Kelly's struggle with triumphalist Anglo-Catholicism in his own Society. The truth is that the interdenominationalism of the ecumenical movement is built on sentences like this famous one from Forsyth:

> I would ten times rather have one man who was burning deep, even though he wanted to burn me for my modern theology, than I would have a broad, hospitable and thin

theologian who was willing to take me in and a nondescript crowd of others in a sheet let down from heaven, but who had no depth, no fire, no skill to search, and no power to break.[61]

Young broad-minded liberals loved this sort of language. But it is a product of liberalism, not of traditional orthodoxy, and its fruits are liberal ecumenism.

Kelham continued loyal to the S.C.M. and ecumenism. When in 1943 the Superiors of a number of Anglican Religious Communities collectively approached archbishop William Temple to try to block the Church of South India reunion scheme, the Society of the Sacred Mission was not among them. It very nearly was.

We now turn to the strand in the history of SSM that, in this and other matters, tried to bring it more in line with other Anglican Religious Communities.

Chapter 7

Kelham and Anglo-Catholicism

Father Kelly was not a typical Anglo-Catholic. The Society he founded was enriched but sometimes handicapped by this.

The very existence of religious orders in Anglicanism is an expression of the Catholic revival. When Father Kelly took his students to Swanwick, they felt, and everyone they met felt, that they were speaking for the Catholic tradition of sacraments and order. They also felt, unlike most Anglo-Catholics of the time, that ecumenism, going to Swanwick, was more Catholic in spirit than refusing to go. The sense of being Catholic is quite properly more than a mere party spirit. In a church where there are other traditions alongside, however, there is a risk of partisanship, and an Anglo-Catholic party developed. It is quite possible to find phrases and practices that will irritate the other side, or the authorities, and then talk about nothing else and do nothing else. It is fun shocking people.

> 'We mean to start Benediction next monf. I should vink it would annoy ve Bishop very much'.[1]

It is also fun belonging to an in-group, over against the drowsy generalities of the rest. Even from the beginnings of the Oxford Movement, with Hurrell Froude and John Henry Newman, some Anglo-Catholics have enjoyed being shocking and partisan.

Most Anglicans in the Catholic tradition were not schoolboyishly partisan. Some were only occasionally. None were invariably: even the most 'spikey' curate was likely to be transcended by the great tradition that his partisanship failed to help. Nor is it wise to take for granted that a moderate Anglo-Catholicism is more desirable than a thoroughgoing sort. Extremists sometimes have right on their side. The judicious episcopal Anglo-Catholicism of bishop Samuel Wilberforce or archbishop Cosmo Gordon Lang was diluted as much by worldly wisdom as by deeper spiritual insight. Bishops were traditionally disappointing to Anglo-Catholics, even when selected to represent them.[2]

Nevertheless, as so much of twentieth century church history comes to us in the shape of biographies of bishops, we tend to get the bishops' perspective on this.

Boundaries of loyalty shifted depending on circumstance. A bishop might be quite fierce in requiring the use of the 1662 Prayer Book, annoying his Anglo-Catholic clergy, and yet in other circumstances be revered by them as a real father in God. This is true of men like E. S. Talbot and Charles Gore. The movement, like other religious movements, needed heroes, to be personal focuses of sanctity. There were problems about this, because an objective sacramental piety makes nothing of the personal gifts of the officiant.

It was felt preferable to gabble prayers than to say them with what was perceived as canting Evangelical unction. (Fr Alfred Kelly, who loved statistics, counted the words per minute in different broadcast services, and it was true, the RCs rattled them off).[3] Some Anglo-Catholics were in fact good preachers, and their sermons were remembered. But preaching was disparaged, and Anglo-Catholics looked elsewhere for images of authentic Catholicity.

In a way they turned to those who confronted time: the vicars, and indeed curates, of slum parishes who stayed there a lifetime; and the religious, who made vows for life. Fr Kelly was part of the tradition when he wrote, in capitals for emphasis, one of his favourite sayings, 'NOTHING COUNTS BUT LIFETIMES'.[4]

It did mean that members of religious orders were in demand. They had given up their lives to Christ's service. This was a mixed blessing for the Society of the Sacred Mission. Young men, no saintlier than others, were deferred to by pious people because they were wearing a habit. This deference brought, for example, memberships of committees. The Anglo–Catholic Congress Mission Sub-committee, apart from the chairman, was completely composed of male religious (Secretary: Fr Tribe, SSM; the others: 2 SSJE, 1 CR).[5] It also brought invitations to preach. Though sermons were secondary in Anglo–Catholicism, there was still a market for guest preachers. (Only bishops appeal as guest celebrants, with the chance of a Pontifical High Mass). Father Alfred Kelly, the founder's athletic younger brother, criss-crossed England on a bicycle, covering 10,000 miles in 1915–16, on preaching engagements.

> On one celebrated occasion he arrived late . . . and finding that the service had already begun, went in and at the appropriate moment made straight for the pulpit. In the vestry afterward, the vicar thanked him for his sermon, adding 'But who are you?' – Fr Alfred having gone to the wrong church.[6]

Fr Wilfrid Hambidge, after the First World War, also peripatetic, though by trains, until his health broke down, was eager for the Society to develop a role as Mission Priests, called in to stir up parishes. It would provide a distinctive field of work for those who lacked the scholarly gifts to teach at Kelham. Fr Kelly, in a modification of this, fancied filling their time between weekends by handing over the routine marking of college essays to the mission priests, a typical lecturer's daydream. There was always preaching to be had, but the great days of parish missions were before the First World War, and itinerancy, though some were suited to it, was at that time felt to weaken the sense of belonging to the Society.

The talismanic role of religious orders also brought money. The Society in its early days had depended very largely on the generosity of the Kelly family, and on challenging its students and novices to live on practically nothing. But by the time it came to build the great chapel at Kelham in 1928, balancing the accounts was no real problem. The big annual Sale of Work in Westminster, with the Dowager Lady Beauchamp as chief stallholder, and all her assistants titled, apart from Miss Kelly, the founder's sister, did not raise vast sums – the total profit in 1913 was £31 – but symbolised a much wider network. There was the Guild of St Gabriel, of helpful ladies knitting for the cause, with ten branches by 1914. The college cost £6000 a year to run in the 1920s, and then £7500 as numbers went up. Kelham was never luxurious:

> gilt lacquer coming off hideous ironwork and bits coming loose from a hideous mosaic pavement . . [7]
>
> There was no linoleum on the floors in A corridor and one jumped out of bed on to the cold concrete, while no amount of sweeping could get it clean. [8]

Kelly contrasted this with the expensive and tasteful simplicities of the Cowley Fathers' house in Westminster: 'all in the severest monastic style but all the same money no object'.[9] Kelham looked grandiose from a distance, but it would be perverse to talk of this Society being corrupted by wealth.

There were, however, other effects of meeting the expectations of Anglo-Catholicism that were to mean trouble for the Society. It is not very important that a lot of the young men who came to Kelham had been brought up in Anglo-Catholic 'party' parishes and came with rather picturesque notions of being monks. A few weeks, or even days, of experience sifted out the utterly superficial, who then left, and the young men selected grew and developed. It is no great clue to the impish and innovative personality of Gregory Wilkins, Director 1962–1972, that he was when young 'a server in the highest church in the world', the Anglo-Papalist St Magnus the Martyr in London.[10] What was more difficult was that the Society could not be, and never intended to be, filled with men whose whole experience since boyhood was Kelham.[11] Some novices came already graduates, and they were desperately needed to teach in the college. There were not many of them: Mirfield was much more attractive to men from Oxford and Cambridge. Kelham, because it took non-graduates, frightened off graduates, who are prone to snobbery. Also the life was very spartan. The graduates who did come were less malleable than the boys, and they had their own ideas, normally more Anglo-Catholic ones than Father Kelly's.

This should not be exaggerated. Father Kelly was sometimes an insecure person, and prone to feel alone and misunderstood. He wrote it all down, and we have these very vivid pictures of the unbelief and hardness of heart of his followers.

> I had an Ideal (Vision) like S. Francis. The Society has turned its back on it, and accepted, not something else, but the very reverse.[12]

The other side of the coin is that it was, in a sense, Kelly's Society they had joined. He had utterly shaped it, and most of the time they revered him.

Consider his relationship with Father David Jenks, the second Director, 1910–1920. Kelly, when fifty, stepped down. The Society, he felt, must be seen plainly not to be a one-man show. Sometimes he looked back, and stressed that the professed brethren in chapter had voted him out. (See the Curriculum Vitae before his *Autobiography*: 'Deposed as Director 1910'). In fact he enjoyed being a 'staff-college lecturer' rather than in charge at Kelham, and also in Jenks's time spent several happy years lecturing in Japan. David Jenks was a Cambridge graduate, and more Anglo-Catholic than Kelly. Thus he had proposed taking ablutions in the Roman place in the eucharist ('tarping', from the initials of the words) rather than as the Prayer Book directs, at the end. Father Kelly would have none of this, so it did not happen. Mildenhall, and later Kelham, was to be straightforwardly Anglican in its liturgy. When Father Jenks succeeded as Director, he did not change the rules on this matter. Such is reverence to founder's intention.

In himself he continued to be more Anglo-Catholic than Kelly.

> [David Jenks] insisted that 'if by his own fault, he had not 'said a mass' (of his own) on a day of obligation, he would feel bound to mention it in Confession.' The idea amazed me, but if folk's consciences do work this way . . . I felt

forced to let them . . . much against my will and judgment.[13]

The man described is the second Director of the Society. He was more typical of the Society than the founder. Even Father Kelly's own younger brother, Fr Alfred Kelly, had his own Mass like Fr Jenks.

Father Kelly stood out against following Roman practices for their own sake. But in any religious community, some practices ultimately Roman almost had to be followed. Inevitably, for there was no other available source, some of the liturgy was borrowed from Roman Catholic models. The Prayer Book provides Morning and Evening Prayer; the services for the other hours came from elsewhere. One can imagine how people trying to live a monastic life came to feel that the Prayer Book rules were fragmentary and unhelpful, and that the Roman material was a well-considered unity. The Prayer Book had other ends in view. We shall look later at how Father Gabriel Hebert in the 1930s, working with the Liturgical Movement on the continent of Europe, had a more dynamic and thinking approach to these matters, handling liturgy as Father Kelly handled dogma, putting the purpose of it, and the understanding of it, before rules for their own sake.

Someone from another tradition might also notice that Father Kelly was taken aback by his successor's scruples of conscience, but took for granted that these scruples should be expressed in terms of what to bring up in the confessional. At Kelham under Fr Kelly, there was the confessional (not obligatory), and there was prayer for the departed, both unprotestant activities.

The priories overseas of the Society, in Korea until 1904, in Zanzibar and South Africa, were in a somewhat different situation. Though the local bishops were likely to carry off individual members for utterly indispensable work, thus making the observance of the ordered life together of a community difficult, their churchmanship was much more clear-cut than that of any English diocesan bishop. These were monochrome Anglo-Catholic dioceses insisting on Catholic practices. Both Korea and the UMCA dioceses were run in ways reminiscent of religious orders, with celibate clergy, under a vow of poverty, with the bishop at the head. The overlap between two contrasting similar jurisdictions, the diocese and the Society, in fact brought trouble.

> Central Africa enthralls: it is no question of a three years' contract.[14]

These priories had strong local reinforcement of their Anglo-Catholicism. Father Woodward, second founder with Father Kelly of the Society in 1893, was for many years archdeacon of Zanzibar. He recruited the young Frank Weston, later to be his bishop, the saintly and extreme star of the triumphalist Anglo-Catholicism of the 1920s. There is no hint of any discord in churchmanship between Fr Woodward and his bishop. Fr Kelly had more mixed feelings.

> There are two Bishops of Zanzibar. One of them quarrelled with me, also with Fr Jenks, and always has his knife in SSM. He wrote *Christ and other Claims*. The other runs UMCA, wrote *God with Us* . . . altogether a most delightful person – backing us for all he is worth.[15]

The difficulties between SSM and Bishop Weston were over staffing rather than churchmanship. Successive Directors of SSM did tend to move people about. If anyone dropped out, it was likely to be all change. When they were desperate for another tutor at Kelham at the end of the war, the Bishop of Zanzibar refused to hand over Fr Whitworth, and that was that. He had only been there a year or two; if he had gone back to Kelham perhaps Father Murphy would not have cracked up as Warden; but the Bishop of Zanzibar had his own priorities. After a struggle, it was the Bishop of Bloemfontein who gave way, and yielded a man.

Father Woodward, in UMCA, was more simply Anglo-Catholic than Fr Kelly, and for the fiftieth anniversary of his ordination, the Society raised money for a Blessed Sacrament chapel. [16] Fr Jenks might have wanted his own Mass on every day of obligation; Fr Woodward

had more regular habits than that.' . . . dear old Fr Woodward says that if he doesn't say Mass his whole day is
spoiled.'[17]

The Korean mission also was Anglo-Catholic. It was a
mission founded with a bishop, as first necessity. It had
nuns before SSM arrived. They always used incense at all
celebrations in the diocese of Korea.[18] There were 21
follow-up conferences round Asia organised by the Continuation Committee of the Edinburgh Missionary Conference 1910. Korea was the only one where the Anglicans
were 'visitors' not members. [19] Bishop Trollope of Korea
had been a novice at Vassall Road, and had then opted for
the mission rather than the Society. He was to go into
print with an argument against 'unreasoning insistence on
the vernacular' in liturgy as

> it must be remembered that the Roman Catholic Church –
> which is the greatest and most successful missionary body
> in the world – has carried on its missions everywhere
> under this handicap, if it is a handicap.[20]

Thus are the blessings of Reformation discounted. Neither
Korea nor Central Africa were as significant in the history
of the Society as South Africa. The Central African province shrunk to one priory, and then the Society withdrew
in 1929. Father Woodward himself went back to Zanzibar
afterwards, dying there, over eighty, in 1932.

The South African province of SSM was more coherent,
with larger priories, more distinct areas of work, and
perhaps with less overbearing bishops. The local churchmanship was also Anglo-Catholic. One must not exaggerate
this. The Church of the Province of South Africa had no
party Evangelical theological colleges or indeed congregations. It had made a stand against the modernist ideas of
Bishop Colenso. The Province was more homogeneous
than the Church of England. But big white congregations
had ordinary Anglican expectations. Anglo-Catholics, with
the blessing of the bishops, and very biddable black congregations, could do much as they pleased.

The SSM, and in this it was very like SSJE and CR, was
determinedly Catholic. 'On Sunday afternoons we have

parts of Evensong, followed by Devotions to the Blessed Sacrament'. [21] There were unkind remarks about the Protestant missions around them, and even more about beginnings of independent African Christianity. 'Oh that the Bible had been kept a 'closed book' to these people'.[22]

But South Africa also provided almost the only possible power-base in the Society against Kelham. This became evident when Father George Carleton was appointed Provincial of the South African province in 1915. Father Carleton had been a tutor at Kelham, and was born to lead. He had great administrative gifts, and there is some evidence that the Society had been rather slackly run in South Africa before he was sent out by the Director, Father Jenks, to tidy things up. He rapidly was promoted to be archdeacon of Bloemfontein.

Fr Carleton was a definite Anglo–Catholic. Here is Father Kelly's description of him.

> Fr Carleton was a typical Irishman ('agin the guv'ment') – a brilliant Trinity College Dublin star scholar – very satisfied with his scholarship – a type of Wilfred Knox – doubtful about the Ascension, but quite sure about 'Our Lady' and 'devotions'. [As Provincial in South Africa, he] substituted devotionalism for the love of God (a very easy and common thing) and ultra-montane 'Catholicism' for faith in a Church ... Two things he demanded: (a) that SSM be re-organised as specifically 'religious' (he meant 'monastic' ...) and (b) 'Catholicised'. The human soul loves a programme and a propaganda. The Province went with him to a man.[23]

Others outside the Society in South Africa found Father Carleton unpleasantly arrogant. [24] But he was obviously highly competent, the sort of man who comes top of the poll in elections to a synod. He could be amusingly sharp, as could Father Kelly. Carleton was the one who, looking at the intake of 1911, asked whether the college was now 'engaged in the reclamation of the criminal classes'.[25] He is unfortunate in being cast as a Lucifer-like leader trying to overthrow all that Father Kelly stood for, failing, after an uncharitable struggle, and then going off in disgust. Those who leave religious orders after a failed putsch, if in the histories at all, get short shrift. Within the small inner circle of the Society, Father Carleton was hated. When he was a candidate to be Director of the Society in 1920, the opposing candidate, Father Gerald Murphy, said he would leave the Society if Carleton were elected, and both previous Directors, Father Kelly and Father Jenks, gave something of the same impression, though Fr Kelly later denied this. [26] Father Jenks, a natural peace-maker, had been driven into a breakdown by controversy.

Consider the case of Fr Rand in 1917. Fr Frederick Rand SSM went on holiday to South Africa, visiting a number of friends. He wrote to the SSM Priory at Modderpoort inviting himself for the weekend of the Society festival at Michaelmas, knowing that the brethren in the outlying stations would all be there. He got this reply from Fr Carleton, then Provincial of South Africa.

Sept. 30 1917

Dear Fr Rand,

Your conduct is very extraordinary, as a member of the Society; . . . causing offence to your brothers.

First, you come into this province without notifying me, and you pay private visits without having come here and placed yourself under obedience. Next you write [inviting yourself] . . . It was not convenient for us . . . We were in the middle of our retreat . . . What you wish for is a hotel, and not the society of your brothers.

. . . I require you to send me such an adequate apology as may atone for your offence; and one which I can read to the brethren . . .

Fr Rand, who was quite a spirited person, wrote back:

4.10.1917

My Dear Carleton,

Have you taken leave of your senses or is the altitude affecting you adversely? Your letter suggests to me an acute attack of what was once called 'Zanzibarbarianism'. Take my advice and run down to the coast for a while, and mix a little with your fellow man; and try to learn that the SSM doesn't teach its members, even if they are Provincials, to be little Popes. I had heard rather extraordinary rumours about Modderpoort but the reality (unless your letter is only funny) surpasses my dreams . . .

Hoping you will soon be feeling better . . .[27]

The unfortunate Director, Father Jenks, had to cope with this. He explained to Fr Carleton that a brother on holiday in South Africa was not ipso facto under his control,[28] and that 'as a matter of fact he [Rand] did what nearly everybody does'.[29] The very slight original discourtesy 'merited that . . . some of the brothers should have pulled his leg'. [30] But Fr Rand's reply was another matter, and he had a formal letter of rebuke from the Director for his 'studiously insulting' language.[31] The South African province, which was completely behind Fr Carleton, never forgave Fr Rand, but one might guess that the Director, though he backed Fr Carleton up, held this episode against him, and did not want him as his successor. The word 'Zanzibarbarianism' might give us a clue why the the Society sometimes found it difficult to work with UMCA bishops.

The South African province put forward a manifesto of Catholic reform in 1917. This took the form of a circular letter from the terminally ill Fr Hubert Hilder, who died that year. He listed the causes of weakness in SSM:

(a) An over-anxiety to increase numbers [leading to] grave mistakes in the selection of candidates.

(b) [In theology, a] failure of the Society officially to keep pace with recent tendencies in the Church.

(c) Lack of proper proportion between the College and the Society, whereby the former has predominated.

(d) . . .placing members in positions of isolation.

(e) The secularising tendency of the domestic arrangements at the Mother House, whereby Seculars and Religious have been mixed indiscriminately.

(f) Laxity of rule and timidity in the exercise of authority.[32]

From the Rand case we might have an idea of what 'timidity in the exercise of authority' means. The 'recent tendencies in the Church' in theology were Anglo-Catholic, 'a movement so strong and irresistible that it must be of God'. Fr Kelly replied from Tokyo, with another circular letter, accepting several of the points but joining battle. 'I never heard anyone say that Eucharistic Adoration and habitual Confession were part of its [the Church of England's] "commonly accepted interpretation".' [33]

The South African reforms particularly stressed the value for its own sake of the religious life. 'We have been thinking of numbers, when we ought to have been thinking of perfection'. [34] Fr Kelly had wanted a Society to be available for work, with a rule of life as a means of guaranteeing availability, nothing more. The Protestant Reformers had had a point in being suspicious of religion for religion's sake, and history suggested, Kelly thought, that orders that did not live for the work tended to corrupt. However, there has been, throughout the history of the Society, a strong pull towards being a Religious for the sake of being a Religious.

Carried through, this would have an impact that was not merely on the self-understanding of individuals. The arrangements of the life at Kelham would have to change. In June 1917, Fr Carleton wrote a paper called 'Counsel with regard to the reorganisation of Kelham offered at the request of the Director'. What is very striking is the emotional charge he puts into the separation of the various groups at Kelham, and the sense of hierarchy.

> . . . one house for boys . . . no man may set his foot therein . . . a house for Aspirants and Associates.. The Associate Master is the sole potentate. He is a great man. The public hear of him as the Principal . . . a novice house, into which sacred precinct no Associate may enter without permission, and that is rarely granted.. the Director [perhaps] . . . with his secretary, in a several house, remote, apart, serene . . . if he deigned to lecture, it would be only in the most superior way, as a special favour.[35]

All these were to be on one site. In fact, as this was a reordering of Kelham, some would be on different floors of the same building. When one thinks of the cheerful bustle of the real Kelham, with everyone mucking in together, there is obviously here a different vision from Father Kelly's.

In the event, the Society did not choose to go down this road. In the Great Chapter of 1920 these issues were argued. Here is Carleton reproaching Kelly there:

> We are a community of 'religious' according to the Constitution. We approach our work with the mind, temper, aspirations, and inspiration of 'religious' . . . This ideal is not selfish. It is personal conformity to God . . . . the preaching against personal religion has hindered the work of the Society by damaging souls.[36]

Always alert for Pelagianism, and aware that the charge of 'preaching against personal religion' was aimed at him, Father Kelly replied that to say 'to love God is to do his will' overlooks 'the Will of God done *in* us'.

The dispute was conducted with some bitterness. Both Carleton and Murphy took three or four years after the election of 1920 to decide to leave the Society. Here is a vignette from Father Kelly's *Newsletter* of July 1923.

> Prior asked G.D.C. [Carleton] to be chaplain of new Associates. G.D.C. refuses. Utter disbelief in the House system. Scrabble! Prior told him – inter alia – that frankly he had much more confidence in Fr Edmund's spiritual influence than in his (C's), to which G.D.C. replied, 'It only shows the incapacity of your judgement.' N.B. one doesn't usually put one's opinion of oneself that way in the Religious Life, but as G.D.C. is our only instructor therein, I may be wrong.

Father Kelly's semi-private *Newsletter*, so open, often so indiscreet, and sometimes so sharp in its sarcasm, gives us a clue of the strength of feeling in the House. It is, however, almost too good evidence. The Society of the Sacred Mission in 1923 had a new young prior at Kelham, Stephen Bedale. Instead of the two gifted and forceful rival candidates for Director, Carleton and Murphy, they had chosen a humble saintly and definitely not very clever missionary, Fr Joseph White. As Director (1920–25), he went out to South Africa, to take over Fr Carleton's work. The Society seemed to run itself; it was growing, and to outward appearance, things went smoothly. Underneath there was still turmoil. There is still extant an eight-page letter from Carleton to White, telling him he would not be welcome in South Africa, and suggesting White should do the sensible thing and resign in his favour. 'I knew all along that your qualities were not those that fitted you for the office'. [37] Fr Carleton was much cleverer and more competent than Fr White, and it was hard on him, as well as on the Society, that his personality and piety were different from SSM. Years before, when he was offered profession, his Novice-Master, Fr Jenks, said 'I hope you will not accept the Society's offer; you would always be a valued tutor, but you never could be one of us'. [38]

Fr Peter Clark, who was a novice while all this was going on, wrote in a note to Alan Jones in 1971:

> whilst the Carleton Affair was raging, the normal life, for students at least, went on – chapel, lectures, meals were not impeded. I should say the majority was anti-Carleton . . . . Gerald [Murphy]'s outbursts were bad enough, but mostly we liked him, admired him for his power of mind. [39]

It was a great blow to Father Kelly that Gerald Murphy, who had come up through the Society, one of the first batch of boys who arrived in 1895, left in 1922. 'He is the last, the only one left, of all the younger generation I trained to be teachers and thinkers.' [40] There is a Swanwick address on 'Unity, Truth, Freedom' from July 1913 given by Gerald Murphy, about truth coming from unity, which is a good piece of Kelly theology done by someone else than Fr Kelly. The quarrel between Murphy and Carleton was a matter of personality rather than party feeling. Gerald Murphy, undoubtedly clever, was unstable and easily led. Left as one of the two priests in charge of the mother house in 1919, when the Director had had a breakdown, as Prior he made sweeping changes in the liturgy at Kelham.

> Murphy had little practical capacity, with men or otherwise. Whitworth swept him along. Between them, they proceeded to reorganise the services to SSPP requirements. [The Society of St Peter and St Paul was Anglo-Papalist].

Notably they introduced 'tarping', priests' masses, six candles and the Roman Angelus. The traditional ideas of
thirty years went in a day without any consultation.. a
most unconstitutional procedure, as Murphy was only
'Prior' in the absence of Jenks.[41]

If one of the two main candidates had been made Director
in 1920, the Society would have been sternly Catholicised.
At the Great Chapter, the other, Fr Gerald Murphy, in fact
proposed that the Society should be disbanded. This was
the man they had to make Prior at Kelham in 1920. The
Society was dangerously short of competent leaders. It is
not surprising that Father Stephen Bedale, professed at
Michaelmas 1921, was Prior by December 1922. Fr Whitworth ('a Cambridge pass-man, utterly incapable of an
idea of any sort . . . who had sold his soul . . . to Band-of-
Hope (or Society of SS Peter & Paul) Catholicism', wrote
Kelly in *SSM, 1929*) had been Cottage Master, in charge of
the boys, and was sent out to Zanzibar, where his sort of
Anglo-Catholicism would be more at home. The Central
African Province had not long to survive. Later he trans-
ferred to SSJE (Society of St John the Evangelist), the
Cowley Fathers.

Cowley was always present as a more disciplined, more
traditional norm. Father Benson himself, the founder of
SSJE, was perhaps not so far in his views from Kelly,
but his Society was more monastic than SSM. Cowley
was the natural precedent. 'I took the House Rule from
Cowley (it was much too high pitched) and the rest was all
fairly obvious'.[42] With hindsight, Kelly himself regretted
much of what he took from Cowley.

> My fear is that the system is itself hopelessly wrong. (a)
> The insistence on obedience and responsible authority cer-
> tainly has utterly obscured the insistence on the responsibil-
> ity (initiative) of the individual. (b) We borrowed from
> Cowley a great deal too much conventional Religious Life
> machinery (e.g. offices). And these two have convention-
> alised men's minds past recognising anything. (If I had
> known of it, I would have followed the Oratory system. I
> do not like CR [Mirfield], but it succeeds just where we
> do not.)[43]

This is the Old Man dissatisfied with the society as it was in its heyday. There was a very strong movement within SSM after the First World War in exactly the opposite direction to Kelly. This in some cases meant 'Roman fever'. In the whole history of SSM, seven professed members have become Roman Catholic, which is not a great number. One was in 1914, one in 1918, and two in 1921, and these conversions are relevant to our present concern. South Africa and the Nottingham priory were affected, rather than the mother house. Non-Roman 'Cartholicism' was much more in evidence. The complaints were that the Society was not sufficiently ordered, not sufficiently monastic in its life. Carleton, touring South Africa, said that the Cowley mission at Tsolo 'seemed to me nearer the ideal Church mission than any other I saw'.[44] SSM was perceptibly less disciplined than Cowley in the field.

More significant than articulated complaints, perhaps, was the fact that there were scarcely observed changes in perception and practice in line with the triumphalist Anglo-Catholicism of the 1920s. The liturgical alterations brought in high-handedly by Gerald Murphy in 1919 were not in fact reversed. Father Bedale was born to rule, and with a compliant Director, Reginald Tribe (1925–43) busy most of the time elsewhere, Kelham was in practice an autocracy. So though Carleton and Murphy had left by 1925, the Society after they had gone continued to be definitely Anglo-Catholic. On the sidelines, Father Kelly, sometimes very fiercely, attacked these 'Cartholic' tendencies.

> I used to be so proud of our Chapel, and its carefully purposed worship. Now I hate to go into it . . . Quite solemnly, as things stand, if I were not a member of SSM, I would not join it.[45]

It may be, as Alan Jones says, that ' " the Old Man" hardly helped matters by making known his own feelings in such a way as to inhibit free discussion . . . His feelings were so strong that his brethren were frankly frightened to inaugurate a discussion with him'.[46] His deafness was worse, so a discussion meant shouting in any case. But it is surely telling that after a time, well into the Tribe-Bedale era, the 'Old Man' got his way, and the liturgy in Kelham chapel returned to Prayer Book Anglicanism, modified in the ways that bishops expect.

The men he was up against, the Director, Reginald Tribe, and the Prior, Stephen Bedale, were neither of them extremist in temper. Fr Tribe was indeed a professional Anglo-Catholic, working in the 1920s, when Director of SSM, almost full-time as Secretary of the Anglo-Catholic Midland Council, but nevertheless he headed for the middle ground whenever possible.

> I was sorry for the Bp of Zanzibar's insistence on the tabernacle . . . to make this the touchstone of the Anglo-Catholic movement is quite wrong. [47]

This refers to the Bishop's provocative slogan 'Fight for your tabernacles' at the 1923 Anglo-Catholic Congress.[48] Certainly the Society had members, and sent priests to congregations, for whom the reserved sacrament was the centre of religious life.

Fr Bedale was very clear-cut and decisive in his running of the College. So when Fr Kelly picked a fight over the chapel services, he got one. But as far as Bedale could be hesitant and willing to learn, he was hesitant over this. It would be difficult to work out his own stance. He inherited the form of chapel services; even as a novice, he had not had any part in the relevant decisions; there had been a Great Chapter (in 1920) between the changes and his installation as Prior, and it had not reversed them; and as head of Kelham he succeeded the last Director, Fr Joseph White, a UMCA missionary perfectly happy with a more Catholic ritual. Bedale's first thought seems to have been to leave well alone. He could claim confidently that he had changed nothing.

There was a lobby for change, for change back to the old ways. Behind Fr Kelly in this matter were several of the lay brothers. Thus, at the 1925 Great Chapter, when the liturgy was discussed,

> Br William Hardwell instanced the growth of Private

> Masses . . . [He] could not understand why people absent
> themselves from the Corporate Communion . . .
>
> Br Edgar Lintott [spoke of] the variety of uses brought
> in by men coming back from the War in 1919 [which]
> made things very difficult for the lay brothers. [49]

The Anglo-Catholic tendency was clericalist; and the lay
brothers tended to resent this. Many of the House had no
great feeling either way. It may be difficult now, but for
many it was difficult then, to have strong feelings about,
for example, when the priest conducts the ablutions in the
liturgy.

> . . . the greater part of this House [says] 'Fr Kelly means to
> get his own way' and watches with amusement or anxi-
> ety . . .[50]

There were moderating decisions in 1928.

> We had an SSM 'Director's Council' on November 3rd re
> Chapel services. I was expecting trouble, but Fr David
> [Jenks] was there. He is not only a very diplomatic person,
> but he is by now a person of considerable standing outside,
> and I think some folk were afraid to let off their rather
> childish anti-K. squirts before him. So when D.J. suggested:
> 'Go on, till the bishops pronounce, then say "We, of
> course, go with the Church."' I said: 'Will you make that a
> motion?" Agreed . . .
>
> On the 10th we got on to Reservation. The Prior urged
> the necessity. We had two cases of sudden illness during
> the last 12 months. There was no question of devotions
> . . . The bishop was asked. He is nuts on us; 'was greatly
> honoured' at being Visitor. Granted permission for reserva-
> tion – with full episcopal formula – aumbry – no organised
> devotions. [51]

The great chapel never had six tall unlit candlesticks on a
shelf behind the high altar after the best Roman model. It
very nearly did: the architect's drawing shows one like this.
Father Kelly told what he called 'The Prior's tale'. Bedale
had come to him 'bubbling with fun':

> 'I said to Thompson: . . . "Must we have these six tall

candles?"' 'Oh yes', said he. 'Certainly we must. Renaissance building. Renaissance fittings'. . . . I tried him again
. . . 'Two short candles and a low cross look much better'.
'Undoubtedly', says he . . . 'These artists' (says the Prior)
'are always dogmatic. I know I am.'

Fr Kelly concluded ' . . . I can only take it as a confession . . .'. [52] The sacrament was reserved somewhere out of
sight up in a gallery. The chapel sums up in a very
impressive way Father Stephen Bedale's type of Catholicism, which did not run on the lines of baroque 'tat'. One
might still have slight misgivings about the continuance of
private masses as the norm. Up in the galleries of the great
chapel there were other altars. But for a religious order
Kelham was strikingly Anglican, no more high-church
than the average English cathedral. Thus the development
which pleased Father Kelly above all was

> the return of this House to its obedience. They had a
> Chapter, Oct. 6th [1932], and passed a resolution: 'to
> recognise the original rationale of the Anglican Liturgy,
> the perfected expression of its idea, guided by (etc) –
> submitting all results to the diocesan . . . before adopting
> them.' [53]

The friendly Bishop of Southwell, already mentioned, in
whose diocese they were, had wanted the 'tarping' (taking
ablutions at the Roman place) stopped. The whole history
of ritualism in the Church of England was one of disobedi-
ence to bishops. Carleton had made a special point of the
independence of the SSM, as a religious order, over
against local jurisdictions. There were precedents in the
history of Catholicism for stands like this. Father Kelly, by
contrast, thought that the Society was there to serve the
Church of England, at home and overseas, at the will of its
bishops. The Constitution says that the Society

> can have no end or aim of its own except the good of the
> Church, and, further, that it should be its aim to take from
> those whom God has appointed to be the Bishops of his
> Church the direction of its efforts. [54]

This included matters liturgical. By 1930 an English diocesan bishop was very unlikely to use any sanction beyond expressing displeasure over ritualist excesses. The Bishop of Southwell in 1922 had refused as Visitor to intervene over 'tarping'; it may well be that his later willingness to lay down the law was stage-managed by the Prior. Anglo-Catholic parishes, and even more, non-parochial chapels of religious orders, were a law unto themselves. (There were Anglican convents with perpetual devotions to the blessed sacrament and the services all in Latin. 'That rogue Bishop Frere defiled our high altar by using English at it'[55]). In any case the whole church, after Parliament had rejected the Revised Prayer Book in 1929, was prepared to turn a blind eye on those who used some technically illegal services. As Brother George Every discovered, Kelham had disliked the 1929 book:

> My interest in Eastern Christendom and my admiration for Bishop Frere as a saint and a scholar made me favourable to the proposals made in 1927, but when I came to Kelham as a student-tutor in 1929 I found everyone against them except, as I later discovered, Father Kelly himself. [56]

The Prior, Stephen Bedale, following the 1932 Chapter, set up a committee of three, including Alfred Kelly and Gabriel Hebert. They revised the Kelham Use in an Anglican direction, and the new use was approved by the bishop. 'So – after 14 years – Kelham has "returned to the obedience of Holy Church". Therein I do rejoice exceedingly, and will rejoice.' [57]

Father Kelly had no direct hand in this; neither had Father Stephen Bedale. The Chapter decision, taken in Kelly's absence, had been unanious. Decisions under Father Bedale tended to be unanimous and he chose the committee. Father Hebert was to go on to have great influence on Anglican liturgy, and indeed beyond, but in this matter it seems probable that he was not the instigator; his Society was moving with him. We can probably say that here Bedale, as omnicompetent Prior of the mother House, built on Kelly's principles.

Turning from matters of liturgy, we find theological contrasts between Kelham and the mainstream Anglo-

Catholicism of between the wars. Here, from Fr Bedale, not from Fr Kelly, in 1922, is a typical statement of the task Kelham theology set itself.

> ... Christianity is not concerned with just one aspect or department of human life, but with the whole of it. The Church is, or ought to be, concerned not only with how men pray, but with how men make boots, with how men fight, make laws, fall in love, play football, and write sonnets.[58]

What has theology to do with the life of lay men and women? The question could not be put more strongly. Here, a few years later, from an address to the 1930 Anglo-Catholic Congress by Father Biggart of the Society of St John the Evangelist, is a possible answer. It is a list of the duties of the Catholic laymen:

1 Hear mass on Sundays
2 Receive holy communion at least three times a year
3 Go to confession at least once a year
4 Observe Fridays as a fast-day
5 Give alms liberally
6 Observe the forbidden degrees in marriage [59]

It may be unjust to pick on Father Biggart, but this dry little list does seem to exemplify the sort of Christianity that does not make sufficient effort to tie in with how people live the rest of their lives. Perhaps Kelly and Kelham theology were needed in Anglo-Catholicism. Were the questions being asked about how belief in God could make sense of how lay people could live their lives now, and about how God is at work there? Nobody would disagree with Kelham theology in theory, but that is not what one would think from that list. It probably was meant to suggest that Christ's yoke is easy and his burden is light. Many thousands of English lay Christians were happy as Anglo-Catholics, but the church that served them had small ambitions for them on the whole. [60] We shall come back to this when we look at Fr Hebert, and 'Parish and People'.

There might be found in Kelham too something of a willed dryness. Father Alfred Kelly, the younger brother, published a book in 1917 called *Values of the Christian Life*. He quoted with delight this comment on it:

> P., who reviews for the Guardian and read the MSS, writes to me (I wish I could come up to his style), 'I like your style, its weariness, its "take it or leave it air"; its "if you wish to be damned, be so" acidity, relieved by sudden yawns; its quite charming bow to the "objector" here and there – "all right, have it so then." . . .'[61]

A 'take it or leave it' air was common in Anglo-Catholicism. It goes with a sense of the objective reality of that with which we have to deal. Fr Alfred Kelly, like his brother, did not sum up the objectiveness of Christianity in Christ being present in the tabernacle. In 1920 he published *The Cultus of the Sacramental Presence*. It is rather an oddly structured little book. He explains the doctrine of Christ's presence in the eucharist and in the reserved sacrament, and spends pages 60 to 118 removing unsatisfactory objections to both. In pages 121 to 130 he disposes of several unsatisfactory objections to the cultus of the reserved sacrament, but then, the sting in the tail, there is the 'final and valid objection', on pages 131–4. 'The cultus of the Reserved Sacrament impairs the balance of worship . . . [because it] forgets his presence *in action*'. It is all briskly logical, and good Kelham theology, but somehow optimistic in hoping to win the reader over with one good argument in three pages at the very end. Perhaps it succeeded. Kelham was within the Anglo-Catholic tradition, argued things through within it, and sometimes came to an unfashionable conclusion as a result of thinking things through. But, as Fr Kelly himself said, 'Our theology is too rational for Catholics, and too trenchant for moderates'.[62]

It is difficult to gauge the status of Kelham in the wider Anglo-Catholic movement. Fr Kelly himself was a member of the E.C.U. (the English Church Union), and spent most of the Twenties threatening to leave it. (He did in the end). He wrote round, looking for more moderate 'Maurician' Anglo-Catholics, urging them to speak out against the ruling clique in power in the E.C.U. He hated Darwell Stone, 'the most mischievous person the church has had to contend with',[63] who had set up a Federation of Catholic Priests, which was even more clear-cut partisan than the E.C.U. To his letters he got either no answer, quite frequently, or bland reassurance (entire agreement, but now is not the time to rock the boat) or sometimes a definite 'no'. E. K. Talbot, Superior of Mirfield, was capable of definite 'no's.[64] Occasionally, quite sensibly, the Anglo-Catholics tried to co-opt Fr Kelly. There are official pamphlets, published by the Society of S. Peter and S. Paul, with large chunks of recognisable 'Kellyism'.

The college was almost certainly, whatever Fr Kelly said, a party college.

> '. . .but you are on markedly High Church lines' – I positively denied it. We were a Church college. (Fr Kelly)[65]
>   . . . we are and always have been a party Society . . . our work is almost entirely supported by one party in the Church . . . (Fr Bedale) [66]

The congregations where there was a Guild of St Gabriel, providing stockings and scapulars, or the twenty-odd London churches where, one chosen week-end a year, right across the city there were SSM preachers, or, not quite as uniformly, but fairly correlated, the parishes from which their students came, would all show up in the *Church Travellers Directory* as Anglo-Catholic parishes. The parochialism of Anglo-Catholicism was its safeguard and also its danger.

> All our parish labour keeps us busy and our people gently interested . . . The 'Catholic' movement has got now into a purely defensive attitude, and has thereby become, like Protestantism, a purely party question of a very narrow kind, holding on to the privileges of elect congregations and chattering about a few spikey doctrines . . . If we can get religion, faith in God, taken out of the hands of the merely pious, translated into intelligible language, we may see something.[67]

Part of the achievement of Kelham is the difference a Kelham training made in the parishes. But the party parishes were already there. Fr Kelly tells an amusing story of archbishop Temple at Bishopthorpe telling him of 'his troublesome parish – there's only one in the whole diocese' while Kelly sat there thinking of how, days before, he listened to one of the Kelham novices:

> Charlie Francis reeled off to my indignant (but totally sceptical) ears, all the sins of Episcopacy towards the parish.[68]

That parish, All Saints, Middlesbrough, where Fr Francis was a curate, is now an SSM priory, and one might hope in good standing with its archbishop. Poor Charlie Francis died within the year, racing to the top of an electricity pylon.[69] It says something about the reckless boyishness cultivated at Kelham that this could ever have happened. It is not part of the picture of stately correctness that would have overtaken the House if Fr Carleton had had his way. There was something different about the Catholicism of Kelham, even in its golden age, to which we now turn.

Chapter 8

The Golden Age of Kelham

Given a building, and a structured routine, and a continuing purpose, religious communities can very easily appear timeless. If the same leaders are in charge, but, as in a school or a college, most of the population moves on in a pleasing blur, this is enhanced. The students of different generations look back, and their memories are assimilated to a stock collective memory. All of them remember being young, in that place, with that routine, and these teachers.

The Society of the Sacred Mission had its college at Kelham from 1903 to 1973, a lifetime. The early days, under Father Kelly himself until 1910, were what one might expect from early days. It is all there in *An Idea in the Working*, the sheer zest of everything, starting with the removal from Mildenhall.

> The men worked, as they always do in such matters, with a speed and energy which left the professionals rather aghast. To load a lorry took 15 minutes, to unload it a great deal less than five. Personally, I thought it a most exhilarating experience. I think I should rather enjoy a move every three years, but my enthusiasm is not universally shared. [1]

It was simply chance that the Society stayed there seventy years, and 'Kelham' became its name. In the early 1920s, when it looked as if the Sugar Beet Company wanted the house back, they hunted round England for a replacement.

The Society put in an offer for Stowe, before it became a public school. But then they had the chance of buying Kelham, and they built the Great Chapel, and new wings, and moving was out of the question before the crash. So 'Kelham' it became.

> For ten years people said – 'Oh, yes, a place for training
> lay missionaries, isn't it?' At Mildenhall they said 'Oh yes, a
> Missionary College'. At Kelham they said, 'Oh yes, a
> Theological College. Branch of Mirfield, I believe'. [2]

As usual he exaggerates a little, but by the 1920s, Kelham
was known. The guest speakers at the Society's annual
meeting in London in 1921 were big names, Studdert-
Kennedy ('Woodbine Willie') and G.K. Chesterton. The
internal affairs of the Society were in fact deeply troubled
at the time. The Prior, Fr Murphy, who spoke at that
meeting, was very near breakdown. The December before
he had asked for release from the Society. But the meeting
was a great success, and the public face of Kelham was all it
should be.

There was no problem finding students. Kelham had
hundreds of applicants to choose from before the First
World War. Perhaps the college expanded too quickly
with the move from Mildenhall.

> We had spent most of our time at Mildenhall growing
> from a House of 20 to near 40. Then we leapt upwards.
> We had expected it, but we did not like it, and got
> frightened. We had been a family, and, moreover, we had
> been a Religious Society. Almost everyone in the House
> belonged to the Society, or wanted to belong to it. When
> we passed 50, we thought we were too big to be a family.
> In our first term at Kelham, 11 new men came at once, and
> we all felt instinctively that it was no use trying to be good
> any longer. [3]

There was normally a new intake every term, not just once
a year, so 11 new men at once might mean more than
thirty in a year, some of them to stay for seven years. In
the 1930s, when Kelham had more students than any other
theological college in England, there were years when
thirty men were ordained. These are not figures in the
hundreds, but enough to be significant in a church which
could find about five hundred ordinands a year. Father
Kelly claimed that if SSM could produce twenty a year
they could change Anglicanism worldwide.

Certainly the Society missed Mildenhall, smaller, homelier, and more beautiful. At Mildenhall it had still been possible to feel that everyone who came was a potential member of SSM. A great many novices did not proceed, but it had seemed natural to try. At Kelham the college swamped the Society, and though the communal life was a great success, there was a spirit in the college, not just a figment of Father Kelly's imagination, that resisted recruitment to the Society.

There was progress, with many novices, under the second Director, David Jenks (1910–20). Nevertheless, a shadow hung over Kelham as a non-graduate college. The bishops of the Church of England, led by Gore, who was not loved in Kelham, explicitly, in a collective statement, planned to end ordaining non-graduates. There was a target date of 1917, though 'bishops smile when they mention 1917' wrote Fr Jenks in 1911. [4] The World War came instead, and very nearly ended Kelham, whatever the bishops intended. Kelham men, on principle, joined the ranks. Their casualties were heavy. 91 enlisted as ordinary soldiers, of whom 24 were killed.[5] The Director, trying to keep in touch with them all individually, worried himself ill. General Kelly, perhaps a biassed witness as he was the Founder's brother, said that Kelham men made excellent soldiers; but some of them were highly strung and physically second-rate, and had a bad time. Others found their faith, or their vocation, challenged. Novices, out of community, found other human support and got married. One cannot overstress the catastrophe a major war is to a religious society of young men. The college just remained open, with the 'Cottage' training boys, who then went off to war. Kelham Hall itself was requisitioned by the army, twice, at short notice, and the college, for the war, was actually housed in Mirfield, the rival establishment. The Mirfield college had then moved across to Leeds, and there does not seem to be evidence of any interaction between the two communities.

After the War, at least the threat from the bishops had gone away. The Church needed as many clergymen as it could get. The Knutsford training school, set up as an emergency measure, processed hundreds of old soldiers

who had felt a call to the ministry. It was not a rival
establishment to Kelham. Some with a more specific call
came from Knutsford to join SSM. Harold Smith, Martin
Knight, Basil Oddie, Sydney Holgate and Howard Preece
all came through Knutsford, and spent the rest of their
lives in SSM.

The Society only just coped with the influx of students.
In the decade between 1911 and 1921 fifteen brothers were
professed, and twenty-six died or were released or removed. That is a clear nett loss. The decision had to be
made to give up the Central African work. The South
African province revolted, and refused to hand over Fr
Hebert, when he was needed for tutorial work in Kelham.
There are letters from the Bishop of Bloemfontein, fighting
to keep Hebert, on the implausible ground that he was
'not particularly a tutor by nature'.[6] Fr Carleton, the
Provincial who had refused to give up Fr Hebert, was
himself called back, but jibbed at teaching elementary
Greek. Some of the teaching at Kelham was at a school
level, to fifteen-year-olds with no paper qualifications. Fr
Antony Snell spent years effectively as a Latin master. Fr
Edmund Couldrey was there for ever. He gave the first
two years Church History lectures, but no further, from
1914 to 1951. He was Sub-Prior from 1922 to 1953, and
Bursar from 1916 to 1952 and indeed later. He could be
relied on in meetings of chapter to quote Fr Kelly when
young against Fr Kelly when old.

A Society running a theological college must have brethren capable of staffing it, and of teaching the advanced
classes. Fr White, the Director at the time, had no preten-
sions of scholarship (he had failed his exams at Vassall
Road) but neither Fr Jenks nor Fr Tribe, the previous and
the following Director, and both on the face of it qualified
graduates, taught at the college in the 1920s. Fr Kelly and
Fr Bedale were indispensable and over-worked. Kelly was
old and deaf and looked older. A workman, asked to guess
his age in 1927, thought he was 80. [7] He was 67. Brother
George Every came straight from Exeter university with a
degree in History in 1929, and took over some of Fr
Kelly's teaching. Changes were very gradual. The new

tutor still used the 'old man's' lectures. Fr Kelly was still delivering nine lectures a week in the late 1930s, when almost 80.

> My *idea* was that each tutor would do his own lectures – maybe 200 copies. After a few years, he would want to rewrite them. *I* always did. But – lo and behold – they kept the stencils, and run off another 200 any old time. They are *all* still using my stuff round 20 years ago. This is NOT my idea.[8]

His colleagues with justice could say that this exaggerates, but there is something in it. The teaching at Kelham was not always perceptibly inspired and helpful. Students are often ungrateful. In 1937 Class 34B drafted a sheet of Complaints about Fr Kelly's teaching.

> 1. *Lectures* . . . . Oral lectures are very discursive, long, and cover little ground.
> The class has always found difficulty in finding relevance . . . many of the connections clear to HK are not made explicit. The difficulty is not met by the question 'D'you see?' . . . further discursiveness accompanied by the symptoms of high blood pressure. .. *Nett result* – 'An hour and a half on a page and a half' . . .
> 2. *Tutoring*. HK marking of essays . . . 'everybody expects to bosh, and few are disappointed' . . . The matter *and* the form have to be HK's . . . parrot-fashion . . . not uncommonly rewarded . . .
> 3. *Lesser fleas*. (a) HK's attitude towards questions and wrong answers is hardly gracious.(b) HK's response to answers following 'D'you see?' is to *give* answers when 'Yes' is returned, and a curt 'Look it up then' when 'No' is returned.
> (c) HK says, 'You know a thing when you have forgotten where you found it and who said it.' In practice, he requires a detailed knowledge of original contexts . . .[9]

Fr Kelly kept this 'Testimonial' (his word), and probably it shows promise in the verbal skills and high expectations of the students. They are certainly not overly reverential.

After the disruption of the First World War, there were problems with discipline and morale. It is true that Fr Carleton had a more rigorist agenda than the traditions of

SSM, but we get a picture of what was worrying to conscientious members of the Society in 1918 in his paper *The Religious Life and the Society*. He spoke of 'temporary dispensations from the *spirit* of the rule' [10], of 'the individualisms of the elders'.[11] Talking of the rule of Poverty, he spoke of 'private pocket-money, private reception of gifts'.[12] Of Chastity, there do not seem to have been sexual problems, though he had slight worries about the risks of meeting women on holidays – he disapproved of holidays – the reproach was that 'many of the seniors habitually over-smoked',[13] and some disregarded 'the decent restraints of civilised behaviour at table'. There were also people playing bridge, and reading frivolous novels. Obedience, perhaps predictably, was Fr Carleton's chief concern. It was 'in practice military external obedience', and there were 'grumblings instead of acceptance of any trivial opportunities of surrender of will'.[14] These are not grave scandals.

When Stephen Bedale took over as Prior in 1923, he found things needed tightening up.

> The Cottage was organising expeditions into Newark after Compline. Professed . . . seemed to come to Offices or stay away at their own sweet will . . . . Senior Associates [that is the theological college students, told him] 'We have no use for Discipline: seen through that in the Army'. [Bedale's reply was] 'I saw it in the Navy and did not see through it'.[15]

He was only thirty-two, and had to deal with senior men, who had been professed years before he was a novice.

> . . . Wilfrid [Hambidge] frankly 'tried it on with me' at first . . . I was (I believe) polite but firm . . . . HHK? . . . Perhaps I was afraid of him . . . and thought he wanted to run me. Perhaps he did. Lots of people say he can't help trying to run things. (He doesn't know himself, any more than I do.)[16]

From its earliest days, the college had been involved in selection as well as training, which meant sending away about half of the students who enrolled. This was of necessity somewhat ruthless. Fr Jenks, in his newsletters as

Director, in the years running up to the 1914–18 War, talked bluntly about named individuals with reasons for why he was putting them out.

> I was obliged this week to send away a boy [named] . . . for much swearing and for not being open with me when I spoke to him. Swearing has increased . . . within the last year and a half at the Cottage . . . got rid of several of the bad culprits at Christmas.[17]

Later Directors no longer had a monthly newsletter, and there was less naming of names. 'Fr Kelly would say when you use 'they' instead of real names it is always an unbalanced judgement'. [18] There was a change, nevertheless. The college was still selective, and people still failed. Stories were handed down of Fr Bedale dismissing a whole class at once from Kelham, because they had dared complain.[19]

A much more serious type of failure was the withdrawal or removal of professed brethren. The SSM Quarterly almost never mentioned anyone leaving. Even if, or perhaps particularly if, they had been professed brethren for many years, their name was just dropped. The silence was perhaps more frightening. In the early 1920s (precise dating is difficult, as a man might feel he left before the Society acknowledged the fact) the Society lost Fr Carleton, Fr Murphy, and Fr Haynes, that is a former Provincial, a former Prior of the Mother House, and the Society's first bishop. Bishop Haynes went on to marry. In each case the break was painful, and they were not mentioned again. They carried on as Anglican clergymen with respectable careers.

Then there were several happy years when no-one left. In 1931 Father Whitworth transferred to the Cowley Fathers, which was the sort of thing that could be mentioned. In 1932 a lay brother got a girl into trouble in South Africa, and was removed. No Society would ever publicise that. In 1933 there was a different question. Fr Conrad Herold thought that he might be able to leave with the Society's blessing. He wanted a little ceremony on Profession Day to wish him well:

> I should be a brother sent out . . . receive Benediction and depart . . .[20]

Perhaps Fr Herold was naive and self-centred. It was like asking for a ceremony of divorce in church. He thought that his way of looking at things had precedents in the Kelly tradition of the Society. Fr Tribe, as Director, was abrupt.

> Although we part good friends, I like every member of the Society feel sore about it. You have given a knock to stability of profession.[21]

Fr Herold was the only professed brother in the ten years between 1925 and 1935 to be granted release; and there was the one removal already mentioned. It would be difficult to show that Father Bedale, particularly in the early years of his rule, was prompt and harsh in putting people out. Certainly some people thought so. In the Brethren file, there are several complete correspondences about individual brethren who had gone wrong. In each case of removal, there were brethren prepared to suggest a gentler line. Fr Buxcy Neate and Fr Jenks, after his retirement as Director, were tolerant souls. But there is no obvious evidence of Fr Bedale taking the lead, or having to fight for rigour. Normally anything particularly serious was a matter of the Director and the General Council, not the Prior of Kelham. Fr Tribe, as Director, wrote gentle letters to sinners, but the General Council, on his advice, tended to be rigorist.

From 1935 to 1938, the Society lost, through removal or release, ten brethren. This was a bad patch, and there is not much evidence for why it happened. They lost many more during the 1940s, but wartime unsettles religious, like everyone else, so there is less to explain. The brethren seem to have thought a lot about the possibility of people leaving. Sometimes, reading the minutes of chapters on various levels, there is the feeling that every time members of SSM got together, they discussed the nature of First and Second Profession. First Profession expressed an Intention, Second Profession made a Promise. What was the difference, and was it inevitably a sin to leave, at least after the Second Profession, or even after the First?

The Anglo-Catholic wing, and Father Bedale himself, wanted a sharper definition of Profession.' . . . as responsible for the Novices . . [I say] They cannot go out without damaging their souls.' [22] And that was only the novices. Father Kelly himself had been pungent about some who left.

> We sent Pigg to Oxford in 1902. By the end of 1904, Oxford had ruined him. To do him justice I do not think it was the ideal of vulgar gentility so much as polished selfishness . . . Life without love and success without sacrifice has many attractions . . . he has failed of us. He proves, not the weakness of the Society, but the strength and reality of what he has cast off. [23]

Even an ordinary worldling might consider that a student educated at Kelham and sent to Oxford at the Society's expense owed it at least some years of work afterwards. But almost everybody became novices at Mildenhall; were they all spoilt monks if they did not continue? As the Great Chapters had full minutes of their debates, we can hear individual opinions. Fr Alfred Kelly, at the Great Chapter of 1925, thought not:

> The failure of more than half was largely due to the peculiar conditions of Vassall Road and Mildenhall, i.e., those of quasi-compulsory Profession. He did not agree that we knew all the Mildenhall boys were 'called and chosen'.[24]

After all, for fifteen years the Society had not actually used a Life Promise. Fr David Jenks, the ex-Director, wrote to say that 'a man may withdraw with a clear conscience because the actual words do not express such finality.'[25] But the drift was the other way.

> Fr Frank Gilks said that leaving the Society had always incurred condemnation in the past and we all remembered Fr Kelly frequently saying of such men that they had turned themselves back in the day of battle.[26]

And though Fr Buxcy Neate replied that it was one thing

to say such things 'under emotional stress' and another to
embody them in the Constitution, the sense of the betrayal
involved in seeking release became stronger in this period.
If anyone in First Profession leaves, said the declaration on
Profession drafted by Fr Bedale in 1925, with muted
menace:

> The Society . . . is not bound to declare him guilty of
> deadly sin or to invoke ecclesiastical censure upon him. In
> the case of the Second Profession, however . . .

Anxious discussions like this might unsettle anyone's profession. It may be that the minutes created their own fields of
discourse. Each year, or each six months, a chapter met,
heard the minutes of the meeting before, and as there was
nothing urgent to decide in an institution that largely ran
like clockwork, talked about the subject of last year's
minutes. The arguments were still there a decade later. The
phrasing of the First Profession is 'so long as God wills'.
Father Alfred Kelly had to apologise to the Mother House
Chapter [27] for the joking suggestion that in Second Profession 'a man promises to stay in the Society whether God
wills it or not'. When Fr Bedale asked 'Can you say 'I was
right to get in – I was right to get out?'[28] it was a question
that expected the answer 'No' but that raised the possibility
of another answer with at least some of his brethren. Why
should not a missionary seek a new sphere of work?

These are matters of the inner struggles of the Society.
The public image of Kelham was quite different. In the
SSM Quarterly for Christmas 1924, we read of the Prior in
a cope, with acolytes and thurifer, going to bless the new
football field. Thus the idea of 'theological football' can be
liturgised. As the college grew bigger, they became quite
good at football, following

> the principle which God has shown us . . . To kick a ball
> with the toe is wrong – to kick with the instep is correct.[29]

The Kelham team could beat Leeds University,[30] and
indeed paid footballers, Notts. Forest Reserves.[31] The town
of Newark turned out in strength to watch. Both the
sacrifice of the boys killed in the war, and the quality of

the football, gave local credibility. The college did tend to recruit from its hinterland.

> ... Fr Carleton said – in hostile mood – that we (including HK) were not only so English, but so midland-and-London English – that we could not understand nor deal with even N. England, let alone Irish, Welsh, or Scotch.[32]

People visited the college. The Bishop of Chester, at the annual London meeting, said that visiting Kelham 'was like being on board ship. They seemed to run rather than walk, and everybody sang'. [33] And Fr Scutt, the Cottage Master, 'was eager to remind his readers that 'one of the strangest notions is that Kelham is a place of holy quiet'. Groups would gather at idle moments with the *Students' Song Book*. He found particularly evocative 'the 'Salve festa dies' sung in procession round the grounds on a sunny Easter morning'. In later years the noisy youthfulness of Kelham, the clattering of hundreds of shoes on wooden stairs, was too much for brethren from other priories home on leave for a rest. The Province of England particularly requested that there should be a Director's House for retreats and grown-ups, away from the noise. [34] It was all very well for Fr Kelly, who was deaf.

There was liturgical singing too. The men were not chosen because they could sing, and less than an hour a week was enough choir practice, but the plainsong at Kelham chapel was memorable. After a broadcast once, somebody said 'the singing had the lightness and brightness of the Dominican, in contrast to the Benedictine style'.[35] People came to listen: the principal reason for the building of the narthex to the great chapel was that

> congregations of anything up to fifty women are now of common occurrence at Evensong, at least during the summer.[36]

Finding seats for men was no problem, but there were definite territorial boundaries beyond which no woman could go. Later generations looked back on these matters rather ruefully. It seems not so much a misogynist theology, as the house rules of a gentlemen's club. Father Antony

Snell, for example, was a creature of habit, and liked the way things were. Here is an extract from his diary:

> Fr Moore from Buxton came with ♀ visitors . . . showed them chapel and had tea in the γυναίκειον.[37]

There we have references to women veiled in the discreet obscurity of a symbol and an ancient tongue. But Fr Snell really enjoyed his regular trips to St Elphin's, the girls' boarding school in Derbyshire. He liked things in their place. Wartime, in any case, was unsettling. There was 'the question of a lady in charge of a railway van who makes incursions into the kitchen.'[38]

The Society had help from and contact with women over many years. The Quarterly reported in Easter 1940 the death of Fanny Wichman aged 72, who since 1910 had lived in the small lodge at Kelham. She was 'largely responsible for the mending', and students kept in touch with her. There were 'cards and letters from her "old boys"'. Earlier, in 1908, one of the students had been given the nickname 'Mary' because he could sew. [39] There were stereotyped expectations. Mrs Duke, Fr Kelly's dear 'Duchess', had as many as 900 helpers in the sewing guild which she ran, each pledged to provide two garments a year. Almost every Quarterly carried lists of donations to the College Fund. In one chosen at random, in December 1950, apart from congregations and anonymous, there were donations from 127 women, and 75 men, of whom 40 were clergymen. Only two others were from 'Mr and Mrs' combined; people did not deal with SSM as couples.

Visitors to Kelham quite soon had a well-rehearsed package deal. There was a difference between day trips and those who stayed for some time. The community, which included the students, grew used to being watched, and to explaining the routine. A time-table is something to hold on to, and it was the utterly planned life that caught the imagination of most visitors. Roger Lloyd, in *The Church of England in the Twentieth Century*, gives up nearly a page of his book to quoting verbatim an account of what happened in Kelham between the Caller arriving at 6.15 am. and the end of breakfast. '. . . it has been a bit of a rush, but we were busy doing God's Will'.[40] Sometimes visitors were surprised to see the students, and the brethren, doing their own domestic chores. The Bishop of Liverpool was

> astonished and amused to see the students sweeping, clean-ing, and washing up the dishes . . .[41]

This surprise sounds rather class-bound to a later genera-tion. One wonders how many of the clergy of the diocese of Liverpool at that time still had domestic servants. Even when it is expressed as a compliment, we should remember that Kelham broke the rules. The Bishop of St Albans said:

> You can't remain respectable and be a Christian, and the great thing about Kelham is that it so abominably unrespect-able.[42]

St Albans is less hidebound than Liverpool, but the norms they measure things against are the same.

Life was full enough to make most visitors peripheral and scarcely noticed. The Society was embarrassed later to think that Dietrich Bonhoeffer came and stayed and got ideas for *Living Together*, and somehow never signed the visitors' book, and there are no memories of his visit. One Continental Protestant with high church notions is very like another. The Society took some interest in what was happening in Germany. Regin Prenter, who was a compe-tent Danish theologian, gave a lecture to the students on 'The Crisis in the German Evangelical Church' in 1935, and explained, in a Barthian way that probably went down well in Kelham, that this new national-socialistic Christ-ianity was really only a revised edition of the old liberal protestantism.

This is what Kelham looked like to Bonhoeffer and his companion in March 1935. They visited Cowley and Mir-field as well.

> . . . in Oxford, tobacco is anathema and smoking strictly prohibited, in Mirfield you may smoke, in Kelham you have to.
>
> And indeed in Kelham we were received by a bearded lay-brother [presumably Br Edgar Lintott] whose pipe

never seemed to go out. The venerable and gifted founder of Kelham, old Father Kelly – sometimes described by the English as a theological precursor of Karl Barth – was a chain-smoker. We smiled when we saw that the front of his monk's habit was covered with cigarette ash. He brought into his lecture-room a medium-sized pail containing an inflammable chemical, and now and then he dipped a wooden stick into it when the cigarette in his long holder had burnt out and a new one had to be lit. A number of his brilliant lectures were for sale in mimeograph, and we certainly did not miss the chance. Many months later Bonhoeffer asked me to send on to him in Germany some of the copies which he had left behind in London . . . I think it was Father Kelly who replied to our question; 'How do you keep it up?' in the paradoxical words: 'I can do it, because I cannot.' . . .

. . . There was the freedom in their community life, which we could not help noticing during our visits – the Anglican monks played tennis or football in their free time.[43]

They also noticed the periods of silence, and how they, as Protestants, were not allowed to receive communion. Marcus Barth, son of Karl, remembered the picture of the pig and the L-plate in Father Kelly's room.

After 1928, some visitors came out of architectural interest. The Great Chapel of 1928 was a masterpiece. It cost £28,000, which was not cheap. The architect, Charles Thompson, was otherwise little known. The interior, rather than the exterior, mattered. It was almost square with a great central dome, the second largest concrete dome in England. This great dark space, vaguely Byzantine in style, was dominated by the great bridge with the rood of the sanctuary arch.

The golden-brown bricks are not uniform, but as bricks should be; some are reddish, so that they melt into a varied texture of colour. The apse is coloured a rather wonderful violetish blue. I do not know if they mean to colour the stone-grey of the dome. The acoustics are very good.[44]

Professional critics approved as well.

Here is a chapel which is a place of assembly, a concourse, majestic, ample, treated with a broad simplicity of handling, its structure of humble materials yet noble in conception. The impression is heightened by the pervading sense of large scale, conveyed by a sure sense of the rightness of sizes and a use, without any kind of exaggeration, of the element of contrast. And to complete the effect of bigness of feeling, of generosity and space, is the dramatic touch of the great bridge-like screen which spans the sanctuary arch. Behind it is the altar . . . In front of this arch is the chapel; the material world. Behind it, the sanctuary, the spiritual world . . .

. . .this central space; but what an achievement, to avoid the pitfalls of this type, to escape the concert-hall or meeting-house atmosphere, and capture under one dome some of the vastness of Westminster Cathedral . . .[45]

There is something of the same spirit as Westminster Cathedral. Some said that it reminded them of Stonehenge. One visitor spoke of 'the altar on the edge of the world, and beyond it there seemed to be the vastness of God's infinite space'.[46] One comment which caught the imagination of the Society was 'This seems the sort of place where they offer human sacrifices'. [47] Brother George Every wrote a poem 'The Rood at Kelham':

This is a place for human sacrifice
And on that altar stone young men must die . .

The Christ with St Mary and St John on the rood were by Sargent Jagger, an expensive London sculptor, not used to doing religious work. For that very reason he put a lot of effort into it, and the Society was proud of the result. Father Bedale told with pleasure the story of the 'perfect little ruffian' whose response was 'Gee, ain't he tough?' [48]

Visitors to Kelham also noticed the tableware, which was 'Kelham plate' of stainless steel. It had been an idea of Gerald Murphy's, arranged by Edwin Cosgrove, who came from Sheffield. From 1925 the ordinary chipped plates were replaced, at 7s 6d a time, which was not cheap, with stainless steel. The Society is still eating off them at Willen; they will last for ever. In some ways they symbolise

Kelham, practical, willing to be different, not at first sight an economy.

There was a full timetable, and the men went to bed tired. It sometimes looks as if activities were found to keep them active. The domestic chores grew less. In 1921 they got a potato-peeling machine, that set some thirty or forty men free for other work. The old slipper baths were replaced by showers in 1927.

> . . . the long-drawn tragedy is at last complete. The bath-room next door was opened for use today. There are 12 shower baths – also basins for washing. All room baths are to be withdrawn. I had not expected that last (What will they do with them?) It has taken just under seven months.[49]

Showers take less work than filling hip-baths. Father Kelly still had his carried north for mountaineering in the Lakes. By 1928 they had electric light.

> The old cooking apparatus [was] superseded by gas . . . cool, comfortless, classic but clean . . all the charm of a tube station, an operating theatre, or a laboratory . . .[50]

The gas meant less work, and so on. None of this means idle luxury. They played football well, among other reasons, because time was set aside for it. Anything but idleness. So, likewise, most weekends there was some sort of theatrical performance in the house. Men must have given hours to memorising parts in plays. Every number of the SSM Quarterly asked for help with costumes; there are hundreds of photographs of groups of young men looking more or less convincing as actors (and actresses). 'The Importance of Being Ernest' was a perennial favourite. They used to read out telegrams of good wishes from famous actors at the annual pantomime. There was also a team of hand-bell ringers, with bells given by T.S.Eliot. Sometimes there are hints of idleness. Fr Antony Snell and Fr Gabriel Hebert stood up for the rights of students to study in deckchairs. There were complaints about people 'sunbathing in worktime in A corridor windows'.[51]

Fr Antony Snell kept a diary for many years, writing three or four lines describing what he had done in the day. He had time, between working in the cabbage patch, and teaching Latin, for a great deal of random reading. The Society noticed how much Victorian biography he had read, but that was a small part of the whole. He also wasted time – it was probably wasting time – on making up and translating funny poems in Latin and English. It is a great gift to be able to tease your colleagues in rhyme. Fr Alfred Kelly joined in with him in the poems. Reading that diary, one has the feeling of an innocent and useful life, that would not have been very different if he had been teaching classics at Winchester, his old school.

Fr Alfred Kelly's interests were impressively wide-ranging. He could write persuasively about modern English literature in one issue of the SSM Quarterly, and in the next one about science (on 'curved space' and relativity), and then again about philosophy. The SSM Quarterly in the 1930s was consistently worth reading, with theology from the 'Old Man', the latest on the liturgical movement on the continent from Father Hebert, and something new each time from Fr Alfred Kelly. For example in the Quarterly for Easter 1933, Father Alfred Kelly, on 'Things New and Old', was discussing Queenie Leavis and classes of literature, how 'the simple despise the clever'. Fr Hebert had left liturgy for economics:

> . . .all human life is redeemed to God, and craftsmanship of every kind is the expression of the principle of the Incarnation.

He wanted a wider meaning to 'church work'. Both articles are interesting though not specialist. In the Quarterly for Christmas 1933 there was 'One Day in Modderpoort Schools', and Father Kelly himself, writing about the 'Group Movement', then fashionable, was discussing inspiration.

> . . .the ideas come at all sorts of times.. I always think of them as inspired (guidance). Sometimes they come readily, and I say, 'God was very nice to me' . . . (I have known people scandalised, but nice and nasty are good child-

> words) . . . the idea that I could make up the waste floor-
> polish into fire-lighters. Is anything too small for God's in-
> terest?

We can never go very far without remembering that part
of the theory of Kelham was that theology had to do with
everything. This encouraged wide-ranging interests. Br
George Every could claim:

> In the religious life I have been able to expand my range of
> interests from modern literature and art through Jungian
> psychology and psychical research to Buddhism and com-
> parative religion as well as liturgics and the sociological
> side of ecclesiastical history.[52]

He thought that within a religious community he could do
this without 'the kind of dissipation of energy' he would
have had 'in the service of the SCM, the WCC, or the
BBC'.

George Every, who took over the teaching of Church
History from Father Kelly, was a lay brother all his time at
Kelham. It was unusual to have a layman in a senior
tutorship, but, apart from that, lay brothers were important
at Kelham. Of the brothers at the mother house, eight out
of twenty were lay, though the Society as a whole was
four-fifths clergy, the 'Kelham Fathers'.

> Fr Huntington [founder of the American Order of the
> Holy Cross], a fellow Maurician, but twisted into correct
> Cattism [Anglo-Catholicism] by his brethren − asked me
> how we managed to succeed with lay-brothers. I said 'We
> don't'. He said 'You do − and you're the only people who
> do'.[53]

When Father Kelly thought about it he concluded that it
was because the Society took on its lay brothers not to
become monks but to do a job: ' . . .what can you do?
Cook? Print? Type?' [54] Some work expanded, but normally by supervising the students, who could be told what
to do.

> The printers have the publication four times a year of the
> 12,000 to 13,000 copies of this *Quarterly* . . . the carpenters
> have been making chapel stalls out of a particularly fine

and obdurate consignment of English oak ... motor me-
chanics ... an electrician ... Typists and duplicators succeed in publishing nearly a thousand books of lecture notes
each year ...

All this work (apart from that of the full-time staff) is
packed into an hour-and-a-half in the afternoon (with
perhaps the odd half-hour after breakfast), each person
responsible doing two afternoons a week.[55]

As time went on, though Kelham still needed men with
these specific tradesmen's skills, lay brothers seem to have
been more middle-class and more versatile.

... another of our lay brothers was a lawyer's clerk with a
passion for amateur dramatics and the history of the odder
kinds of religion. Another was a librarian and then a
market gardener, who was business manager of an anarchist
literary paper, and now combines cooking, and some gar-
dening, with running a political club for the students.
Another, who is a very good carpenter, does our housekeep-
ing and shopping and travels about the country lecturing
on plainsong.[56]

Kelham became a very civilised place. There is a newspaper
interview with Fr Tribe as Director, and the image he put
across of charming sophisticated worldliness, the sort of
monk who has a nose for a good wine, is almost self-
parody.

'He was the only one of the "bosses" who treated students
as human beings. (Stephen only learnt to unbend toward
the end). He knew a lot of people, and was always name-
dropping – a bit of a social snob. He had been a gynaecologist, and would read out Lady So-and-So's engagement
notice from the *Times* and add, "I was the first man to slap
her bottom!" '[57]

Important people came. The poet T.S.Eliot, Anglican and
royalist and traditionalist, all of these by an act of will,
liked to visit. He was a friend of Father Hebert. There is a
slight incongruity in a down-to-earth college for working-
class boys being a focus of fashionable conservatism.

If our society takes the opposite road, of materialism in
education, then the modern religious communities will be

like the monasteries in the dark ages, self-contained fortresses, keeping alight the Christian lamp of learning and
civilisation.[58]

Several of the brothers were correspondents of interesting
people. There was a correspondence between Father Kelly
and Dorothy L. Sayers. George Every was a friend of F.R.
Leavis, who, without any personal rancour, sent him a
very sharp put-down of the sort of literary criticism from a
Christian standpoint that he and Fr Alfred Kelly had been
doing.

> ... the establishment of the Christian Critic is a miscon-
> ceived and illusory undertaking; ... you are all more
> dependent on the mere Literary Critic than you have ever
> acknowledged or appeared to know ... in taking over the
> Literary Critic's work you all show yourselves unable to
> use it with real understanding ... ('pillaging' – a mild
> word).. when you attempt first hand judgment you all
> betray calamitous critical inadequacy ... [you] foster com-
> munally an assertive consciousness of superiority that is
> a very dubious recommendation for militant Christian-
> ity ...[59]

Leavis was famous for his tartness, and dismissed most
professional literary critics as brusquely. But his critique,
not aimed specifically at Kelham, had a point. Christians as
such were amateur literary critics. The admirable Kelham
breadth should not be over-praised as polymathic perfection. They kept up to date and they touched on a lot, but
no more.

Kelham in its glory was a very great theological college.
The next generation of wardens, Victor Ranford and
Theodore Smith, were both products of the college. Admittedly, to Father Kelly's disgust, Father Ranford was sent to
London to get a theology degree. But they, and Roland
Walls, were competent academic theologians, who came
up through the system, without the benefit of a public
school and an Oxbridge college behind them. It could be
done. More important, perhaps, was the steady flow of
well-trained clergymen into parishes. Kelham was fulfilling
its purpose. Though the vision was Father Kelly's, much of

the credit should go to Father Stephen Bedale, who was indisputably the leading light in Kelham from 1923 to 1952.

Fr Bedale was intense and masterful. People remember discovering with surprise in his later years that he could cope with being teased and disagreed with. He was too busy to write books, but his lectures on Paul were on fire with theology, and it was Kelham theology. Kelham in its glory was in some ways a strange expression of Fr Kelly's vision, but it was not a betrayal, and the credit for this should go to Fr Stephen Bedale.

Contemporary with Fr Bedale was Fr Gabriel Hebert, the most well-known member of SSM in the world at large, and it is to him we now turn.

Chapter Nine

The Work of Father Hebert

If there was one member of the Society of the Sacred Mission with an international reputation, it was Gabriel Hebert, liturgist, New Testament scholar, ecumenist. But a prophet has no honour in his own country. His fame came as a surprise, and in some ways almost as a threat, to many of his brethren.

When a young man, Fr Hebert did not make a strong impression within the Society. Listing the graduate recruits from Tribe to Snell, Fr Kelly would forget him.

> After the war Bedale joined SSM. Before the war Tribe ditto. This is all I can remember of grown priests, since I don't know when. (Oh yes, Hebert.)[1]

He seems to have been gawky and self-effacing. Not everyone with a public school education instinctively takes the lead. On paper, he had the qualifications for a bishop: Harrow, and New College, Oxford, a First in Greats (1908), another in Theology (1909), and then trained at Cuddesdon.

He came to Kelham as a tutor in 1914, and became a novice in 1915. 'His ecumenical interests had brought him into contact with Fr Jenks on one of the latter's visits to Oxford'. [2] The first idea was that he should accompany Fr Kelly to Japan.[3] In the event he was turned down for that 'on the ground of nerves'. The nerves went, yet he was always somewhat odd. I have seen mimicry of the way, harumphing like an elephant, he would throw his scapular up over his head.

He rarely kept the same rhythm as his brethren when

reciting the Psalms in chapel, and he usually sang out of tune – but with gusto . . .[4]

With age comes permitted eccentricity. Religious societies even elevate these things to be part of the collective memory. 'Remember how Fr Ranford was obsessed with slamming doors'. Often people's little ways were mild or understandable. It was repetition and non-familial closeness that made them a test, something that had to be defused with humour. It makes it difficult to gauge the weight of sentences like this:

> I think it is most extraordinary how some of us began by regarding [Hebert] as a rather harmless figure of fun and then progressed through admiration to love . . .[5]

When a relatively young man, he was sent out to South Africa in 1920 with Father Carleton. He was professed in South Africa. In his letters home there is no hint of disquiet over the way the province was run. He drafted a very Catholic Baptismal liturgy for them in 1922 ('Then the Minister shall breathe on the candidate, and say: 'Unclean spirit, go forth, and give place to the Holy Ghost the Comforter''), and for a man who was later to be a great ecumenist, his view of other Christians was not always very kindly.

> . . . the church of the faith-healers or Bafolisi . . . no windows . . . holes in the grass roof . . . stay inside for hours.. weird howlings . . . One of our church men . . . deserted his wife and taken to himself two other women . . . Such 'churches' I think one can safely say are churches of Satan. When our people go off to Protestant places of worship they are always put under censure or excommunicated – and isn't it right? [6]

He may have been less at ease in the South African province than he let them know at home, as within a year or two he had some sort of breakdown. However, when a decision was made to transfer him back to Kelham, Fr Hebert was completely on the South African Provincial's side in resisting it. He wrote to his father:

> There is a scheme on the part of some of the Kelham

> people to get me home to do tutoring at Kelham again. I
> don't fancy it is coming off. Fr Carleton won't let it
> happen easily ... simply abandoning the work that we
> have undertaken here ... There is a lot that needs to be set
> right at Kelham, but this isn't part of a scheme for doing it
> – it is simply an expedient to keep things going.[7]

He had in fact accepted the South African party line.

> I feel very sore that Kelham has more or less stood out of
> the Anglo-Catholic show. I fancy it is an idea of old Fr
> Kelly that the Anglo-Catholic Congress was a *party* thing..
> The SSM had rather a bad name out here, till Fr Carleton
> took it over in 1915, for general slackness about the Reli-
> gious life etc ... it's not changed altogether as regards
> Kelham [8].

The Director, planning the move for Fr Hebert, first got in
touch with Fr Hebert's father. 'It is very strange that the
Director should have written to you, and not have written
to me or to Modderpoort'.[9] The young man was probably
biddable and easily led. Certainly when Fr Carleton had
gone, and the Director, Fr White, had come out to South
Africa to take his place, there was a complete change in Fr
Hebert's views. The letters are now full of hero-worship of
the saintliness and insight of the Director, 'the most wonderful person you had ever met',[10] and of sharp comparisons
with the Carleton regime.

> We are slowly realising what we have been delivered from
> by the coming of Fr White out here [11] ... I'm slowly
> learning from Fr White how much it pays not to pull
> people up ... leave them to see for themselves that they
> aren't doing right ...[12]

It may well be that this change of perspective, which he
calls slow, but others might not, did him harm in the
Society, and underlay such phrases as 'His sensitiveness to
changes in the theological air was always acute' in George
Every's balanced rather than generous obituary in the
Society's own Quarterly. [13]

Under Fr White he came to see there were other ways
of dealing with slackness than Fr Carleton's rigour. He also
blamed Fr Carleton for giving the people the catechism

instead of the bible.[14] He would go on to be a biblical theologian.

When in 1926 he did come back to Kelham, in a furlough that became permanent, he fell more under the influence of Father Kelly. This might not have won him favour. He took Fr Kelly's side in liturgical matters when battles were being fought. For example, in the 1930s he wrote, for internal use in the Society, papers on 'Priest's Masses' and 'Forms of Service', that are lively and full of pungent phrases that could doubtless give offence.

> 'Every day [at Modderpoort] there are five masses'. Why this rapture?
>
> Tarping [is] a pure FCP – Halifax invention. Every missal in the world, except the Roman, has the Ablutions at the end.
>
> [On the liberty to have priest's masses] Liberty does not apply to the server.
>
> Transubstantiation is not, as I used to think, merely a piece of crude or materialistic metaphysics.

This is not the way to win friends in an Anglo-Catholic religious house, where Priest's Masses were the norm until the sixties.

> Gabriel Hebert was present in the house throughout this period, but had little direct influence on Society affairs. It was only after he had been recognised by the world outside that his ideas were accepted in the Society; at the time, they only aroused the Anglo-Catholics within the Society to violent reaction. [15]

When Fr Herold left the Society in 1933, he said 'We should be less "Catholic" and more catholic (to use Fr Gabriel's distinction)'. Like the 'Old Man', Hebert was becoming something of a focus of dissent.

From 1926 to 1952 he was a tutor at Kelham. Most of his teaching was on the New Testament. But he also travelled and published books, though Kelham did not pay much attention to this. It is easy to understand that someone busy in international ecumenism might seem marginal to life at Kelham. It is harder to see how a leader of liturgical reform in England did.

HEBERT AND THE CHURCH'S LITURGY

Liturgy and Society came out in 1935 and was a very influential book, in the Church of England and even beyond. Jocists [Young Christian Workers] in Belgium wrote to say they were reading it. There was an Italian edition in 1938. It was full of good sense about lay participation, about the basics of what happens in liturgy, and about practical change for the better. Liturgy was not primarily a matter of printed rites in books.

> ... the things that people do in church leave a deeper impression than the words they hear or the doctrines which are taught [16]

This was an age when people became aware of non-verbal subconscious communication. Kelham was ahead of other theological colleges in actually teaching psychology. They talked of the way Christians' minds work in coming to belief, a discussion anticipated by Newman's *Grammar of Assent*. When Father Kelly says

> The man who can only see opinions to agree with has plainly no least idea of what I am talking about. [17]

he sounds rather like Newman. But if actions speak to us more than arguments, then what is the message in a non-communicating High Mass? With one of these connections between systematic theology and liturgy which throw light on both sides, Hebert said that leaving the liturgical action to the professionals is like leaving what one believes to the professionals. In what sense can we say that the laity, with implicit faith (fides implicita in Aquinas's phrase) believe the official teaching of the church though they do not understand it?[18]

> ... the individual lays his hand on the *Summa Theologiae*, and says 'All this I steadfastly believe'. [19]

The same thing is true of what happens in liturgy. The believer's own religious life is left to its own poor devices, provided the professionals are trusted to get on with the business. Because people cannot just be passive, and need to do something in their religion, they find individual things to do alongside the liturgy.

> The whole raison d'être of extra-liturgical devotions to the Blessed Sacrament is that those present may perform individual acts of adoration. [20]

Individualism destroys liturgy. Like Dom Gregory Dix, the Anglican Benedictine liturgist, Hebert points out that an individualist piety had been common in the West since before the Reformation. [21] Medieval liturgy needed reforming, and the liturgy of the early twentieth century needed many of the same reforms. On the face of it, this might be expected to come from the churches of the Reformation.

> The ideal Protestant would be a keen sacramentalist, and his vocation would to be hold a mirror to our conscience, bearing witness against all and every mechanization of the spiritual life. [22]

But modern Protestantism was awash with liberal subjectivism. *Liturgy and Society* begins and ends with the corrupting influence of liberalism. It does however set itself to move forward, not backward, from liberalism. 'Forward from liberalism' is one of Hebert's catchphrases. Anything backward-looking, such as the Victorian Gothic Revival and all that it implied, was a mistake. What is required is a timeless objectivity. In matters aesthetic, this is easier said than done. A reviewer in the New Statesman [23] spoke of 'the horrible illustrations of modern ecclesiastical art' in *Liturgy and Society*, though 'it is better than they are'. It is something for a religious book to be reviewed, even with a critical review, in the New Statesman. There is a page of favourable reviews from more likely places in *Earth and Altar*.[24]

In *Liturgy and Society* and *The Parish Communion* (which he edited), Hebert provided the text books for a reformed understanding of Christian liturgy. It was not all his own work: he caught a trend, in Catholic and Protestant thinking. The liturgy was a communion, a sharing, of the people of Christ, not just a sacrifice wrought by a sacrificial priest. It constituted the congregation as the people of God, and was a focus for all of their life in the world. With stresses such as these it became possible for the Parish Communion to become the central act of Christian worship in a way in which the 'Solemn High Mass' of Anglo-Catholicism never could for more than a minority of Anglicans.

Hebert's view of Christian worship is heavenly-minded. In the liturgy

> All is seen as from the eternal point of view[25]... The visible Church on earth ... is the projection of the eternal into the present. [26] Her ground-plan is that of the Celestial City.[27] The vision of the heavenly worship in Revelation chapters IV and V is a liturgical vision: its background is the eucharistic worship of the church.[28]

Nevertheless, he sees it as a starting-point for a changed earth. 'Can anything but this common faith and this organic life re-create our secular politics?'[29] It is not a retreat into individualism, but it is local, parochial, face-to-face, dealing 'ultimately with persons and personal relations'.[30] The Christian congregation has real possibilities. He later quoted wistfully from Hans Ehrenberg:

> The English regard our [German] Church conflict as something which is carried on by individual heroes of the Faith ... But the confessing, witnessing congregation is something strange and unknown to them. [31]

Images like this underlay the Parish and People movement, and Fr Hebert was one of their gurus. It is a great step forward from the type of piety that was alone with God in private devotion at the 8.00 celebration, to the experience of the eucharist as itself a sacrament of the common life of the People of God. There were losses on the way. The change to a Parish Communion later in the morning has in practice meant the end for most of the laity of the rule of fasting communion. Hebert himself, unlike, for example, Dearmer, struggled to keep the rule going, though it was a lost cause.

A religious community is not a parish, and in striking

ways Kelham achieved more of a family feeling than any parish ever could. None the less, people noticed that the liturgical changes advocated in *Liturgy and Society* and *The Parish Communion* were not put into effect in Kelham, where a traditional High Mass remained the norm. (One of the Society's phrases to describe the old service at Kelham was 'High Mass at Wellington Barracks'.) Hebert, nearly quarter of a century later in Australia, thought that Kelham never changed. He grudged quaint phrasings justified because they were there in the Roman rite, and the way that Kelham still had no sermon at the main celebration.

> I think you are 'medieval' in accepting the Propers as they stand . . . horrors like the first words of the Gradual for a Bishop–confessor – 'Behold a mighty Prelate' (!!)' . . . There remains one rubric which is being disregarded . . . a Sermon or a printed equivalent (a Homily) of suitable pithiness and brevity. . .[32]

Hebert was never in charge of teaching liturgy at Kelham. In the files of his lectures there is one rather swift and perfunctory course on liturgy, dating from 1954 when he was an old man in Australia. It is largely on the Book of Common Prayer. There are some good things in it. A liturgist would understand the quick sketch of Anglican liturgiology in this paragraph:

> It became something of a 'dogma' in our liturgists, down to Frere, that the Epiclesis is primitive . . . various other 'dogmas' or 'tendencies' – to regard *Ap. Const.* [a 4th century Syrian liturgical work] as primitive; to glorify the 'Great Entry' of the Eastern rites . . . It has been easy to assume that things which seem very good must be primitive.

Here is the confidence of a scholar who knows how to weigh his sources. It perhaps assumes knowledge in his students.

In 1939 he drafted the syllabus on liturgy for the Central Society for Sacred Study, with *The Parish Communion* as a set book, and with set questions all on his preoccupations, many of them Father Kelly's too.

Is there not a danger in the modern emphasis on 'experience', and a need for a stronger grasp on theology?

Is our eucharistic devotion too narrowly 'religious'? It
should be the lifting-up to God of the whole life of the
people.

How far are the people (both in Church and in Chapel;
and RC too) 'onlookers'?

How far do they attend 'a service' purely to get spiritual
benefit for themselves?

So, without great paradox, one might well say that students
at other theological colleges were more influenced by
Hebert on liturgy than those at Kelham. On the other
hand, Horton Davies is not wrong when he says that 'the
consecration of certain Anglican religious communities to
the primacy of worship and spirituality' produces great
liturgists like Hebert and Dix. [33]

The cool objectivity that Kelham strove for was Hebert's
ideal as well. There is a Report of SSM (Kelham) Committee on BBC Services, from March 1936, with several
telling sharpnesses about BBC religion.

There is a BBC prayer in which we confess that we have
often fallen below the higher levels — it suggests that we
are usually on them.

There is another which asks that we

'may go forward with the light of hope in our eyes and the
fire of inspiration in our hearts' . . . [i.e., says the Report]
looking forward to the pleasure of being very good —
picturing ourselves as such.

Kelham as usual rejects pleasing subjectivity and sweetness.
A favourite French quotation was used again. 'If the salt
hath lost its savour, wherewithal shall it be salted . . . Avec
le sucre'.

This strand is certainly there in Hebert, if slightly less so
in the 'Parish and People' approach to liturgy that he did
so much to further.

HEBERT THE ECUMENIST

Hebert's family had private means. He was sent to Harrow and Oxford, and his parents carried him off with them for holidays on the Continent, justified by calling in at religious houses on the way. So his 'deep water fishing' in the ecumenical movement was, seen from one angle, a middle-class Englishman's continental trips. It is different, however, because of what he found on the continent. After all, Anglo-Catholic clergymen of independent means had been touring the continent since the 1830s, inspecting convents, interviewing friendly Roman Catholics, and bringing back ecclesiastical fitments. There was a great deal of finding what one wanted to find, and Anglo-Catholics found Tridentine certainties, and peasant simplicities, and occasional Victorian fripperies. Fr Hebert wanted to find lay participation and liturgical reform, and successfully hunted them out. As often happened with religious tourists, he was looking for authentication for ideas already in the air in England, rather than for something utterly novel. The parish communion was not copied from continental usage, the idea was already there. [34]

Cosmo Gordon Lang, in 1904, not yet an archbishop but a go-ahead suffragan, was arguing for

> one great parish communion every Sunday in which the aspect of the fellowship of the body can be realised . . . at, say 9 o'clock or even 9.30. [35]

It is one thing for bishops to have bright ideas. There were parishes doing it. Thus it is relevant to Hebert that St Mary, Horbury Junction, the next parish to the one he served his title in, and St Saviour, Poplar, a Kelham parish whose vicar was Mark Trollope, formerly of Vassall Road and later Bishop of Korea, both were Edwardian pioneers of parish communions, with no Roman Catholic models for precedent.

> The Parish Communion certainly was not copied from Roman Catholic usage on the Continent. It is very

common now in France and Germany, but I am sure we were first in the field here. [36]

Nevertheless, the Liturgical Movement on the Continent deeply influenced Hebert's thought, and he made it his task to spread news of it in England. Those who read the SSM Quarterly could rely on regular articles in this field by Hebert, for example, the detailed description of a Liturgical Mission at Mont César in June 1938.

By the late 1930s, Kelham was involved with French Roman Catholic ecumenism. Fr Couturier talked about his 'cher et venéré Père Tribe'.[37] Hebert belonged to an organisation for prayer called the *Invisible Monastère de l'Unité Chretienne* in 1941, but the list of communities, Catholic and Protestant, prayed for every week, included Mirfield and Nashdom, but not Kelham. Fr Curtis of Mirfield and Fr Dix of Nashdom were more prominent in France than Fr Hebert.

> L'hôtel est *modeste* mais *excellente* [double underlined], il a ravi le F^{er} Curtis . . .[38]

Hebert also visited Protestant Europe, Germany and Scandinavia, mixing with High Church Lutherans, and here he had great influence and reputation. Fr Tribe, as Director of SSM, had gone to the Stockholm Conference of 'Life and Work' in 1925, and some Swedes had asked him to send another Anglican Catholic. A young Dane had visited Kelham, so Hebert went to Sweden via Copenhagen. There is a handwritten Logbook of his visit to Sweden and Denmark in 1928. In Denmark he found himself talking 'about Kelham and the sanctification of sport', and met a Danish Lutheran pastor

> a refreshingly familiar type – a real Priest, devoted to spiritual things, with a nice little oratory opening out of his study, fond of boys, musical, interested in railway engines.[39]

The shared interest in railway trains is the final touch. And Fr Hebert decided, even then, that churches cannot be summed up on the one issue of the apostolic succession. The bishops of the Swedish Church were in the succession, those of the Danish church were not.

> For myself, I cannot but conclude that . . . if the Swedish
> Church is 'all right' the Danish church can hardly be 'all
> wrong' on account of a historical accident in the XVI cen-
> tury.[40]

Sterner Anglicans like C.B.Moss [41] kept up the resolute
distinction between the Church of Sweden, which was a
church, and the Church of Denmark, which was not.
Hebert was more likely to look at the whole life of a
Christian tradition, and not be blind to what was there.
The marks of the church are not summed up in an apostolic
succession of bishops.

> . . . if both sides of Christendom are still providing saints
> and martyrs, it is clear that the truth of Christianity does
> not lie exclusively on either side.[42]

To begin with in Sweden Hebert was an observant liturgical tourist. He went to Choral Ante-Communion, 'very
like an English High Mattins', but the Swedish Communion service was different.

> . . . while the Agnus Dei was sung the two priests stood
> holding the Sacred Elements, in silence, facing the people.
> It was a sight that I shall not forget . . . It was all most
> impressive; very un-anglican and un-roman.[43]

Hebert was a good linguist, and he learnt Swedish, and
went on to attend many of the talks between the Church
of England and the Swedish church. More importantly, he
translated works by several Swedish theologians into English: Gustaf Aulén's *Christus Victor*, Anders Nygren's *Agape
and Eros*, and Yngve Brilioth's *Eucharistic Faith and Practice*,
as well as his history of the Anglican Revival. It is thus
directly due to Gabriel Hebert that a major strand of
Protestant neo-orthodox thought became influential in Britain. Aulén and Nygren are still in print in English, the
Swedish theologians with the greatest impact on British
theology. Brilioth, son-in-law of the great archbishop Sod-
erblom, and himself later to be primate of Sweden, was an
ideal Protestant to have unity negotiations with, a man
who rediscovered the catholicity of the church of Sweden
and steeped himself in Anglican history. On the other hand

he was an establishment figure. Hebert confided to Tribe in 1936 that he found in Brilioth 'a strain of officialism.. the official mind which accepts and tolerates the existence of various parties in the church'. [44] This was not, as we shall discover further, in Hebert's reckoning the first step towards ecumenism.

Fr Hebert, trained by Fr Kelly, was a positive and listening negotiator, and the Swedes liked and trusted him. His own understanding of the basics of liturgy was enriched by work on Protestant liturgies, and he was not anxious to put people in the wrong.

> Positive denials of anything are rare. In controversy, we are always trying to fix a denial on to the other man, and it is almost invariably resented. [45]

Apparently the Swedes found Dom Gregory Dix, another Anglican monk and liturgist, more down-putting, and compared him unfavourably with Hebert. [46] In churches there is a risk that external relations are carried on as a means of point-scoring in internal conflicts. The High Church movement in the Church of Sweden was one party competing with others, and its Anglican friendships were in part a gesture against other Swedes. There were also rivalries between the High Church theological faculty at Lund and the more liberal one at Uppsala. By the late 1940s Hebert's connections in Sweden were less ecumenical in spirit than they had been in the days of Brilioth. Hebert had greatly admired Bo Giertz's memorable novel of the religious history of a parish, The Hammer of God. But he found himself translating controversial writings by bishop Giertz that were less palatable. The bishop, describing the church history of his own country, spoke of 'tainted sources', and lists them as, first, Liberal Theology, then, Christian popular literature, 'based in Anglo-Saxon revivalism', then, 'the 1919 scheme for Christian teaching in our schools' which made 'the great mistake of setting up the Sermon on the Mount as the primary document of the Christian faith'. [47] This is a hard orthodox Christianity demonising softer forms, and Herbert tired of translating him.

The High Church movement in the Church of Sweden, though it had its harshnesses, in fact enriched that Church's liturgy and thought, and Hebert, as a friendly and unthreatening spokesman for the Catholic tradition of Christianity, played a significant part in this movement.[48]

Hebert had links with Germany as well as Scandinavia. In Germany, external friendships were more likely to rouse suspicion, as the totalitarian Nazi state cut links with abroad. Fr Hebert admired the Confessing Church:

> We often wonder what sort of witness the Church of England would have borne if she had been put through the *trial* that has come upon some of our fellow-Christians on the Continent during these five years.[49]

He did not have many close links with the Confessing Church. Bonhoeffer is always the exception to this, with his high doctrine of the church, and interest in the values of monasticism, but he can scarcely be presented as a close friend of Hebert.

German theology, aware of being the great tradition, was insultingly dismissive about theology done in English. So it is rather impressive to discover that Barth was discussing Hebert's theology (the rigorist Anglo-Catholic response to the Church of England Doctrine Report) in his seminar in Basle in 1939. Seen from the continent of Europe, Hebert was a leading Anglican theologian. He earned this by his openness to the real insights of other Christian traditions. It is unlikely that any English theologian ever became a household name in Germany. After eight years in Australia, writing to Bornkamm, Hebert shyly introduced himself as a friend of Davis McCaughey.

Gabriel Hebert was a New Testament scholar and a liturgist, more than a systematic theologian. His systematic theology tended towards Thomism. When in Australia he had to teach the *De Deo* course, he found he could not use Fr Kelly's scheme, because it was not Thomist enough.

> HK's scheme. I can't make it my own. Very different from T.Q. [i.e. Aquinas]. HK is trying to see the thing in the light of modern knowledge: anthropology, physics etc in our post-Christian world.[50]

In 1936 Hebert had brought out a volume of selections from Aquinas. Kelham was often more Thomist than Kelly. The Roman Catholic Blackfriars, reviewing his *Memorandum*, spoke of Kelham as a place

> which aims at combining freedom of thought with true deference to the authority of traditional Christianity, and exact theological teaching based on the study of St Thomas.

This was as ecumenical a statement as one was likely to get in a British Roman Catholic publication of the period. They did review Protestant works, but almost invariably in a very negative tone. SSM and the go-ahead English Dominicans (OP) under Henry St John had talks in 1936 at Laxton. SSM thought they were perhaps getting somewhere in the talks, but then the minutes came back with the Dominican amendments:

> ... for 'OP thought' read 'OP said that it had been maintained by some theologians that' ...[51]

In the climate of 1930s English Roman Catholicism, it was impressive that talks were held at all.

Ecumenism was hard work in Britain. Hebert went, for example, to the Friends of Reunion Conference at High Leigh in May 1933. It was quite an effective conference, with dignitaries, and competent theologians, and foreign missionaries, and a few women. A week or two later, Fr Hebert wrote manuscript 'subsequent impressions': 'Horrors of High Leigh'. He took notes of what people said, with occasional asides: '(The Scottish Presb. humbles himself with a distinct purpose of being exalted)'. The horrors were largely liturgical.

> But the prayers! They were awful. On the first evening we had the Bishop of Croydon. In the address it was all 'Don't you think? ... ' not 'Thus saith the Lord ....' The prayers consisted of a Litany drawn up by him rather in the Dwelly style, which I regard as a model of what ought not to be. The liturgical prayers of the church speak of the greatest things of all in simple 'objective' language.., refraining entirely from intruding the ego and its views of the

cosmos. When the ego is brought in, it is in the language of humility and penitence. ... If it tries to move about with angels and archangels like a 'young man carbuncular', like a nouveau-riche registering his impressions ... the result is dreadful.

Dwelly was the Dean of Liverpool, and in the wonderful space of his huge new cathedral he had liturgies which were adventurous for their day. Hebert's response, quoting his friend T.S.Eliot, was classical and Augustinian, against the diluted romanticism of made-up liturgies, and subtly snobbish.

To show that he is not snobbish about nonconformists – he genuinely was not – he continues:

When a Free-churchman – say a Congregationalist – conducts prayers according to the tradition in which he has grown up, I like it – the thing is sincere and good of its kind. It is personal, and does not profess to be more. It expresses the approach of human experience to the Divine Mystery: it is humble and truthful.

... But the 'Grey-book' style [a modernist draft liturgy of the 1920s] is neither the one thing nor the other. It apes the liturgical forms of the church; it expresses – not God's coming in power, but our co-operation with God, our high ideals, our spirit of friendliness, *our* purpose to make all things new. It tries to express the beautiful feelings that we think we ought to have, and our own firm intention that God's will is done .... we confess the sins of the other people who are not, like ourselves, keen on Reunion.

This is Kelham. Like Father Kelly, he turns savagely on the impulse to substitute human idealism for what God has done. Sometimes, again like Father Kelly, he is too dismissive. Dean Dwelly did good work. When Hebert goes through the modernist *Songs of Praise* with blistering scorn, one feels that some good has been missed. (See the detailed footnote in *Liturgy and Society*[52], using words like 'unforgivable'). It may be, again like Father Kelly, his sternness comes from being watchful of his own tendency to sentimentalism. He was capable of sentimentality. His own favourable picture of Scots Presbyterianism was based on

J.M.Barrie's rather sugary *Auld Licht Idylls*.[53] He was easily moved by children:

> . . . it was for me a marvel when for the first time, ministering at a Parish Communion in America, I saw the little unconfirmed children coming up with their parents to the altar rail.[54]

There is a rational case that children should not be outside the circle of God's people together, but the emotion is there.

He was more likely to take up stern positions. At High Leigh, he wanted to return to the idea of 'heresy' (and specifically used the word).

> We must make it plain that there can be no Christian unity with Theosophists or Christian Scientists: here I think they will agree now, most of them. Then we must ask them what to do about our non-Christians in the Church of England: *what would they do* about 'The Modern Churchman'?

This is one side of what 'Friends of Reunion' are for, to help put down other Anglicans. (He left 'Friends of Reunion' when they seemed prepared to admit occasional intercommunion). It reminds us that Fr Hebert was commissioned by the Church Union to write a critical Memorandum (published with the authority of their Council) on the *Report of the Archbishops' Commission on Christian Doctrine* (1941), chaired by William Temple. SSM, along with the other male religious orders, had formally deplored the publication of the Report. Though it was in his view satisfactory on Church and Sacraments (the primary concerns of the Church Union) 'on Revelation and Miracles and Resurrection and Virgin Birth one sees traces of liberalism', 'an alarming symptom of a progressive deterioration'. The Report, as might be expected, was careful and middle-of-the-road, and, because they worked hard on it, in many ways rather a credit to the Church of England, as Reports go [55], so Fr Hebert sounded alarmist and ungrateful.

He had already crossed swords with Archbishop Temple about the Virgin Birth. Temple wrote to him in 1939:

> ... you say that the Virgin Birth can only be a symbol if it is in fact a fact. That is quite true; but belief in the Virgin Birth can be a symbol even though the Virgin Birth is not a fact.[56]

Temple thought that Archbishop Davidson was right over against Bishop Gore in not wanting things to come to a clear issue. It made men commit themselves unnecessarily to what might turn out to have been the wrong side. [57] This resembles what Hebert found 'a strain of officialism' in Brilioth in Sweden. In these days, he, and very largely Kelham, where they spent time discussing the Archbishop's letters, were clear-cut anti-liberal, quite ready to confront apparent heresy. This was why T.S.Eliot liked Kelham, and George Every was turned to as a spokesman for traditional values. Kelham was at its most sternly traditional in the later years of the Bedale era. The striking thing is that Hebert was as successfully ecumenical as he was.

It is very difficult being loving and positive in every direction. Fr Hebert, very unusually for someone from an Anglo-Catholic background, could win the confidence of Free Churchmen.

> ... not one wounding word, not a sentence that makes a Free Churchman feel 'how hopelessly far away he is from understanding us!' And I could not say this even of a recent attempt of ... our dear William Temple himself![58]

This Methodist comment refers to Hebert's short book on *Intercommunion*. Hebert opposed intercommunion, whereas Temple thought it the way to unite the churches, but the Methodist trusted Hebert. Anglicans, even very pleasant Anglicans, could be wounding. Temple, writing to Hebert in the last year of his life, found this somewhat odd way to describe the real ministries and real sacraments of churches which have 'lost the Apostolic Ministry':

> ... much as a man who has lost his hands may learn to write with his toes![59]

Hebert had his own blind spots. Alan Richardson, reviewing the same work, *Intercommunion*, in the Modern Churchman[60], picks out 'unkind remarks about Modernists (especially his bitter sneer at Bishop Barnes..)'. Richardson found
Hebert's use of an argument against open communion
based on the customs of English polite society engagingly
naive. Hebert had contrasted turning up uninvited for a
formal dinner party with dropping in any evening of the
week for a chat.[61] There was no ecumenical feeling between the Modern Churchman and Hebert. One might
mention that Alan Richardson was later Professor at Nottingham, and his, not very modernist, type of Biblical
theology took over at Kelham in the new régime under
Simon Mein, Warden of the theological college from 1962.

Fame in Europe led to fame worldwide. Michael
Ramsey, the archbishop of Canterbury, was on Christian
name terms. In 1948 Hebert went as a visiting lecturer to
Berkeley Divinity School in the United States. The Old
Man told him

> Tell the Americans that Theology is not like the twin
> pillars of Solomon's temple, which at a great height above
> the ground carried elaborate decorations of carved tracery;
> Theology gives you the ground on which the pillars
> stand.[62]

On that trip he visited Chicago. In the morning of December 5 1948 he preached the university sermon, and in the
evening spoke at the Chicago Sunday Evening Club. The
other speaker that evening was the Moderator of the
Presbyterian Church USA.[63] When we compare the red-
carpet treatment of Fr Hebert with Fr Kelly's earlier visit
to the USA in 1912, we can see how the reputation of
SSM had grown.

THE LITURGICAL MOVEMENT AND POLITICS

A question arises about the relationship between the Liturgical Movement and politics. Anything that involves lay
participation might be expected to have democratic

instincts; anything that says that the liturgy is tied in with the whole of human life might be expected to have political overtones. A possible pedigree is plain to see, of 'sacramental socialists' through the years. Stewart Headlam, the firebrand of the Guild of St Matthew in the 1890s, could preach in Westminster Abbey about Holy Communion as a pledge 'to be Holy Communists'.[64] Conrad Noel, after the First World War, in his Manifesto for the Catholic Crusade, tried, like Fr Kelly, to see theology in human life.

> 'If you believe in the Blessed Trinity and a Divine Commonwealth steeped in the worship of the Social God, in the Blessed Trinity, One-in-Many, Many-in-One, VARIETY IN UNITY, not as a senseless dogma for Sundays only, but as the basis and meaning of all human life [you will join the Catholic Crusade]'[65]

The Catholic Crusade was pugnacious socialism. There were more moderate approaches. Fr Tribe, Director of SSM, was one of the founders and a leading light in the Anglo-Catholic Summer School of Sociology. Sociology had a wider sense then: as Tribe himself wrote 'Every Act of Parliament . . . is an act of practical sociology.' [66] His book, *The Christian Social Tradition* (SPCK 1935), deals with political and economic questions, but much more cautiously than the Catholic Crusade.

When Fr Hebert wanted a lay perspective to interpret society, he turned to T.S.Eliot.

> He was a great friend of T.S.Eliot, who loved coming to Kelham, where he could speak freely without fear of being quoted. His *Idea of a Christian Society* originated in lectures at Kelham, and was discussed with Gabriel.[67]
>
> It has been said of [Hebert's] *Liturgy and Society* that 'the 'liturgy' was Hebert and the 'society' was Eliot.[68]

Eliot was on the right politically, fighting the cold war against communist materialism.

> Either we should find a new, but a real, object for education, as the Russians have done, or we must revert to the Christian wisdom and Christian ideal of education. If this path is taken, at Kelham and at places like Kelham a lead

can be given and a standard can be set. On the other hand, if our civilisation takes the opposite road, of materialism in education, then the modern religious communities will be like the monasteries in the dark ages, self-contained fortresses, keeping alight the Christian lamp of learning and civilisation.[69]

Like Eliot, Hebert's mind sometimes ran on dualist lines. Their perspective on the past is similar: he saw the beheading of king Charles I as 'the great dividing line in English history'.[70] George Every, teaching history at Kelham, was Cavalier too, but pointed out, fairly, that Eliot moved to the centre as time passed.[71] And like the seventeenth century Anglican divines, Hebert's image of Christianity was one of passive non-resistance.

> Quite properly [unity] will not come till we have all been compelled to suffer together at the hands of a secularised state.[72]

At other times, writing on political matters, his stance was more easy-going. It is world-seasoning, rather than world-shattering. In devising a 'Picture-Book of the Holy Eucharist', he wanted to use

> 'a picture from no.13 of the French *Albums liturgiques*, of the blessing going out from the altar and reaching all sorts of men in their several occupations'[73]

There is a whole section on 'Social Idealism' in *Liturgy and Society*. 'Whatever new social order may emerge must grow out of the old; Utopia cannot suddenly appear from nowhere'.[74] He is cautious in his phrasing, as even-handed as a bishop. He tried, riskily, to be fair-minded about Nazism:

> We may well be cautious about accepting the criticisms of the Nazi régime so commonly made in this country, in the name of the Liberal ideal of individual freedom; for with all its faults, the Nazi state has actualized the unity of the German nation, as the Liberal-democratic régime which preceded it was powerless to do.[75]

This is not a Barthian theologian. As time went on, he was

influenced by neo-orthodoxy. In one of his lectures, talking about eschatology, he sounds like the young Barth, radically undercutting human religiosity.

> Bp – a cheap-jack. Dogma and sacraments his stock-in-trade . . . Perhaps our church-practice is (almost) a blasphemous parody of what the Church is . . . The Church is itself an eschatological reality, in which Christ the Tiger is present . . .[76]

His pamphlet 'The Natural Law and the Reign of God' (undated, c.1944), though predictably full of quotations from Aquinas and Hooker, does say 'It is a radically false method to begin with natural theology as if that could stand on its own feet'. But in *Liturgy and Society* natural law reigns unchallenged. Some social institutions are undercut by the radical questioning of Christianity, but others, like the nation, are let alone. The contribution of the Church

> . . . includes a firm upholding of certain institutions, above all that of Marriage according to the Divine law, as the basis of society. It includes also a radical criticism, in general, of the Liberal-democratic theory of government, namely that the best form of government is that of an assembly in which various interests meet in conflict, and the vote of the majority prevails.[77]

As an example of a system where majority voting does not prevail, he cites Kelham. Ultimate responsibility lies with the Director. 'The Chapter has its defined rights of free discussion'.[78] Most religious societies, including SSM, looking back on ages when Superiors were Superiors, have moved nearer to democracy since Hebert was writing, so here his views have dated somewhat. We need many careful caveats before saying 'There is no freedom for man except in acknowledging authority'.[79] Fr Tribe spoke similarly of

> the Christian idea of freedom as liberty to do God's will and not liberty to do one's own will.[80]

In saying *nisi dominus* to all cheerful liberal optimism,

Hebert does not really forget the real goods that liberalism stood for.

> While the Bible and the Sacraments stand, man *cannot* be trimmed to the shape required for him to be just one item in the purpose of a system, or State, or race.[81]

On the whole, his discussion of the institution of marriage, while making real positive affirmations, has also dated, as has Tribe's. There is a paper for the Mothers' Union on 'The Incarnation and the Problems of Sex', where one of the problems is 'Lustfulness, and the cult of nudism generally'. In 1961, when he was an old man, the BBC turned down a script called 'Man in God's Image', a dramatic reworking of the Genesis story.

> GOD'S VOICE: And now I am going to unite you in Holy Marriage. Adam, wilt thou have . . .?

The stage directions say 'Adam is to think of his part as a boy's part; he should have a fresh, clear, merry voice'. Eve is vain about her personal appearance, in the way that girls are. Celibates often find it hard to pitch it right talking about sex.

Gabriel Hebert's stance on political and social questions was moderately reformist, consciously Christian rather than a child of the times, and perhaps best seen as the forerunner of the 'Social Democratic party at the parish eucharist'[82]. In this, he fairly expressed the position of SSM in his day.

THE BIBLICAL SCHOLAR AND AUSTRALIA

As a biblical scholar Hebert did good work. He was eager to find the theology in the bible, just like Father Kelly, and it was there to be found. He published *The Throne of David: a study of the fulfilment of the Old Testament in Jesus Christ and His Church* in 1941. It was an unfashionable theme, as much good biblical scholarship had gone into teaching us not to read the New Testament back into the

Old. He argues that Christians can read the Old Testament and rightly find a Christian meaning:

> there is a sense in which mystical interpretation is obligatory for all Christians'[83]

and that we should not be bound by what the writers understood at the time. 'Those who shaped and carried out the rituals in the dim past were themselves groping in the dark'.[84] After all, God is in charge, and they may well not understand what he is doing. Only with the perspective of God's history can sense come.

> They [the New Testament writers] need the old Testament story in order to see in their true context the events which had lately happened . . . The terrible events of the Passion, and the experience of the first Easter, were a Crossing of the Red Sea . . . the Pillar of Cloud had gone before, leading the Israel of God to salvation and freedom.[85]

The *Modern Churchman* was sharply unpleasant about Hebert's 'effrontery' in warning his readers against 'reading in preconceived ideas',[86] when that was what he did himself. In these books on the relationship between the testaments,

> He finds in the Old Testament only what he wants to find, and it is always what Catholic dogma demands.[87]

There is something in this rather predictable assault. His students, by contrast, thought him modernist. There is a rather silly student cartoon from about 1930 'Fr Gabriel persuades St Matthew that he could not possibly have written the first Gospel'. He became an effective populariser of modern scholarship, unthreatened by novelty, but capable of being scathing about scholarship misapplied.[88]

The risk with many scholars is that they compartmentalise their lives, often in the name of scholarly objectivity. Hebert, as befitted a Kelham man, tried to hold things together. So when he read the bible, he read it as relevant to the theology he believed. This might lead to anachronisms, but it raises real questions. One cannot read Hebert, as one cannot read Barth on Romans, and forget that this book has to do with almighty God. It may have been irritating to modernists, but an orthodox theology is likely to find more resonance with the bible than one freshly constructed of the best spiritual impulses of the twentieth century.

One of the most commonplace ways of compartmentalising a Christian's life is to separate the liturgical and the scholarly reading of scripture. When scholars notice this, they tend to disparage the liturgical. But 'the liturgy of the Church is the best school for the right interpretation of the scriptures'.[89] He could normally manage to convince people whose piety was centred on the bible that he was reading it seriously as well. One of his recurrent tasks was to defend the cursing psalms against mealy-mouthed modernists.

> It has seemed to many people shocking that the psalmist should so curse his enemies: particularly to people who have lived sheltered lives, and have always tried, and have usually been able, to believe the best of everybody. But there come times in the world's history when satanic evil unmasks itself: ours is one of them.[90]

Hebert had the useful skills of the popularist, and became well-known. He was chosen to address the Lambeth Conference of 1948, and indeed that Conference was full of references to him.[91] So it was news when in 1952 the SSM sent him to St Michael's House, Crafers, their Australian theological college. He was then in his late 60s, and he stayed there until 1961, two years before his death. He was tempted to be a theological lion in a new country, 'as though I was Somebody and as though my ideas and insights were Mine',[92] but Basil Oddie, the brusque Australian Provincial, soon put a stop to that. There were occasional personal sharpnesses in the House. Fr Antony Snell and Fr Hebert were the only two real scholars, and one was famous and the other was not.

With his fame, the Society took more notice of him. When he wrote his *Fundamentalism and the Church of God* in 1956, the Director, Fr Paul Hume, did not leave it to Gabriel Hebert's colleagues in Australia to approve it. He had to see it himself, and passed it on to the Visitor, the

The Company of the Servants of Christ, the SSM native community.

Miss Wright
at Modderpoort.

Two South African styles –
Fr Cecil Hemsley and Donald Hiscock.

Fr Hector Lee on horseback in Basutoland.

Round the altar of Willen church.

Bishop of Southwell, for a nihil obstat.[93] The SSM had no history of censoring its authors.

Fundamentalism and the Church of God was an attempt at 'a rapprochement with the Conservative Evangelicals . . . our primary ecumenical task'.[94] Father Kelly had set himself to do the same thing. The actual result of the book was somewhat different. Perhaps because his analysis of fundamentalism was rather close to the bone, it earned a formal reply, as well as a lot of letters from evangelicals. J.I. Packer's *'Fundamentalism' and the Word of God* (1958) went into far more editions than Fr Hebert's book, and became a standard handbook among conservative evangelicals. Many people only heard of Fr Hebert as a critic who tried to pin a charge of scriptural monophysitism on fundamentalists, as an exponent of a 'biblical theology' which was really liberal, even though he said it was not, and as one of those who said it did not matter whether Peter wrote his Second Epistle or not. Some good critics liked Hebert's book. Martin Marty, a very competent American historian of doctrine, agreed that

> deviations to the right are ultimately as dangerous to the claims of Christian truth as are those to the left.[95]

Hebert's later ecumenism loosened up. In *Apostle and Bishop*, published the year of his death, 1963, he says that he has moved on from the theology of bishop Kirk's *The Apostolic Ministry* (1944). The South Indian scheme had worked. Anglican doctrines of the church are too high and dry. It is

> . . . a common fault among us Anglicans to present the Episcopal Office as if it were primarily a matter of the Law and Constitution of the Church[96]

He quotes the Roman Catholic ecumenist Yves Congar:

> 'Hierarchy' is not a New Testament word, nor is the word *arché* ever used of Church Authority.[97]

His habitual approach was 'both-and' rather than 'either-or'. The Protestant churches would add forms of ministry, rather than being recognised as, or changed into, Catholic forms. When the question of the ordination of women came up, his answer was to look for 'more fluid and less formalised ministries'.[98]

When *Honest to God* came out in 1963, he said that the questions it raised would serve 'for the more confirmation of the faith',[99] and passed on a favourable review in the *Catholic Worker* to John Robinson.

But though in his old age, the old Father Hebert was less intransigent than in his youth, and the SSM too felt the spirit of the 60s, the continuities are more important than the changes. In one of his last books he goes back to Fr Kelly's beloved F.D.Maurice:

> . . . every man who is doing the work he is set to do, may believe he is inspired to do that work . . . inspiration is not a strange marvellous ['anomalous' in FDM] fact; it is the proper law and order of the world; no man ought to write or speak or think, except under the acknowledgement of an inspiration.[100]

It is not in the strange and marvellous but in the commonplace choices before ordinary people that God is ordinarily at work. Here Hebert is expressing something central in Kelham theology. He did so before a wider audience than any other SSM writer. He cannot be understood without SSM.

We have already followed Fr Hebert to the SSM college in Australia. We now turn to look generally at the work overseas of the Society, an international missionary society from its beginnings.

Chapter Ten

Asia and Africa

KOREA AND CENTRAL AFRICA

SSM began as the Corean Missionary Brotherhood. Corea[1] was a missionary diocese, only just founded, which meant a bishop and a block grant and almost nothing else. Christian missions were just beginning to penetrate the country. Earlier Roman Catholic missions had been crushed in the Great Persecution of 1866–71, but in the 1880s a weak monarchy was anxious not to offend foreign powers, and lent its patronage to missionary hospitals and schools. Perhaps more importantly, the young progressives in the country were also pro-missionary. There were Koreans wanting what they thought the missionaries could provide. In the next twenty years, Korean Christians did not wait to be given missionary schools, but set up their own Christian schools. In consequence, the Protestant missionaries, led by Dr John Ross (1842–1915) from Scotland, but predominantly American Presbyterians and Methodists, could report real progress. By 1910 1% of the population of Korea was Protestant. (Compare Japan, where Protestantism has never yet reached 1%). The Roman Catholics, made nervous by their history, held back from founding hospitals and schools, and their growth, though genuine, was less spectacular.[2] Korea was, though this might only be evident with hindsight, an open door, where a mission might well prosper.

The Society for the Propagation of the Gospel gave the money, and the bishop had to find his team of workers. His idea was to have a diocese run as a missionary brotherhood. There was a precedent in Central Africa, to which we shall return. If he could have single men, under a vow of poverty, willing to do what they were told, he could run a missionary diocese as a tight little ship. In 1889 the newly-appointed Bishop Corfe had two priest volunteers, Fr Kelly and Fr Trollope, both with some private means. He himself had been a naval chaplain, and had found some naval ratings to volunteer for lay work. He would have taken them out and trained them there, and had to be persuaded that it was better to test their vocation in England, and then send them out. So Fr Kelly was left in England in charge of the Corean Missionary Brotherhood. The name was soon changed, and as SSM discovered its own purposes and momentum, it became less and less useful to the diocese of Corea.[3]

In 1892 one of the first students went as a printer to Corea. Most of the candidates dropped out. Of those who remained, four out of the five were being trained for ordination. This in itself was a change from the bishop's expectation. One of the first three novices in 1893 was Badcock, who was training for Corea.

Mark Trollope, the senior priest of the diocese of Corea, was looking for some sort of community life. He thought of joining the Cowley Fathers, but that would mean giving up Corea. Instead, rather hastily on furlough, in September 1895 he became a novice of SSM, and in January 1896 went back to Corea with Badcock and Hillary, the two senior students, to set up a priory of SSM. They were all three still novices: it was a very grave risk, and it did not work. The bishop could not leave three of the staff of his under-manned diocese in one place. He moved Fr Trollope away,[4] and Badcock and Hillary, both young, not speaking Korean, were left to be a priory by themselves. The bishop found less use for laymen than he had expected, and proposed shipping them to Japan to learn Japanese. [5] The Kilburn Sisters (Community of St Peter) four of whom had gone out in 1892, were more fortunate.[6]

Perhaps the Anglicans were spread too thinly. The various American Protestant missions, first informally and then formally in 1908, agreed on spheres of influence.[7] In fact they went on to negotiate a united church, but were overruled by their funding bodies at home. Though SSM's own commitment to ecumenism was never an easy pan-Protestantism like this, nevertheless what happened in

Korea might properly raise questions for an interested observer like Fr Kelly. There was there a small amateurish Anglican mission, unwilling to co-operate in any way with large friendly and successful Protestant missions. 'Our men *do not attend social functions of any kind.*'[8] The Anglican mission was determined that its Korean adherents would not be rice-Christians, half-understanding and supplementing the faith with their own superstitions. It was a very disciplined Christianity. For example, no Korean was allowed to communicate on Sunday who had not been to Evensong and preparation for Holy Communion on the Saturday night, and the Sunday service began at 7am.[9] The diocese was happy to see slow growth, thinking it more genuine. In practice, the Anglican church became marginalised, in a country which is now one-fifth Protestant.

This is to look ahead. Over the years another four SSM recruits went out. There were two little priories, one at Mapo, just outside Seoul, and the other at Kanghwa, an offshore island. Br Hugh Pearson, who would go on to be factotum for many years at Kelham, while in Korea superintended the building of a hospital, and then a church, and, as so often with SSM lay-brothers, operated a printing-press. The lay brothers, however, were measured against a clerical missionary standard and found wanting. The bishop thought they were dirty and ill-mannered.[10] There was a problem of social class: the mission would have liked graduates; it certainly did not want social-climbing Cockney clerks.[11] From the first there were boundaries.

> . . . the clergy 'keep their own mess' and the laymen feed by themselves – the chapel being our only common meeting ground – unless we go out for walks together or invite one another to smoke after dinner.[12]

Fr Henry Drake was sent out to succeed Trollope as SSM Provincial in Korea in 1898. He was a professed member of SSM, and something of a new broom. He was eager to explain what the rule involved, largely in terms of renouncing private property.[13] Both he and Fr Trollope were strong personalities, and they clashed.[14] With hindsight, Fr Kelly thought that much of the damage was done by Fr

Trollope stirring up the anxieties of the others before Fr Drake's arrival. In consequence

> the novices found the pressure of the rule too much for them, and we were reduced to two professed priests and one layman. One of the priests was invalided home in 1901 ... We hung on for some time ... At the Bishop's suggestion, we finally withdrew in 1904.[15]

Of the seven SSM professed and novices there in 1898, four withdrew from the Society in 1899, including the original three. It had been a very grave gamble trying to run a novitiate in a missionfield. Fr Trollope, a natural leader, was a serious loss. Fr Firkins was invalided home, and another withdrew in 1901. Most of those who withdrew carried on working in the diocese. None the less, there was ill-feeling. Bishop Corfe, himself disillusioned and unhappy, felt that SSM (Fr Kelly) had pointed a gun at his head: either the brethren could live together or they would be recalled.[16] Fr Drake was not a conciliator. Fr Kelly wrote to him:

> Do not go telling people 'Of course if you order it I shall obey'. It puts people off dreadfully. Both the Bishop and Fr Trollope refer to it.[17]

It was too late to retrieve the Korean province, and it was clear the bishop did not want them back. This sad little episode damaged the confidence of the Society, and they learned something about the dangers of putting young untrained men into solitary work miles from support. They also learned something of the ways of bishops. Much of the story was a matter of personal interactions in a very small and rather inward-looking group of people. The bishop, Fr Kelly, Fr Trollope and Fr Drake were all potential leaders of men with very few men to lead. The Vassall Road boys whom they led were not ready for missionary work in Korea. Everything was rushed. The pity was that Koreans were ready for missionary work; for example in the 1890s the Roman Catholic church in Korea was training a handful of Korean priests. If the Society had successfully set up priory life, they might have found Korean novices.

The next bishop of Korea abandoned the attempt to run the diocese as a missionary brotherhood, but in 1911 Fr Trollope became bishop of Korea himself, and tried again. He brought back Fr Drake, so the difference between them cannot have been lasting. (There may be some significance in the fact that they both were old boys of Lancing). Fr Drake, after being SSM Provincial in South Africa from 1906 to 1911, returned to Korea 'on detached service' (a familiar technical term in the history of the overseas missionary work of SSM) for many years. He was still there in the Second World War till 1942, vicar-general of the diocese.

Fr Drake was probably too stern as a Provincial. In Fr Alfred Kelly's file labelled 'Scurrilities', there is a poetic skit lampooning all the leading lights around 1920. It includes this character's speech.

> THE MAN FROM THE FAR EAST : I've broken up one province and it's at peace. That's why it's called 'The Land of the Morning Calm'.[18]

They could only tease because they were relaxed about the memory. For someone on the other side of the world, Fr Drake kept in touch with his Society, writing articles for the Quarterly, turning up for Great Chapters, and settling in to Modderpoort in 1942 when he had to leave Korea.

In 1922, Bishop Trollope induced SSJE, the Cowley Fathers, to set up a short-lived house, and in 1925 he invited SSM back to run a theological college. They refused.

In Korea, the SSM had been there at the founding of a missionary diocese. In Central Africa, where there was an SSM Province from 1894 to 1929, they played a small part in an existing Anglican missionfield. The UMCA (Universities Mission to Central Africa) was set up in response to David Livingstone's appeal to the English universities in 1857. Though Livingstone was not himself an Anglican, these were Anglican missions. After a false start, the first UMCA diocese was set up in 1864 with its bishop in the offshore island of Zanzibar. From 1873 there had been work on the mainland, and in 1892 the second UMCA diocese, Nyasaland, was founded. Unlike the other major

Anglican missionary society in East Africa,[19] the CMS (Church Missionary Society), the UMCA was Anglo-Catholic in churchmanship, and eager to work at once through dioceses rather than through a missionary society. So the UMCA dioceses were run like missionary brotherhoods, under what were in practice temporary vows. Thus SSM had much in common with the UMCA.

Fr Kelly was training men for the missionfield, not necessarily for Korea. So, when an appeal for volunteers to the Church Times in October 1891 brought more men than Corea could pay for, he offered six men to UMCA who 'found a friend willing to pay for their training'. Travers, Secretary of UMCA, was sympathetic to SSM. [20] Only three arrived, but they got three more by the end of the year, all destined for lay work. In fact, Kelly noted ruefully, five of the six were to draw back. In 1892 'Bishop Smythies [the bishop of Zanzibar] visited the House and arranged for Mr Russell to proceed to Magila as printer'. (He went in 1893). The first novices (May 9, 1893) included Cyril Chilvers, who had arrived only two months before, a UMCA candidate. Fr Woodward, priest-in-charge of Magila, came on furlough in March 1894, and was noviced. He and Trollope (in Korea) had appealed to Kelly for some sort of 'Brotherhood'. He wanted a rule of life, and to be under vows. Woodward was professed in October with Fr Kelly. In November he went back as SSM Provincial of Zanzibar and Nyasaland. Magila was a well-established mainland mission station. The mainland of the diocese of Zanzibar was Tanganyika, which was a German colony, though this created few problems until the First World War. The Roman Catholic missionary orders, not predominantly German, had far more converts than the Anglicans.

Joseph White went out to Magila in 1897 as a lay brother, having failed his ordination exam. They sent him back in 1899 for more study, and he was ordained in 1902. Fr Kelly himself visited Central Africa in 1902, and was full of plans for a catechists' college taking 16-year-olds.[21] The SSM had a very happy experience with African schoolboys, starting at Magila. By 1910, when he was moved to Mkuzi, not far away, Fr

Joseph White had reorganised the whole schools system in the district. 'He used to be very autocratic', said Fr Kelly.[22]

The grant from the UMCA was indispensable in the early years for the funding of the college at Vassall Road, but this money stopped by the end of the century, as it became a self-sufficient theological college for England. Nevertheless, SSM still saw itself as a missionary order. By 1902 five of the total 22 professed members were in Central Africa. As 10 of the 14 in England were students, that means more adult SSM in Central Africa than in England. But five is not many, and there were only four there in 1906 and 1908, two of them lay. For health reasons, there was nearly always someone away on furlough, so the practical numbers were lower yet. Between 1894 and 1904, 14 men were sent from SSM to East Africa, several for a very short time.[23]

Most of the Society's work was in the senior diocese of Zanzibar, though Br Ronald Moffatt, after being treasurer of the UMCA in Zanzibar for 10 years, joined Bishop Hine in 1909 in pioneering the new diocese of Northern Rhodesia.[24] From 1908 the bishop of Zanzibar was the great Frank Weston, who had in fact been recruited for UMCA by Fr Woodward. One of the most memorable figures in UMCA history, in his dealings with SSM he was frequently autocratic and unhelpful.

In 1911 Fr Woodward was Archdeacon of Zanzibar, where he was based, and Vicar-general of the diocese, as well as being acting archdeacon for Shambala and Bonde. Fr White was at Mkuzi, Br Arthur Makins at Msalabani (Magila), Br Robert Carroll was doing odd jobs for the Bp of Lebombo, and Br Ronald Moffatt was Bp Hine's secretary, based at Livingstone. The lay members had low status in the missionfield. Fr Kelly had thought of sending out laymen as assistants to the clergy. In 1908 Bishop Weston of Zanzibar visited Kelham, and was 'completely at one with my old idea of the secretary or *socius*'.[25] A missionary would have a lay helper, a *socius*. In the event, some bishops got lay assistants for themselves. If the lay workers were ordainable, in practice they ordained them. Hence SSM tended to mean unordainable lay workers whose all-too-human flaws had been observed by the

bishop in person. There was obviously very little community life, though Fr Woodward and Fr White had been
together at Magila for several years, and Fr Woodward got
back to Mkuzi when he could.

In 1912 the bishop of Zanzibar allowed SSM to have
Mkuzi as a priory. Until then they could be moved around
as he chose. Mkuzi was an ordinary mission station, on the
mainland about 30 miles from the coast a little north of
Zanzibar. The district had ten native schools and teachers,
and these teachers were the key to its work. Fr White had
no very high opinion of his teachers.

> Native teachers, however well educated, have not the
> intellectual resources of the European; their teaching tends
> to become stereotyped and lifeless . . .[26]

For Africa, Mkuzi was a compact little parish. No parish-
ioner lived more than five miles from the church. Fr
White listed what had to be done: first, the care of themselves, the European missionaries (some services in English
instead of Kiswahili), 'second in importance' came the
African staff, third the parish in general, and 'finally the
grappling with the whole problem of the unconverted
heathen'.[27] Somehow it does not sound on fire with mission. On the other hand, we should remember the pressures
against any community life, that had destroyed the Korean
province. Fr White was being realistic about keeping the
community going.

For members of a religious community, it was a lonely
life. There was the hope that they would have three at
Mkuzi in 1912: 'we shall be quite a crowd'. Within ten years
the three lay brothers had left the society – two of them had
been removed (the SSM technical term for putting a man
out, unlike 'releasing', when it was his own decision).[28]

Then the work was disrupted by the Great War. Fr
White was interned by the Germans, and was marched 200
miles cross-country inland.[29]

More testing than the Germans were the religious stresses
of sharing an internment camp with other Anglicans. There
were CMS missions in German East Africa as well.

After a few Sundays we found them admitting a Noncon-

formist, not once but every Sunday. So I made a protest to
the Archdeacon (Rees). He said 'Yes it was pity for one
cast off as he was and being a Christian he felt it right to
ask him' . . . Consequently we withdrew from their Communion . . .[30]

Fr Woodward and Fr White were priests of the diocese of
Zanzibar, whose bishop had excommunicated his neigh-
bouring CMS bishops for allowing intercommunion with
non-Anglicans at Kikuyu in 1913, so this was to be expected
when UMCA met CMS.

Fr White, whom internment actually mellowed, re-
opened the Mkuzi priory in 1917, but in 1920 was called
back to England to be Director of the whole Society, a
surprising stopgap appointment. Then in 1921 Archdeacon
Woodward was in trouble. One of the first two professed
members of SSM, he had followed his own career as a
missionary more-or-less detached from SSM. He had been
in the diocese of Zanzibar since the 1870s, a great linguist,
and a gentle and loving person, now an old man. But some
complaint came to the bishop (Frank Weston) that the
archdeacon had been fondling girls in the confessional, and
asking them too probing questions about their sexual lives.
The bishop presumed him guilty.

> . . . your overworked brain, combined with your keen
> interest in sexual affairs in connection with Africans, has
> disturbed your moral judgment, and landed you in very
> serious indiscretions.[31]

To avoid scandal, he could retire at once with a canonry.
Fr Woodward refused it; he did not feel he had done
anything wrong. He was quite sure that he had never shut
and fastened his door with a girl; that on one particular
case, when the girl had denied any possible breaches of the
seventh commandment two weeks before her baby was
born, he had asked her again if she had broken the commandment; all his life he had been hugging African children, and he was now an old man.[32] What made matters
worse was that the Archdeacon belonged to a religious
order, and so the question was not simply between him
and his bishop. The bishop found himself at once making

formal charges to the Director of SSM. It is difficult to tell
how damning they were. On the one hand he says 'His
admissions would have fully justified . . . a silent resigna-
tion'[33] and one wonders, as Fr Woodward did, if they
really would. On the other hand, in a thirteen page letter
the next day, the bishop says that touching girls is

> forbidden, by custom, not only to their fathers but even to
> their grandfathers . . . I do not see my way to calling the
> eight girls who have complained liars and slanderers.[34]

Fr White, the new Director, was not the sort of person
who could confront Frank Weston, his own diocesan, in
full flood of righteous indignation. So the Society at once
moved Fr Woodward to Modderpoort in South Africa,
and, to fill the breach, Fr White himself and Fr Tribe set
off for Zanzibar. (The journey was presented in the Quarterly as a visitation of the Foreign work of the Society).[35]
The Director, after all, had only left the diocese of Zanzibar
the year before, and Fr Tribe (the next Director) was a
qualified medical doctor. It was the best they could do, but
it failed to please. There was an angry letter from the
Bishop.

> My first duty is to enter a most earnest protest against your
> treatment of my diocese . . . your so planning matters that
> I have had no say at all before you arrive with Fr Tribe.[36]

Obviously SSM was unhappy about its dealings with Zanzibar. Most of the African work was now in South Africa,
and they had already given notice to the diocese of Zanzibar
that the UMCA work would have to be wound down,[37]
though there were still three SSM priests working in
UMCA parishes through the 1920s. Fr Kelly said 'Whitworth took White's place in UMCA, where things are
now much worse than they used to be'.[38] He meant more
Anglo-Catholic, as he was then fighting his private battle
against party Anglo-Catholicism at Kelham, and Fr Whitworth had been a ring-leader in Romanising changes there.
Though he had his flaws, being impetuous, too eager to
dismiss teachers, 'tactless and unsympathetic with Europeans', Fr Cyril Whitworth was a successful missionary, and

Mkuzi prospered. The diocese felt that the SSM way of working was rather extravagant of men (and of money). SSM felt that the work given them was too parochial in its nature.[39] The closure of the SSM province came in 1929.

Quite soon the bishop repented about driving out his archdeacon.

> I believed nothing against you that could have made your withdrawal necessary ... at its worst nothing more than indiscreet conduct. The terrible mountain that has arisen from the molehill seems to have been due to the official reception given to my original letter by your Director ... [God] knows I never intended you to leave the diocese: and never intended you to be put on your defence before fellow priests of SSM.[40]

This was almost an apology. Fr Woodward did not return. A little life of him, *Father Woodward of UMCA*, was published in 1926. In 1928 Oxford University gave him an honorary MA for his work on African languages, of which he could speak at least eight.[41] At last, in 1930, with a different bishop of Zanzibar, and on doctor's orders, he returned to the canonry he had earlier refused. He was delighted to be back, and died within two years. He had outlived the SSM province that he had founded. Fr Kelly, a much more complex man, said of him:

> I have a feeling that I knew – that anybody would know – all there was to be known, the moment we met him.[42]

He was transparently good and simple.

Magila, where the first SSM brethren had worked, became from 1910 the mother house of an order of nuns, the Community of the Sacred Passion. Fr Harold Smith of SSM, who had worked with UMCA, went back to Zanzibar in 1939 on detached service, until 1964. He was the last link. UMCA itself was merged into USPG a few months later. Over the years, twenty SSM brethren had served in UMCA.

Good work was done, both in Korea and Central Africa, by individuals. But the attempt to run SSM provinces failed. Some of this is because bishops could not handle a society which wanted to work as a body. Paradoxically, things might have been easier if SSM had been more stereotypically monastic, and had presented itself as a power-house of prayer, or as a model of the religious life to be copied by native Africans or Koreans. As it was, it fell between two stools, and a society for work was worked too hard and then, sometimes very politely, found inadequate.

SOUTH AFRICA

The very first Anglican missionary order for men was the Society of St Augustine, founded in 1869. They went out from England, and found a base for their work at Modder-poort, in the Orange Free State. The newly founded missionary diocese of Bloemfontein had few English people, and the bishop was unhindered in his plans for a Catholic missionary order. Modderpoort was chosen be-cause the Society had asked the bishop of Bloemfontein to buy them a farm. He could find nothing cheap near Bloemfontein, but there was land available newly ceded to the Free State from Basutoland. Modderpoort was, and remains, a village near the border; the nearest town was Ladybrand. The two farms that were bought, 7000 acres, are held in trust by the bishops of Bloemfontein.[43] For thirty years the Society of St Augustine worked among both the black and white populations in the Free State. They had also promised the king of Basutoland, but had been unable to fulfil the promise, to start some work across the border there. The king had perhaps some notion of playing off the Anglicans against the Paris Mission (French Protestants) and the Methodists who were already there. The Society of St Augustine showed with pride the cave which was their first base in Modderpoort.

> . . . a cave formed by three or four 20-foot boulders which chance falls from the kopje's crown of cliff have rolled together. The main part of the cave was their oratory; at one end some rude steps have been cut and there stood the altar; round this are some shallow recesses, where there were sleeping quarters. It is from this cave that they carried the Catholic faith to the Basuto people . . .[44]

But the brethren grew older, and had no recruits, and when there were only three left, not that there had ever been many more, the Bishop of Bloemfontein in 1902 invited SSM to take over the work. The bishop's secretary was an ex-novice of SSM, who had left with TB and six months to live, and found South Africa suited him.

One practical inducement was that several of SSM's members needed to go to a warmer healthier climate. As almost always in the history of the Society, it was difficult to find enough men to go. The opening of the South African province probably sealed the fate of the Korean one, and perhaps in the long term Central Africa as well. Fr Kelly went out with three lay brothers in August 1902, and stayed a month. His brother Alfred went out in 1903, as Provincial of South Africa, with another priest, a deacon, and a fourth layman.

The Orange Free State had recently suffered the Boer War, and most Christians there were, and remained, Dutch Reformed. It was not very promising territory for an Anglican mission. In 1904 73 per cent of the Europeans in the Free State were Dutch Reformed, 12.5 per cent were Anglican, and 2.3 per cent were Roman Catholic.[45] It was not part of SSM's ambition to be allocated easily successful fields of work, so it scarcely fair to say they should have tried to get somewhere more interesting, like the Rand, where the Community of the Resurrection worked. There were very few hints that the Society might have been seen as the church of an occupying power. In May 1905, in Ladybrand, there was 'a raid on the Church by the Police during a Native Service'[46] which was perhaps a foretaste of troubles to come.

With hindsight, SSM took over too much from the Society of St Augustine, and largely repeated the same pattern of lifetimes of expatriate work with no local recruitment, tied to the place where they owned land.[47] They inherited Fr Sanderson and Fr Carmichael from SSA.[48] The reputation of SSA was high:

I remember how the drunks, stiffs and on-the-makes, who

peopled Ladybrand just after the war of 1914–18, had nothing but good to say of Sanderson and Carmichael.[49]

SSM inherited also from SSM the promise to staff a mission in Basutoland. Fr 'Tommy' Wrenford, the ex-novice mentioned above, ordained, and back in SSM, was in charge of that mission from 1906 to 1951. This was at Teyateyaneng, 'T-Y', a very familiar name in the Society,[50] only fifteen miles from Modderpoort, if one was prepared to ford the River Caledon on horseback. They were given bigger stations in Basutoland, such as Hlotse in 1907, but 'T-Y' was the one they stayed with. In fact quite soon the Society made a conscious decision for work in the Free State instead of Basutoland, and for more than thirty years Fr Wrenford was the only Anglican priest in Basutoland. An intransigent Anglo–Papalist patriarch, and a saint, he would probably have found it difficult living in community. Fr Cyprian Thorpe, sent to assist and, it was hoped, succeed him in 1946, had amazing stories to tell. The old man used to sit there at night throwing his assegai at the rats; and there were dead rats in the drinking water.[51] There were a couple of thousand of Easter communicants at 'T-Y', and all of them had to make their confession; 'fortunately the people had got used to waking the priest when he fell asleep'.[52] When the new diocese of Basutoland was set up, and the priests made their oaths to the bishop in 1951, as customary they swore to use the Book of Common Prayer and none other 'except as shall be allowed by lawful authority'. 'Fr Wrenford added in each case, in a low whisper "such as the Pope"'.[53] The bishop allowed him to do what he liked: every now and then Sir Ernest Oppenheimer used to send his car and chauffeur from Johannesburg to collect him for a holiday: and his people loved him. Here is Fr Phoofolo, one of his boys:

> Compare Modderpoort to living with Fr Wrenford; at TY we lived with him, we ate together etc . . . we boys bathed with him every morning. We felt he was our father . . . Was it the same at St Patrick's [Bloemfontein] ? . . . at Modderpoort? No, it was more formal and all magnificent.

No cup of tea was offered. As teachers we could never go and read the newspaper . . .[54]

So, in one corner of Basutoland, without many outstations, because confessions at 'T-Y' took so much time, there was a timeless piece of London Edwardian Anglo-Catholicism, utterly paternalist, and a delight to the memory.

In 1906 Fr Drake replaced Fr Alfred Kelly as Provincial. There were ten members of SSM in the province, most of them at Modderpoort, though two were looking after black and white work respectively in Ladybrand nearby. Fr Alfred, from 1907 somewhat underemployed on the staff of Bloemfontein Cathedral, found time to work off his surplus energy. He was a mountaineer, the first to climb various peaks in the Drakensberg, and a lawn tennis champion. There are newspaper cuttings about 'Fr Kelly in Great Form'. He could beat anyone in the Orange Free State at tennis, and was runner-up for South African champion in 1911. He was also a successful boxer, 'the "parson" who knocked out the local terror of the troops at boxing'[55]. He also wrote a great deal for the local papers in Bloemfontein. Fr Alfred Kelly, in his multifarious activity, was what SSM was best known for in South Africa before the First World War.

In 1911 the Provincial was Fr Stanley Haynes, who had a black congregation of 600 at Modderpoort, while Fr Firkins had 230 at Ladybrand.

Fr Firkins's flock are located in the native compounds, where he spends most of his time, only leaving the compounds to sleep at St John's Vicarage in town.[56]

The Society, in Dutch Reformed territory, had fewer white members, though two priests were working full-time with them. Fr Rand was three days' trek away in the far north of Basutoland. Rather like Fr Drake, whom no weather could frighten, he did not greatly need community life,[57] and was happier on horse-back visiting outlying white farmers. He talked of Modderpoort as being 'as dull as a Dutch dorp'.[58] There are slight hints that the province allowed men to go their own way, and some did.

In 1914 Fr Carleton was sent out 'in order to survey the general conditions of the work of the Society in that Province, and to consider the organisation of a college for native catechists.'[59] He found, as he thought, much that needed tightening up, and came back with plans to the 1915 Great Chapter. Fr Alfred Kelly, who was out of sympathy with these plans, stayed in Britain after the Chapter, and Fr Carleton went back as Provincial. The story of the clash between Fr Carleton's rigorist monastic reform programme and Fr Kelly has already been covered in chapter 7. The South African province followed him in wanting 'Religion for its own sake', apart from Fr Rand, with his informal Bush Brother style, who clashed with the new leadership.

Fr Carleton was a go-ahead expansionist Provincial. By 1919 the province had four districts, Modderpoort, Kroonstad, Harrismith, and Thaba 'Nchu, as well as the work in Basutoland. Great distances were covered: Kroonstad was 120 miles north of Modderpoort, and in the 1920s had 40 mission stations, covering 16,000 square miles; Thaba 'Nchu was fifty miles to the west. The SSM missions were a small province, sternly administered. Even the farm was making a profit.[60] The pattern of work, with a team living in community, and journeying to their various mission stations, seemed rewarding. It coped with distances that would challenge a Bush Brotherhood, and celibacy was of obvious practical use. There were nevertheless recurrent problems. Some of them stumbled learning Sesuto, and the diocese formally adjusted to priests granting absolution who understood *most* of a confession;[61] it could create tensions having one brother working with whites and another with blacks; it could be very lonely for the odd lay brother left doing the housework while all the priests were out visiting the locations.

Fr Carleton had a high profile in South Africa, and was respected for his abilities but disliked.[62] There was the refusal by the South African province to allow Kelham to take back Fr Hebert, and then the recall of Fr Carleton himself in 1922. The Director, Fr Joseph White, left Kelham and appointed himself as Provincial of South Africa in

1923, to bring the province back into line. The young Fr Hebert (see chapter 9) was won over by him. Fr Haynes, former Provincial of South Africa, became Assistant Bishop of Bloemfontein in 1923 ('We've got a Bish. SSM has got a Bish . . .'),[63] but then scandalised the Society by leaving to get married. When Fr Norton had married in 1918, they squirmed and said 'It is the joke of the sub-continent'[64]. This self-consciousness was itself a problem.

The most distinguished work of SSM in Southern Africa was the 'Modderpoort Schools'. It began with Edwin Bradbrook, then a lay-brother, running a village school at 'T-Y'. When he was recalled to Modderpoort in 1916

> Br Edwin was instructed to draw up a simple syllabus for elementary schools, and to prepare to act as school inspector for all schools maintained in missions administered by members of the Society.[65]

This developed into the Modderpoort Training School for catechists. Under Fr Carleton they added a class to train Africans for the diaconate, and in 1925 six native deacons trained there were ordained. Fr Hebert was then in charge of ordination training at Modderpoort, with four students. Fr White started a boys' school, St Cyril's, in 1925, the year that he gave up being Director of SSM. He continued as Provincial, dying at Modderpoort in 1934. The schools were to be his most significant work.

There was only one secondary school for natives in the whole of the Orange Free State. In 1927 the Society decided to open schools at Modderpoort.

> . . . we have a magnificent site, an ample water supply, and are right away in the country from the squalid locations and their undesirable influences . . . A school for 200 Basuto boys and girls is likely to prove as important in the history of South Africa as the great monastery and school of Glastonbury in English history.[66]

SSM, here, as at Kelham, believed in removing adolescents from their homes in towns. And in the Tribe-Bedale era they saw themselves as in the great tradition of monks.

There were separate schools for boys and girls. The hostel for the girls' school would be served by the Community of St Michael and All Angels. As often has happened in the history of men's religious orders, nuns were available to supplement their work quietly. The sisters also went on to run St Raphael's hospital at Modderpoort. Minnie Wright, an ex-novice of another order, ran the girls' hostel throughout the history of the Modderpoort schools. Her obituary[67] quotes words like 'indispensable', 'dominating', and 'dictatorial'. She was much loved, both by the African girls and the brethren. It would be utterly misleading to describe the human interactions involved in being male religious at Modderpoort without saying how much they turned to her. There are happy stories of how food was sparse early in term, until the girls had eaten up the hidden stores from home, but then improved.

> One of the proud traditions of our schools has been that we never had any riots, especially any food riots – a trouble which (alas!) beset many training institutions.[68]

The Society superintended the building of the schools themselves, grumbling that Africans did not understand straight lines. In 1928 Fr Basil Oddie was appointed Warden of all the schools together, primary, secondary, normal college, and theological college. 'Thus Modderpoort aspires to become a Basuto Oxford or Cambridge'.[69] After Fr Hebert went back to England, the theological college petered out. But there was still real work to be done in the field of education.

> Manual work is to form a large part of the training of the natives . . . there are considerable grounds for hope that the intellectual development of the African is going to come through a scientific training of the practical mind.[70]

This could ring true, because manual work played its part in SSM's own theology. There were brothers with appropriate certificates in teaching and agriculture, and a waiting list of potential students. By 1930, when Fr Amor replaced Fr Oddie, the waiting list was nearly 2000.

The Modderpoort schools got bigger. There were seven blocks to the secondary school by 1940. It was a boarding school for about 140 students, by the 1950s 170. These are still not very large numbers; the Society wanted to give individual attention to students, so that they could grow in character, and there was to be no rote learning. By then four of the five native teachers on the staff were graduates. Nearly all the African priests of the diocese of Bloemfontein had come through the Modderpoort schools. The primary school was rebuilt with government money to hold 350 pupils, more than was needed for the local community, so it too had pupils boarding, in native huts to start with.

There is a description from June 1933 of 'One day in Modderpoort Schools (Through the Eyes of a Boy'). It takes us through from the 5.45 rising bell. They were in silence till the 6.05 chapel bell. On 'Monday or Friday half of us must go to the parade ground at the double for our PT'. 'Never a day passes but some of us go to mass, but there is no rule to make us go'. Then they went to their jobs, which included cleaning the drains: he mentions 'the smell of the stuff the father makes us put down them'. Breakfast was at 7.15, then at 8.05 they were on the parade ground. 'Father only allows us one minute from the first stroke of the bell, and so we have to run'. There were lessons 8 to 10.30, and 11 to 1.30. Then there was dinner at 1.45 and at last a lull. 'We go and sit about under the oaks or have a little sleep on our beds'. They were back to work at 3.30, some 'industrial' training. '[We] are generally happy and noisy about it, and of course sometimes we steal little rests'. On Wednesdays and Saturdays there was football; the teams naturally were invincible. At 5.30 there was the chance of a bath and a rest before tea at 6.30. Then, if they got permission, a boy might talk to a girl. At 7.30 there was evening prep., and at 8.30 'we give a big cheer'. They spent the next half-hour practising their songs. At 9.00 there was compline and night prayers followed by silence. He also tells us about Sundays. Mass was at 6.45. In the afternoon they played tennis or went walks, to 'gather (and eat) prickly pears',[71] or they went to boxing. After solemn evensong there would be singsongs and debates, and then compline. 'Every night at 9.30 one of the fathers comes round the dormitories to say "good night" and put out the lights'. There is a note by the Warden at the end saying that he then has to start the marking.[72]

Kelham was clearly not the only 'total institution' in the

history of SSM. Modderpoort was very consciously another
college of the Society. It was

> teaching laymen, but fundamentally 'theological' – cp Prin-
> ciple VI – 'and the Principles are more fundamental than
> the constitution'[73].

Principle VI, 'Concerning Knowledge', said:

> ... Be not in haste to know many things but to understand
> one; since for all things there is but one efficient cause,
> even the will of God. As many sciences as there are, so
> many are the roads to that knowledge, but it is well if you
> reach him by one ...

If Fr White's memorial was the Modderpoort schools,
Arthur Amor, who was Provincial of South Africa from
1935 to 1951, left his mark on native education throughout
the Free State. In large towns, like Bloemfontein and
Thaba 'Nchu, it was quite possible to run successful SSM
schools. But most of the Free State was thinly populated,
and there was a variety of religious denominations. Fr
Amor, working hand in glove with Mr Kuschke, a government inspector of native education, brought about a network of united Christian schools, in an ecumenical scheme.
Local schools were run by any one of the contracting
churches, with a school committee on which both Africans
and Europeans served.[74] Mr Kuschke was serious and
paternalist. There is a letter from him in the first number
of the Modderpoort Schools Magazine in 1934, quoting
Mr Gladstone. He advised the Director, visiting South
Africa in 1940, to tighten up on discipline at the Schools.
Students did not stand when the teacher entered the room,
and rushed pell-mell out of classes when the bell went. The
SSM staff were too familiar with students, and not enough
of them could speak Afrikaans.[75] The advice was acted on,
and the schools became more formal. Later, however,
there was a change of heart, and Br Patrick True in 1952
decided that students need not stand when he entered the
room.

Fr Amor had great administrative gifts. Always in a
hurry (he crashed his motor-bike twice) in dealing with his

brethren he roused the suspicion that he preferred the typewriter to personal contacts. On the other hand

> the government inspectors and the ministers of other churches found his friendliness quite irresistible[76].

It was a real achievement to work together with Presbyterian, Methodist, Dutch Reformed, African Methodist Episcopal and Ethiopian churches, and with Afrikaaner civil servants to set up a school system. It was a good practical expression of the SSM commitment to ecumenism.

Should a Society, working in black Africa, recruit black members? At the Great Chapter of 1925, Fr Rand, speaking candidly among his brethren, had doubts:

> To force the Native into social proximity to the White Man would do infinite harm . . . the Native is naturally very lazy and very imitative.[77]

Fr Rand was not a white supremacist: he had stirred up the diocese of Pretoria to stand up for native rights, and *Ons Vaterland* had called for his expulsion. He represented a continuing mood in the Society. Instead, therefore, in 1928 there was set up at Modderpoort a native community for men, with its first two postulants. Everything was under the direction of the South African Provincial, but with the prospect of independence.[78] The first postulant, Patrick Maekane, one of Fr Wrenford's boys from 'T-Y', had already been testing his vocation for three years at Modderpoort. Standards were set high for potential black religious. One of the two died in 1934,[79] but others came. Only in 1942 were the first two brothers professed of the Company of the Servants of Christ. They were given an old school building and land to farm, and a mission to look after, at Masite in Basutoland. They had land to farm but nothing else.

> As the Mothaka (the company) has no stock and implements for tilling the lands, [Br Benedict] has offered himself to the churchwarden to be the driver of his team of oxen in order to be able to plough the lands belonging to the Mothaka.[80]

The community at one time had thirteen novices and

postulants, but the novices were illiterate servants, and remained so. Fr Maekane, though 'a successful Mission Priest with a developed prayer life'[81], was autocratic and too often absent. The Society had felt that though he would have coped in SSM, less educated blacks would not have done, and it was to give them a chance that the separate CSC was set up. In the event the Bishop of Bloemfontein and the Father Provincial decided to disperse the novices in 1952. The three Anglican orders for men in South Africa, SSJE, CR and SSM, even when they compared notes, could not work out a good formula for training black religious. SSM's happiest efforts in this field came in 1962 to 1968, when Fr Ernest Ball was chaplain and tutor to the Melanesian Brotherhood in the Pacific. He devised their short and sensible 'Constitution and Rule' (1964), and then left them to it.

In the 1930s more white congregations, at Heilbron and Ladybrand, were entrusted to the Society. This was largely because these congregations were dwindling. There was migration to Rhodesia, and British officials in the Orange Free State were replaced by non-Anglican Boers. Monks were a cheap stopgap. One of the disadvantages of working in the Free State was that the Society did not recruit from the local whites. Up to 1950, the diocese of Bloemfontein in all its history produced one white ordinand.

In 1935 the Society took over the native congregation in the city of Bloemfontein, and in 1937 the 'coloured' one, with all the mission stations in the southern half of the Orange Free State. With half its members overseas, SSM could find manpower: there were twenty members of the Society in the diocese of Bloemfontein in 1935.

> The Bloemfontein mission work grows beyond all expectation because of the large staff we have been able to supply.[82]

By now SSM was running nearly all the native missions in the Orange Free State. It was a field of work as large as many Anglican dioceses, and very competently run.

In 1907, SSM missions included 615 communicants: in 1945, there were 20,380 on the rolls of membership. In

1907, we managed an area of 3,200 square miles, with three mission stations and five farm centres; we are now looking after three quarters of the Free State, an area of some 37,800 square miles, with 71 mission churches.[83]

They were accustomed to big churches packed to the doors, like All Saints, not the priory church but the mission church in Modderpoort, which could hold 800. St Patrick, Bloemfontein, regularly had congregations of 1200. It was quite normal to hear fifty confessions before mass on Sunday morning. Perhaps the people were too deferential: Fr Kelly thought missions like these brought out the authoritarian streak in Anglo-Catholics. Fr Hebert, as early as 1924, said 'Our missions here are full of rabbits . . . scarcely a single outstanding native'.[84] These congregations were kept sternly in order. There is a 25-page pamphlet, published in 1918, of *Regulations to be observed in all Missions under the charge of the SSM in the Orange Free State*. It has an interesting list of 'cases which call for public discipline':

1. Elopement, Fornication, Adultery, Polygamy, Incest, Bestiality.
2. Obstinate Schism, as e.g. becoming a declared member of a sect.
3. Participation in, or abetting, heathen circumcision.
4. Organising beer-drinks.
5. Conviction by the criminal courts for serious crimes.
6. Serious and persistent quarrels.[85]

It took two years in the penitents' class after sins like these. There is a similar set of Missionary Regulations published by the diocese of Bloemfontein in 1937, when most of the mission work was in the hands of the SSM. 'Habitual drunkenness' had replaced 'organising beer-drinks'. They were cautious about native customs.

A priest shall never deal with heathen customs as sin until he has taken council with the older men and women of his congregation . . . Some Native Customs provide most valuable social helps.[86]

This lattitude did not include withcraft or 'children attending heathen Circumcision schools'.

Most native Christians were in practice looked after by

local catechists. The SSM priests were always on the move:
at Modderpoort itself there were celebrations of communion on only two Sundays of the month; three outstations
had celebrations once a month; three once every two
months; and two others once a quarter.[87] As early as the
late 1920s, there had been talk in the province of the risk of
effectively handing over the pastoral work to lay catechists.
Fr Felix Macintosh wrote to Fr Kelly in 1929

> We are bringing these people up in a non-sacramental
> Christianity. And we are asking these catechists to do a
> priest's pastoral work.[88]

Fr Kelly himself had thought about these matters when in
Japan, and felt that there were problems in making catechists priests. His friend Roland Allen had influential ideas
on this. Kelly wrote:

> It appears that SA [South Africa] has been Roland-Allen-
> ising and is hankering after the possibilities of a 'lay'
> priesthood – i.e. unpaid. What a thing it is to have a name
> (like R-A). I do not think Bp Carey (certainly not Roland
> Allen) quite realizes the complexity of the conditions in-
> volved.[89]

In the event, things went on as before. After the Second
World War, the Society appealed for £15,000 'to build 25
churches now'.[90] They had been given sites on condition
they built quickly. The bill for travelling, by road and rail,
in the Heilbron priory was already £400 a year. They
could build a large church for £800.

It may be that an itinerant ministry is always second-best
to a local one, but certainly a celibate order comes into its
own when itinerant work is needed. It is so easy to underestimate the distances in the Orange Free State.

The Society kept to familiar formulas of work, but was
not complacent. They watched with mounting misgiving
the move towards racial segregation in South Africa. They
could see that true separate development was a nonsense.
After all, at least 40 per cent of the natives were working
in close contact with Europeans, many of them 'practically
in the position of serfs'.[92] In 1938 Fr Charles Martin was
writing about 'The Black Man's Burden',[93] describing life

on a location at Kroonstad. He talks of the miseries of the pass laws, of poor housing, of work away, of the collapse of tribal custom, with nothing to take its place.

> The African child is baptised to temptation as he is born to adversity ... that atmosphere must continue while the present social structure, or lack of structure, is allowed to exist.[94]

The fact that there were newly developing gold-fields in the Free State did not help matters. The Society started work at Welkom, among the gold-fields, in 1952. By 1959 Welkom was the largest town in the Free State. Kroonstad had gold-mines too. The conditions of black African life became worse with the apartheid under the Nationalist government of 1948. The work at Welkom was very difficult. No visitors were allowed at the compounds after 4.30, but the men were away at work until then. Men from the compounds were not allowed to visit the villages, so unless they got round the policeman on duty, they could not go to mass. The language spoken was

> patois Fanagalo ... a vocabulary more suitable for mining than the truths of the Gospel.[95]

The schools at Modderpoort had some (14–17 year olds) doing the Junior Certificate, but mostly served to train teachers (17+), using the local primary school as a practising school. But in 1954 the Bantu Education Act stopped this work. If the Society had been prepared to change the teaching in the schools to 'Bantu' education, the schools could have remained open. Instead, rather than 'deny the true ends of humanity'[96] they closed the schools in 1955.

> The Modderpoort schools were of greater importance in the total South African scene than Kelham ever was in England, owing to the large number of Africans in public life who had been educated there.[97]

There had been 700 teachers trained at Modderpoort. This closure was a very great blow to the work of the Society. They were left with a campus of buildings to find a use for. They ran a farm school; from 1957 to 1965 there was a preliminary Test School for African ordinands. Not many came, and in the end the government forced them to close it. Modderpoort was a 'white' area, even though the white population was about one a square mile. The buildings continued as a somewhat under-used conference centre;[98] Minnie Wright ran an SSM bookshop. The farm at Modderpoort could make a profit, as long as there was someone in the Society to run it.

The Church of the Province of South Africa set up in 1950 a new diocese of Basutoland, where the new laws did not run, and the Society decided to develop the work at Teyateyaneng in Basutoland, in the hope of matching there what had been done at Modderpoort. Fr Paul Hume was the new prior at 'T-Y', replacing the elderly Fr Wrenford[99] but was quickly moved to Modderpoort to be Provincial and then to Kelham to be Director in 1952, all within a year or two. Teyateyaneng became a priory with several staff, and dispensed with Fr Wrenford's Latin ways. Out went the sanctuary lamp, the altar of Our Lady, the statues, the confessional box; and Evensong replaced night prayers.[100] They opened a church secondary school at 'T-Y', being careful not to hint to the South African authorities that this was Modderpoort reborn. There were boarding pupils at St Agnes School who had come from the closed Christ the King School in Johannesburg; there was some feeling that St Agnes's was not sufficiently a local school. As a church school, they had endless trouble with it.

> African teachers are crammers and increasingly anti-white, and the principal of Teyateyaneng was hard to convince of our ideals. The teachers do not go with the school to mass and hardly ever appear at evensong.[101]

The Society also founded a mission at Chooko's, remote in the Basutoland mountains, so there were still monks on horseback in the 50s.[102]

The Society began to retreat from some of its South African work. The priory at Kroonstad was closed in 1957, and that at Welkom in 1965. As numbers fell, community life was threatened: the members were scattered in ones and twos keeping distant priories going. The statistics of church practice and membership dropped sharply in their congregations each year between 1958 and 1960.[103] There were questions about the payment of the 'kabelo', or church dues, which had been part of life in mission congregations.

The very word 'mission' now had unhappy overtones.

> The Constitution [of SSM] still uses the word, but it is fast disappearing in missionary circles because of its close connection with colonialism and imperialism . . . Is it the African alone who needs conversion?[104]

Brethren had misgivings about what had been done and what they were capable of doing. The SSM missions seemed out-dated, dealing too much in terms of master-servant relationships, turning out mere conforming Anglicans, unable to come to terms with the place of marriage in African society. For the first time, there is reference to 'the low standard of the education' at Modderpoort or at the secondary School at 'T-Y'.[105], though they were convinced it was no worse than other mission schools. They talked now about the feelings of the Africans. Br Patrick True said that

> It was impossible to criticise Africans without inflicting humiliation on them . . .[Africans would be formalists who would be] scrupulous about the observance of the office and leave the dinner to burn in the oven . . . He doubted if we were fit to train Africans.[106]

Though the Director thought that '*boys* of all races' were like that, he agreed that radical change was needed.

Some of the brethren left the Society. The South African Provincial left in 1972, and the new Provincial was an Australian, Fr David Wells. In 1973 SSM withdrew from their biggest congregation, St Patrick's in Bloemfontein, handing it over to native clergy.

For seventy years, the South African Province of SSM had been staffed by expatriates. Latterly, there were whispers that difficult brethren were shipped off to South Africa. Consider Fr Victor Ranford. Fr Ranford had been head of the theological college at Kelham in the early Forties, when the Director, Fr Tribe, briefly deposed Fr Bedale. Afterwards, Fr Ranford found it difficult to work with Fr Bedale, the new Director, and was sent first to Australia and then to South Africa. He was a wonderfully gifted person, 'always talking, arguing, lecturing', but the brain trouble that was to kill him made him quite a handful to his brethren in South Africa, where he died in 1961.

With the collapse in England, the South African province had to face the fact that unless they recruited in Africa, the work could not continue. In practice they scarcely recruited, and the work continued on a reduced scale. A lot of effort went into building a dam at Modderpoort; the estate was probably better run than ever before, with great fields of wheat. Agriculture was one possible work for the Society. On the other hand, some of the most radical ideas in SSM came out of South Africa in the 1960s. They rebelled against the authoritarian traditions of the Society.

> The Report bears the shadow of Fr Stephen [Bedale] on every page . . . the South African chapter did not wish that type of government to be perpetuated in the Society.[107]

The South African province was now more informal then England. They were not very studious,[108] but they were politically aware. Fr Austin Masters contrasted the money spent on the new carpark at Kelham with the salaries of teachers in the schools the Society had started in Basutoland.[109]

One ambitious new move was out of rural work in the Orange Free State and Lesotho to the coastal city of Durban. Two of the brothers were appointed as chaplains to the universities of Natal and Durban-Westville (at the latter often with Hindu congregations, as this was a university for Asians). St Bernard's Priory, Durban, was the new-style SSM.

> The apparatus of rules, permissions and reports belonged more to the world of school-children than that of adults . . . preventing some of us from becoming mature and self-reliant men.[110]

Four of the five brethren were doing degrees, and so were not much in the priory, and the routine of the Office was curtailed. But it seemed to work well: brothers reported 'a relationship with one another on a very deep and telling level'.[111] But the priory also was radical in public affairs; there were seminars on 'Black Theology', and in 1977, the New Zealander Fr Michael Lapsley, who now had the wider role of National Chaplain for Anglican students, was told that his residence visa would not be renewed. The priory at Durban broke up; they lost the university chaplaincy work; two of the brethren left the Society; Michael Lapsley had to finish his degree at the university of Roma, in Lesotho. The prior, Fr Anthony Perry, stayed on a little longer in an informal community in Durban, doing hospital chaplaincy work. Fr Michael Lapsley had made enemies, and made more as Anglican chaplain at the National University in Lesotho, where once again he was dismissed in 1983, for his work in black 'consciousness-raising'. In 1990, working in Harare in Zimbabwe, he lost both hands and the sight of an eye when he opened a letter bomb. It is probably fair to say that his very political work and style were his own; the Society supported him, but no other brother ran such risks.

In the so-often-deferred hope of starting an African novitiate, SSM closed Teyateyaneng in 1975, and set up a new priory in 1976 at Masite, in the lowlands of Lesotho, with three SSM brothers and two Basotho aspirants. There was a community of nuns next door, as well as Fr Patrick Maekane, whose earlier Company of the Servants of Christ had come to nothing, running a village of orphan boys.[112]

> Since the arrival of William and Judah, we have all been concerned in the elementary and basic courtesy of trying to speak clearly and simply in order to make real contact with one another . . . We try to use both English and Sotho in our daily life, although it is a struggle for all.[113]

In 1979 William Nkomo was the first African professed member of SSM.

In that year they decided to move from Masite to Maseru, the capital. There had been a number of new starts in the '70s, and the brethren were moved about a lot. For example between 1949 and 1975, there were nine priors of

Teyateyaneng, an average of less than three years each, and
none of them over five years. It was four years before the
new priory in Maseru was opened. It was purpose-built,
rather small (the 'Sardinery'), with room for six brothers
and two visitors. Like other SSM houses, it had magnificent
views. It also had

> a ready-made atmosphere redolent of the Society. The
> common room might always have been there, with the
> impression of relaxed bookishness, pipe smoke, conviviality
> – whatever it is that is characteristic of our houses.[114]

It sounds pleasantly nostalgic, but the future was less certain.
The brethren were getting older, and there had never been
a pattern of local recruitment. The dwindling English and
Australian Provinces made it plain, at successive Great and
General Chapters, that they could not foresee themselves
continuing to send men to South Africa.

In 1987 the Director, Fr Edmund Wheat, visited the
South Africa, and agreed with the Provincial Chapter there
that the Province should be closed down, gradually. In
1988 Anthony Perry and Frank Green were withdrawn.
Some brothers would remain in South Africa. In 1992
there was still a priory at Maseru, with Fr Wells, Fr
Mullenger and Fr Nkomo. Fr Wells was the local archdeacon, Fr Mullenger and Fr Nkomo both had parishes, and
Fr Mullenger was also acting Warden of the Theological
College at Roma. Br Andrew Longley was still farm and
estate manager at Modderpoort, and Michael Lapsley had
returned to Southern Africa, this time to Cape Town.

The South African work of SSM suffers by comparison
with others. No-one in SSM wrote a book like *Naught For
Your Comfort*; a teaching order, they never ran a major
theological college in South Africa; their work in black
education, good after its kind, cannot bear comparison
with Lovedale and Fort Hare. They were perhaps unlucky
to be tied to a large farm in a remote corner of the Orange
Free State. But much of what they did was workmanlike,
larger in scale than one might think from an English
perspective, and good team work. The Society rightly has
good memories of South Africa.

dents doing house repairs at
Michael's House, Australia.

Fr Gabriel Hebert.

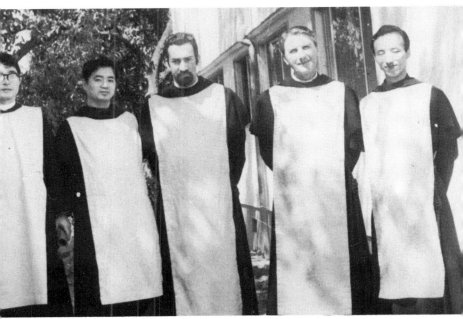

SSM in Japan – including, on the right, Fr John Lewis and
Fr Moses Kimata.

Quernmore.

Fr Antony Snell and Fr Edmund Wheat at Durham.

JAPAN

From 1913 to 1919 Fr Kelly was in Japan. His title was Professor of Apologetics: 'I have not the remotest intention of defending the faith. My faith has got to defend me'.[115] He was teaching at the central theological college, Ike-bukuro, newly set up, of the Anglican church in Japan, Nippon Sei Ko Kwai. Three strands of Anglican mission had entered Japan, the high SPG, the low CMS, and, most influential, the Americans. The missions were not very successful. Fr Kelly wrote home about 'a crush of Anglican parsons . . . without a scrap of religion to them'[116] and miserable little replicas of Mattins and Evensong Anglicanism, done on the cheap.

There was genuine Japanese interest in Western culture. In the theological college this meant 'talk about "religious experiences", Ethical ideals, spiritual Resurrection, ingeniously hiding empty platitude . . .'[117] Students had too many courses, with 35 lectures a week, which is too much for any students, though they were all given good marks. Fr Kelly, as he did for most of his life, wrote every week pungent letters commenting on what he was encountering. This paints a dark picture of the liberal theology of the time, too dark a picture. Shailer Mathews, for example, the modernist professor at Chicago, was one of an impressive tradition. There may have been resonances in that tradition for Japanese thought, but it is also possible the students were just lost, and turned to Kelly with delight.

What was particularly dangerous in Kelly's view was the way a human-centred Christianity became self-centred. Christianity can not be boiled down to ethics, even the noblest ethics. Here is an argument from Kelly, skilfully condensed and paraphrased by David Holmes.[118]

> This American 'Personality' twaddle' was dangerous for Japan. 'You may play ducks and drakes with the "traditional faith" in England, as much as you like' because the traditional faith is strong there, but 'out here there is no traditional Christianity to trust to, and we have certainly not brought it with us'. For him [Kelly] Christianity had

sacrificed the three ways of doing ethics – (I) subordination (of one's own will to that of another) (II) self-seeking . . . (III) self-sacrifice (the self is only allowed to be sacrificed for others in order that it may achieve something self-fulfilling and appealing such as acclaim, or an heroic status) – as self centred. This self-choice had been superseded by the righteousness of Christ.[119]

There must be a gospel, not merely ethics. 'We can only convert Japan to faith in God by telling Japan what God has done, not by talking about ourselves.' [120] So Fr Kelly talked about God, was humble and comic, and his Japanese students were his for life.

The Japanese suffer from an inferiority complex, and are proportionately touchy. I insisted this was their country and their Church; 'I was only a foreigner.' My very helplessness was a help – notably my ignorance of the language. I paraded it laughing . . .

I laughed at the fine language which attracted them so much, imitated it, made them see its absurdity, and brought them back to the plain issues of faith in the reality of God. I threw my best Maurician Catholicism about in all directions . . .[121]

He teased them for their 'hai kora' ('high-collar', i.e. smartly genteel) taste for the latest fashions in theology, but himself, in a way, became a fashion. At the time he wondered about the meaning of his popularity with the Japanese. He fought against 'Kellyism'. There were obvious overtones of the Buddhist master gathering his disciples. Though in many ways he simplified the teaching of the college, and laid into high-flown modernist nonsense, yet in some ways he was the hai kora dream, because he was spontaneously paradoxical.

I can no more keep off rhetorical fireworks than I can keep off rocks when I see 'em . . . Everyone is filled with admiration as they watch you wriggling out of impossible positions. The wild cheers are given solely for what they take to be your cleverness. What you mean goes for nothing.[122]

He attacked the modernist American missionaries, and they (the modernist American missionaries) loved it. But the staider, more orthodox, English missionaries were much cooler. We need not go to trouble hunting for parallels with Zen Buddhism. Anything quotable might be said to sound like a koan. One might have doubts how well he understood the Japanese, or how well they understood him. However, he gave them something. 'Give us another Fr Kelly. Even if the students don't understand a word he says, they will get from him something that will last them all their lives.'[123]

Kelly was a friend of Uchimura Kanzo, founder of the 'No-Church' movement, a real Japanese theologian. Kelly had a lasting influence within the NSKK, the Anglican church in Japan. In effect he trained a generation of bishops. (In 1960 five of the bishops were his former students). Michael Yashiro, at Kelham 1928–9, was the most distinguished of a string of Japanese Anglicans who later came to Kelham as students.[124] A key experience of his life was Kelly's response to a broken arm rock-climbing: 'Funny'. Later, as a young bishop, Michael Yashiro led his divided church when half the bishops went into a forced pan-Protestant union during the Second World War. This is one of the cases where an ecumenically-minded Kelham theology refuses what it sees as false ecumenism. Fr Kelly himself called it 'a very godless affair'.[125]

The NSKK is a small church and a little set in its ways. There is some evidence that some of Fr Kelly's disciples, the 'Kelly-kai', held tightly to his teaching of man's dependence on God, without any of his fireworks.

> I remember Bishop Michael Yashiro talking about the 'Kelly-kai' . . . and saying 'The trouble is they've all concentrated on Fr Kelly's strong point of dependence on Almighty God – but he is so almighty they don't have to do any work at all, they feel'.[126]

Bishop Yashiro, even on his death-bed ('I hate Anglo-Catholic ways'),[127] remembered Kelham. The unworldly reality of his faith made an impression on more worldly souls, and other Anglican primates spontaneously deferred to him.

> Committees – slogans – resolutions – policies – you understand? All are secular, secular – ordinary business world – no good to the Church . . . Only way is to speak straight to each soul.[128]

In 1960 a Japanese, Fr Barnabas Yogata, was professed at Kelham. One or two more followed, and in 1969 the Society opened a priory at Kobe in Japan, the Kobe Shudoin of the Seisi-shushi-kai (that is, priory of SSM). They chose the west side of Japan, partly through links with bishop Yashiro, partly because most Christian institutions were on the east, around Tokyo and Yokohama. There were in the priory four Japanese and two Australians. [129] The Japanese had certain misgivings about being sent home; was this because they were useless in England? The Society had felt guilty for years about stealing recruits needed for work in Japan. The first prior was John Lewis, followed by Barnabas Yogata, but for most of its history, Fr Moses Kimata[130] was in charge, as prior and provincial from 1978.

There was a steady stream of Japanese students at Kelham in the 1960s, paid for by the Kobe Trust. There were four there in 1971. In 1972 the first SSM profession took place in Japan. The Great Chapter of 1977 decided to set up a Japanese province.[131] The Society was filled with determination not to be intrusive, and not to strike a false note.

> We ought not to substitute Japanese antiquarianism for English antiquarianism, e.g. the kimono for the cassock, the pagoda for Victorian Gothic.[132]

Real power was in the hands of Fr Moses Kimata, in some ways rather an old-fashioned superior. Perhaps there was nostalgia for Kelham; there were definite overtones of England. The illustrated brochure of the Kobe Shudoin shows a portrait of the queen over the fireplace. The little priory carried on with its work in schools, and its scout troop, and its visitors on retreat or studying. Fr Moses Kimata worked at the International School in Kobe. They were chaplains to two universities at Tarumi. When the Cowley Fathers left Japan, Fr Simon Yamada moved across to SSM in 1976. Already old and ill, he died in 1982. Fr Vincent Hara had been released in 1979, and there were no novices. SSM publications in England carried regular reports from Japan, written by visitors from England or Australia.

In 1990 the local bishop gave the two remaining brethren notice to move. Effectively, this was the end of the Japanese province. Fr Moses Kimata died in 1992, and Revd Brother Andrew Murumatsu, still a member of SSM, in 1992 joined the staff of Yokohama cathedral.

The Nippon Sei Ko Kwai is not a very flourishing branch of the Anglican communion. It would have been a surprise if an English religious order for men had blossomed in Japan. Such surprises are possible.

When one looks back over a hundred years of SSM work in Africa and Asia, it is difficult to speak as if a new and more glorious century is dawning. Where there were provinces there are now scattered individuals. The SSM was a missionary society: in the 1930s, even before the Australian province existed, half its membership was working overseas. Despite attempts, the Society never became thoroughly indigenised; Andrew Murumatsu and William Nkomo are in 1993 the only non-white brethren. When SSM thinks, quite naturally, of going back to its roots, it thinks of pre-theological education, and of small brick terraced houses in South London, but scarcely of overseas missions.

Both the diocese of Korea and the UMCA put money into SSM. In all fairness one must say they got their money's worth. One might have a sense of failure if one dreams of SSM institutions and native SSM novitiates, but if SSM is primarily there to fit men to serve the church, then it did its work. Often very young and utterly ordinary men, who would have otherwise been clerks in offices, became useful Christian missionaries. It was hard doing this as well as living a life under vows. One thinks, for example, of Ronald Moffatt, one of the lay brothers in Central Africa, who left SSM in 1918. He wrote to the Director in

1955, speaking with shame of when he 'fell away' (his phrase).[133] But Fr Moffatt was then an 80-year-old priest still in work in South Africa. In any fair measurement his life was not a falling away. The SSM helped shape usefully more men than those who died as its members. If it had been more like a Bush Brotherhood, it might have fitted more easily into existing missionary structures. If it had been more monastic, it would not have tried.

> We never knew whether we were monks or missionaries, and in trying to be both we did neither very well.[134]

In South Africa, the Society had large institutions and packed churches. With the hindsight common to white missions, they might regret some paternalism and some opportunities missed. There is nothing upsetting in the thought that the Church of the Province of South Africa now has black priests successfully running what had been large SSM parishes. Missionaries were there to do a job, and should then move on. It was sadder to see church schools closed by government action, or, when continuing, adopting a new lay ethos. The other religious societies, CR and SSJE, have also seen their South African work shrink since the days of its glory. CR now lives in three little bungalows in Turffontein.[135] There is inevitably regret that no sturdy indigenous order for men emerged in South Africa. There are two new black postulants of SSM in 1993.

The attempt to run an SSM province in Japan was not foredoomed to failure. When one thinks how small the pool of Japanese Anglicans is, the proportion of them having an SSM link becomes more impressive. The Society tried to learn from past mistakes, and there was a common life in a priory which was well sited, and could serve as a focus for a wider group. But it was rather late to start; few orders flourished in the 1980s and 1990s.

One reader of an earlier draft of this chapter was struck by how 'amateurish' the SSM missions in Asia and Africa sometimes were. There is something in this, though particular pieces of work, like the Modderpoort Schools in their heyday, seem professional enough to me. Some of the amateurishness is not only endearing but commendable, as the Society tried to be open to God's will, instead of settling for familiar formulae.

We now turn from relative failure to the most successful of the transplantations of SSM, the province of Australia.

Chapter 11

SSM In Australia

In 1947 SSM founded their second theological college, St Michael's House at Crafers in the diocese of Adelaide. Australia was not a mission field, and the Society went in response to an invitation from the Australian House of Bishops.

Australian Christianity owed much to Britain. The Church of England in Australia confronted the same familiar range of Protestant denominations as in England, Methodists, Baptists, Congregationalists, Presbyterians. As in England, the statistics of Roman Catholicism in the first half of the 20th century were more encouraging than those of other churches. There were great regional variations in the strength of the different churches, but Anglicans in most places made up about a third of the population. This was without the benefit of being an established church.[1]

In South Australia no religious body had had public money since 1851. Public money was not needed: Adelaide was a 'city of churches'. There had been an Anglican bishopric in Adelaide since 1847, its jurisdiction shrinking as new dioceses were carved out of it. The city of Adelaide dominated the colony of South Australia, with more than half the population of the colony living within the metropolitan area. The population was rising rapidly through immigration. In 1947 there were about 650,000 people in South Australia. The number of at least nominal Anglicans grew by 19% between 1947 and 1954, in line with the general growth of the population. The Anglican cathedral, built by Butterfield and later adapted, was on a conspicuous site beside the River Torrens. Though the free churches were relatively stronger than elsewhere in Australia, the Church of England was larger than any of them and its institutions, like St Peter's Collegiate School and the Anglican St Mark's College in the university, had considerable social prestige, somewhat reminiscent of being an established church. The Christian churches were in competition with each other, and seldom worked together. The usual Anglican churchmanship was Prayer Book Catholicism, which unchurched other Christians, but did not upset the laity with ritual innovations.[2]

The worst that could be said of South Australian Anglicanism in the 1940s was that it was somewhat stuffy and self-satisfied. There had been no change of bishop from 1906 to 1940, and things were going well. The new bishop chosen in 1941, Bryan Robin, coming fresh from outside, in this case from England, not unnaturally found his diocese inward-looking and set in its ways. One of its settled habits, incidentally, was to choose bishops from England. He was to be the last such choice in Adelaide, and even he, though appointed from an English parish, had previously served most of his ministry in Australia. Most of his clergy were Australian-born and Australian-trained. This had been true of the diocese since the 1920s. The bishop was a man of initiative and wide plans. He felt the Australian church needed fewer, larger theological colleges. Most of his clergy were non-graduate, so he thought of SSM, who were running a large successful non-graduate college. He also wanted a religious order to replace the Community of the Ascension, the only order for men in Australia, which had just disbanded.

Australia is a federation of former colonies, and only with jet planes is it easy to move from one state to the next. At one time West Australia formally voted to secede from the rest. One cannot overstress the separateness of South Australia from New South Wales, and so on.[3] For the Church of England in Australia this has resulted in great local autonomy for bishops. Unlike the Anglican church in New Zealand, where the provincial synod ruled, in Australia dioceses went their own way, which for Anglicans meant that they chose their own monochrome churchmanship. This was modified only by the weakness of some of the rural dioceses, which were satellites of the nearest major city.

Bishop Robin, recently returned to Australia, and the

SSM, scarcely knowing the country, misjudged the possibilities of a genuinely national role for an SSM college. The
larger dioceses of Australia, including Adelaide, each had
their local theological college. He went to trouble, under
pressure from his Dean and Chapter, to have the invitation
come generally from the bishops of Australia. In November
1943, twenty of the twenty-three bishops, including the
primate and all but one of the archbishops, signed this statement:

> In view of the cessation of the Community of the Ascension
> and the consequent disappearance from the Church in
> Australia of any religious Community for men; and recog-
> nising the very important and manifold contribution of
> Religious Communities to the life of the Church, we
> cordially approve the proposal of the Bishop of Adelaide
> to invite the Society of the Sacred Mission to establish a
> House of the Society in Australia and within his Diocese,
> with a view to the strengthening of the Religious Life, the
> training of men for the Sacred Ministry, and any other
> work to which the Society might in due time be led.[4]

Each bishop must have made a mental exception for his
own college in accepting Bishop Robin's scheme. Nevertheless, SSM set up its college in Australia on the invitation of
the bishops, not just of the diocese of Adelaide.

Bishop Robin took perhaps slightly less trouble to persuade his diocese of the wisdom of his rather impulsive
move.

> . . . although the ultimate decisions and actions concerning
> the training of the ministry are my responsibility alone, I
> am nevertheless something of a democrat. . .[5]

He had consulted his Dean and Chapter, and they had
voted with him overwhelmingly, but there was something
of a feeling that he had bounced them into it. What
particularly rankled was the fate of St Barnabas' College,
Adelaide. As soon as the new college was under way, in
1949 bishop Robin carried out his plan to close the existing
one. St Barnabas' College, Adelaide,[6] was a diocesan college, and at least half the clergy in the diocese had been
trained in it. Every college has its pride and its grateful

alumni. St Barnabas's was very small: even the two full-time staff normally had cathedral duties as well; it produced about two ordinands a year, normally non-graduates; and the course was short, with a lot of time spent on student attachments to the city parishes of Adelaide. One former principal, Philip Carrington, went on to publish quite well-known books and to be archbishop of Quebec. There were some scholarly clergy in South Australia, but the church generally was not bookish. Theology was not taught in the universities of Australia, through fear of sectarian strife, though individual clergymen had often been leading figures in universities, confidently lecturing on wider fields than modern academics dare. The locally trained clergy were somewhat in awe of Oxford and Cambridge graduates. The bishop specified that some of the staff should be 'men of public school and university study . . . to confute the few doubters'.[7]

SSM also had to be persuaded. They thought Adelaide might be a backwater, that the Australian church might have no real place for a new largely non-graduate college, that the bishop was asking them because he had been left 'just the right kind of house'.[8] The decision had to be made to close two English priories to staff the new province. Once the college was founded, the Englishmen and Australians running the new province were largely left to go their own way. A later Australian Director noticed that 'Great and General Chapters 1894–1952' did not mention Australia. They 'sent copies of all changes to mother house and *once* got an acknowledgement'.[9]

The SSM college was to be a Kelham in Australia. The long course of rigorous theology, the students living in a community under rule, scarcely distinguishable from novices, the sheer size of a full-scale college on the Kelham model, the professionalism of the training that made social class an irrelevance; all these were selling points, and brought many enquiries from potential students. Fr Stephen Bedale, the Director himself, was there in 1946 with Fr Basil Oddie and Fr Antony Snell. By the end of 1946 there were already 80 applicants.[10]

The bishop was offering a house, which had been left to

the diocese. Adelaide lies on a coastal plain, with a range of wooded hills behind the city, not dominating it, as if this were mountainous country, but certainly a welcome feature of the view throughout the city. Rich people built themselves summer retreats among the trees, away from the heat and dust of the plain. The diocese had been given[11] a large villa near Crafers, just below the summit of Mount Lofty, more than 2000 feet up (the reports home to Kelham keep adding a hundred or two feet), with predictable views across Adelaide to the sea beyond, and on a clear day to the Yorke Peninsula beyond that. The Society had always dreamt of windswept heights and regretted that Kelham itself was on low-lying muddy river-flats. The symbolism of a holy place, high above the city, utterly visible (certainly once they repainted it white), and yet remote, summed up dangerously what the Australian church was looking for in importing a religious order for men. The Society was also visible because everyone at St Michael's House went around constantly, including when out in the city, in habit. It was not customary for Roman Catholic religious to go about in public in habit, so SSM was even more conspicuous.[12]

There were striking inconveniences. The house was in poor condition, and had been designed for family use, not as a large college. They needed the accommodation in the lodge, but it was occupied. It was cold in winter, when the mist came down, and the view disappeared, and fuel bills were a problem. Everything had to come up the long haul from the city, and in the 1940s the roads were not smooth tarmac designed for tourist trips to Mount Lofty. How could they carry on the Kelham tradition of team games with no flat ground for football or cricket pitches? It was all the sort of fun that setting up something new with enough money, though not wealth, and a lot of local goodwill, normally is. They were bowled over by the universal friendliness and curiosity. There were hundreds of 'friendly gatecrashers' at the first Visitors' Day in October 1947.[13] The Visitors' Day became part of the social calendar of Adelaide, with thousands coming in the 1950s and 1960s.

Bishop Robin personally chose which Kelham Father would lead his new college. When he was a vicar in

Cheshire, he had known Basil Oddie as head of the SSM priory in Liverpool. The choice was challenging to Kelham on academic grounds. SSM safeguarded its scholarly tradition by what were called the 'theological privileges', an inner group of Rectors and Sub-rectors (earlier Masters and Bachelors) qualified to teach theology. On the whole, those who staffed the smaller priories in England were not considered up to the academic work of staffing Kelham. The Society gulped, re-considered, and made Fr Oddie a Rector.

As the first Australian Provincial, Basil Oddie (born 1894, professed 1924) had the chance of shaping St Michael's House, the new college, opened in 1947. In many ways he did transplant Kelham, including the hierarchy of command, and came to be looked back on as larger than life and somewhat fierce. If something were broken, there might be a ten minutes harangue before breakfast.[14] But he could catch the imagination of young Australians, who accepted roughness if it seemed authentic. In the SSM way, he was panjandrum, being Provincial of the Australian province, Prior of St Michael's House, and Warden of the college. There were precedents for setting up provinces of a single priory.

There were already some Kelham-trained men in Australia. There had been Kelham-trained Bush Brothers. Reginald Halse was in the St Barnabas Bush Brotherhood in North Queensland before becoming Bishop of Riverina and later Archbishop of Brisbane.[15] In the next diocese to Adelaide, Willochra in South Australia, Bishop Richard Thomas (bishop 1926–58) was also from Kelham and a Bush Brother, though the diocese did not prosper under him.[16] Though the Kelly tradition transcended party Anglo-Catholicism, the Kelham priests in Australia were Anglo-Catholic.[17] Party churches greeted the new college with proprietorial friendship. There was a nasty little skirmish in 1952 when Fr Oddie was invited to preach at Christ Church St Lawrence and a few other churches in Sydney. The Archbishop of Sydney, which is the largest and most clear-cut Evangelical Anglican diocese in the world, gave his consent with grudging suspicion, specifying that

there will be no reference to the work of your society and
the training of men for the ministry.[18]

There was to be no touting for trade at the expense of
Moore College, Sydney. It had not helped that the *Anglican*
had had a headline 'Sacred Mission to raid Sydney for
more priests'. Of course the handful of Anglo-Catholic congregations in Sydney sent ordinands to St Michael's House;
but no ordinand ever went sponsored by that diocese.

It is a question how far the Kelham course could be
transported. These were the late 1940s, and Stephen Bedale
himself, as Director, had came out to Australia for a few
months to supervise the opening of the new house. Bedale
had been in charge for quarter of a century. With hindsight,
one might think that his autocratic way of running a 'total
institution' at Kelham could not have lasted much longer.
However, in much of Christianity, traditional ways of
doing things had an Indian summer in the 1950s. Numbers
seeking ordination went up, religious orders had large
novitiates, and congregations flourished. Thus confirma-
tions in Adelaide went up in the 1950s from 700 to 2400 a
year.[19] The statistics for St Michael's House were impressive, but the number of men in training in the Wesley
(Methodist) College in Adelaide rose in the decade from 18
to 34.[20] They were lucky in their period. People did not
feel that this was a surprising success for an old-fashioned
product; at the time they thought they were usefully up-
to-date.[21]

St Michael's House, throughout its history as a theological college, had a minimum of five full-time members of
staff. There are theology departments in the universities of
England that have taught degree schemes with less. The
bound series of Kelham lecture notes, typed and duplicated,
were shipped out. There were some quiet adjustments.
Church History, so central when the Old Man taught it,
was taught at first by a local clergyman, Kelham-trained,
who came in.[22] It became a chore to members of staff who
did not see themselves as historians. There was never a
Cottage, for 15 or 16 year-olds, though there was a year's
course provided with elementary grammar etc, for those

who had not reached matriculation standard. St Michael's House could never be quite as cavalier about preparing for official church examinations as Kelham had been.

Two of the lecturers were a match for any theologian in Australia. Gabriel Hebert was known beyond Anglicanism as a New Testament scholar and a liturgist. Antony Snell, though not a great name, wrote books, enjoyed encyclopaedic learning, and built up at St Michael's House a theological library of 40,000 books, much larger than most Anglican theological college libraries in Australia, then or since. Part of the folklore of the college is that neither of them was much use as a lecturer. Fr Antony, with, after all, a prepared text in front of both him and his hearers, was likely to say 'But you know all that', when it would have been more profitable to have read through it.[23] They had the obvious handicap of coming as middle-aged (or older) public-school Englishmen to teach young Australians. English brethren, later than Fr Hebert and Fr Snell, could give the impression that Australians would never make real scholars.[24] But the college in time recruited from its early students novices and then professed members of SSM who, having completed the course, were capable of teaching it. By 1958 there were 12 fully professed Australian members of SSM.

The appeal of the Society to new recruits lay more in the life than in the scholarship. Br Aidan Honey, a lay brother, who did dangerous things with gelignite and ran the dispensary, was impressive as a religious with his sanctified commonsense, quiet deliberation, and ability to stand up to Basil Oddie. When Australians talk about why they thought of joining SSM, they are quite likely to mention him.

Gabriel Hebert came from a world of ecumenical encounter. He had been a key go-between in negotiations between Anglicans and Swedish Lutherans. His liturgical work had brought him in contact with reforming movements in European Catholicism. Adelaide was rather different. The local Catholic leaders were in the anti-Anglican tradition of Irish Catholicism; the ancestors of the distinctive local Lutherans had left Germany in protest against the early

19th century ecumenism of the Old Prussian Union[25]; and the local Anglicans disputed the word 'Catholic' with the Romans and refused the word 'church' to the rest. There was an existing theological circle, where thay honed their positions by reading out, in sequence, prepared statements round the table. There was no discussion, because it would have led nowhere. Fr Hebert had come out on the boat with Davis McCaughey, an Ulster Protestant with a difference, fresh from work with the Student Christian Movement, that nest of ecumenists, on his way to teach at Ormond, the Presbyterian College in Melbourne. Between them, and quickly finding a go-ahead Roman Catholic, they started the Week of Prayer for Christian Unity in Australia. (It had to be a different time of year, as January was too hot). Hebert continued to be active in the ecumenical movement. He was remembered and quoted:

> I didn't come here to relax. I came here to worship Almighty God.[26]

Students from the college went to SCM conferences. It is difficult, in such a slow-moving business as church unity, to make anyone's work sound exciting, but Hebert was undoubtedly significant. He could sometimes win the confidence of traditionalist protestants:

> ... here a wonderful thing happened: some who had come ... thinking we are all 'liberals', and determined to do battle for the fundamentalist position, had learnt to their great surprise by the third morning that the people whom they suspected and feared were 'full Christians' after all.[27]

Locally, ecumenism meant at first brothers from SSM mowing the lawns for Catholic convents. It worried Anglo-Catholics.

The Anglo-Catholics had not much cause for worry. Many students became in their turn old-fashioned Anglo-Catholics. We should not overplay the claim that the college made men think, and so helped them move beyond party catch-phrases. Students mature, and students think, under almost any regime. The real evidence of what challenged students is that every year some of them became novices. Imaginations were caught by living the life. In the

next quarter of a century, from the first Australian novices
in 1947, the Society professed nearly a hundred Australian
novices. There was no year between 1947 and 1971 when
the Society did not profess an Australian novice. This is a
significant number in the whole history of Anglican religious orders for men. Three-quarters of them did not go
on to full profession. The Society was traditionally less
tense than others in letting people go without guilt. They
could imagine why men became novices:

> sales-resistance to protestant argumentation, sex repressions,
> just a vague longing to get away from the council estate
> suburb . . .[28]

Nonetheless, it could be embarrassing to carry on in the
college as a student having been a novice, and, as in almost
any religious order in the 1950s, the handful of ex-professed
were almost non-persons.

There are statistics of the intake of St Michael's House
over the years. In the beginning they were all ex-Navy
men. This was soon after the Second World War. They
took to the regularity and the chores and the private
jargon and the isolation, as perhaps might be expected of
sailors. The college grew, sprawling out in army huts; the
chapel was an old army building. Later they converted a
stable into rather a fine library block. They learnt plainsong
after the Kelham tradition, and the services, with sixty
voices, were impressive. There was pig-keeping, in honour
of the founder. The students helped dig the underground
water tank and build the dining room. Student memories
seem to mingle real poverty with hints of gracious living:

> We boiled water in a copper in the courtyard so that we
> could have hot baths in the one and only enormous zinc
> bath! We worshipped and prayed together in a Chapel that
> seemed to become an increasingly Holy Place – we enjoyed
> chestnuts in the common room fire – read copies of
> Country Life – played chess, basketball (the likes of which
> might have made the Geebung Polo Club pale with fear) –
> learned a little fencing – milked the cow (those of us who
> let on that we knew how!) – worked on the wood gang
> (under the watchful and encouraging eye of Sub Lt John
> Lewis and Able Seaman Len Goggs)[29].

Fr Oddie was a disciplinarian. In 1955 he sacked three students at once.

> The House is in a chastened and very much happier mood since the moral cleaning-up ... there was secret drinking going on, including some wine from the sacristy, and threatenings of homosexual vice. Fr Basil is a man who acts very vigorously.[30]

He could be a difficult person to work with. He was touchy about status. How far were they priests of the diocese of Adelaide? He thought that being 'licensed to officiate' had overtones of being 'under some sort of continued censure'. Should they attend synod? He tried the patience of an eagerly positive bishop.[31] Fr Oddie was a strange man, given to fantasy – you could not believe all his stories – but his work in Australia gave SSM a new lease of life. When he left Australia in 1956 this was news on the national ABC television network.[32]

He was succeeded in 1957 as Prior and Warden by Fr Nicholas Allenby (born 1909, professed 1933), a reserved English consolidator. This time, incidentally, the 'theological privileges' refused to give Fr Allenby the status of Rector. It is not surprising that the whole system was soon dismantled. Fr Allenby went on to be bishop of Kuching. In Anglicanism, a college has arrived when its principal is chosen to be a bishop.

The next Prior and Warden, in 1962, was John Lewis. He had been one of the first two Australian novices, and had come up through the system. There was a sense that the Society was giving the young ones their head in making an appointment like this, but not much changed. People who rise quickly through the only system they have known are often conservative. There was a somewhat philistine tone, and the college was uneasy with intellectuals. On the other hand the intellectual Fr Hebert noticed with approval that 'at our "concerts" he [Fr Lewis] always used to get up an item by the lay-brothers'.[33]

A catchphrase often used to describe the college under John Lewis was 'jockstraps and axe-handles'.[34] He had been a naval lieutenant. 'He says he ran the house as you'd run a ship'. There was a lickspittle atmosphere, and a student would fall asleep at nights tired out. It was not formal: 'you, you, and you', like running a gang, and John Lewis treated everybody in the gang as his mates, including the giving of nicknames.[35]

In an age when degrees in theology were becoming more common, a Principal, and other staff, without a degree looked strange in Crockford's Clerical Directory. The five years Kelham course, and then the experience of teaching the subject, objectively were a fair equivalent to a degree, but the doubts were there.

There had been a false start in north Queensland. This was the first new work beyond the college in Australia. In the late 1950s, under the same Fr John Lewis, the Society set up a priory at Ravenshoe, running a boys' school. It lasted from 1958 to 1960. The St Barnabas Bush Brotherhood was already there, and the idea was that SSM would take over their school while the Bush Brothers, guided by SSM, became a regular religious order. In fact this did not happen, so SSM found itself running a school. Australian numbers were high enough to look for extra work; there was a nostalgia, perhaps more at Kelham than in Adelaide, for open spaces and Bush Brotherhoods; and the Society toyed with the idea of being a teaching order. It may be that they were influenced by the Jesuit prototype, in this as in other things. It is one of the obvious comparisons between Roman Catholic and Anglican religious orders that by the 1950s the Catholics had practically managed to staff schools for all the Catholic children in Australia with members of religious orders. The clear-cut extrovert games-playing Christianity of Kelham looks as tailor-made for school-mastering as the Christian Brothers.[36]

But it did not work; one image of the Society of the Sacred Mission must be misleading. The school, for all this was a Bush Brotherhood, was the prep school for one of the few expensive fee-paying private schools in Queensland.[37] The Society sent some good men there, but most of them were unsettled, and the local recruits disappeared.

The Society found much more congenial work, not in the outback, but in the capital city of Perth, Western

Australia, in 1960. The Archbishop was eager to have them: the Society made two conditions:

> The two things you will see that are *not* envisaged are that we should do parish work, or be engaged in any kind of theological education.[38]

They found chaplaincy work at the university and hospitals, and a parish which included exciting and important people. There is an irony about an order designed as troops for places where ordinary clergy cannot go, being most useful hobnobbing with Governors and Vice-Chancellors. The Society was known publicly: the opening of the priory was on television. Locally they waved to everybody, who waved back. There were athletic achievements: Dunstan McKee became a student leader at the university of Western Australia, and had a boat named after him for the rowing club, as did Douglas Brown later. The priory could also hold its own intellectually. Flew and Macintyre's *New Essays in Philosophical Theology*, an influential book still on reading-lists in England, came from a circle in Perth with a strong input from SSM. Fr Dunstan McKee became a competent philosopher. When he was Director, in 1974, he was writing on 'Mind and Matter: monism or dualism?' in the journal *Theoria to Theory*.[39]

The work in Perth showed that the Society could do other things than run large theological colleges. It came to an end because the Society had no prescriptive right to interesting and pleasant work. The Archbishop of Perth wanted to make his own appointments; the Society would go wherever the local bishop chose to send it. So he moved them in 1979 to a dismal remote suburb called Girrawheen working among immigrants. Australian cities are very thinly spread, and remote housing estates are inaccessible and desolate. (That is one image of the priory; another is that they were surrounded by a pack of noisy, if often delightful, children. Fr Jonathan Ewer called it 'iced-lolly evangelism'.) Some honourable work was done, but perhaps different gifts were needed, and the Society wound up the Perth priory by 1981. As often happened, one brother was left behind, engrossed in his hospital chaplaincy work. Brethren looked back on the Perth priory with enjoyment, but the Society recruited no members from Perth, and there was a perception that novices sent there tended to leave. Small priories, like Perth, or even more St John's Adelaide, meant novices alone in a house. 'No novice has yet survived two years at St John's', claimed Antony Snell (incorrectly, as it happens).[40]

By the late 1960s, Kelham had declining numbers and a changed approach to theological training. St Michael's House also had problems. Fr Hebert, at his ecumenical best, could find common ground even with different types of Anglican. But later the college came to lose the confidence of a number of the bishops, who stopped sending candidates.

There was gossip about homosexuality. Perhaps we should look at this. The Kelham regime gave scant opportunities for misdemeanour; living in groups with regular changes of room-mates and a full time-table they all learnt celibacy together. There would be a loss of solidarity when new relaxed customs permitted week-end breaks, and men came back quietly proud of their girl-friends. (Kelham, at the same period, fought a totally unsuccessful battle to discourage engagements.) What about the homosexuals? With free week-ends, some may have found their way to whatever there was down the hill in Adelaide; some used joky camp talk, that meant nothing, of course; most avoided sharp definitions of themselves, were very chaste but still felt guilty, and were quite likely to disapprove of other homosexuals.[41] The college leadership was divided on how to deal with them. Should they have taken the sort of student whose parish priest wrote:

> a rather typical example of a brittle, rather shallow, modern city-dweller . . . not the type of material you would normally accept . . . he gets around with an 'odd' group of young fellows from S. James who come here for Evensong and 'the extras' – however this does not necessarily mean that he is effeminate in any serious degree.[42]?

There is a later letter to a bishop describing in close detail an investigation into the matter.[43] The conclusion

seemed to be that one of the married students had homosexuality on the brain, poor man, but that there was
nothing happening beyond silly lines of talk. Nothing of
what was going on seems out of the ordinary for Anglican
theological colleges. It deserves a mention because the
gossip did harm the college.

But there did seem to be something else more disquiet-
ing. The calibre of students rather disappointed the staff.
The number of graduates coming to St Michael's House
had fallen. The students seemed to want spoon-feeding in
their courses; not to use the library; to grumble a lot, and,
as this was after all a democratic age and country, to feel
that as the majority they should decide on changes in St
Michael's House. It felt less like a religious community,
and more like a routine rather second-rate college. The
staff were worked off their feet, scarcely met each other,
communicating through notes in pigeon-holes, and some
of them were teaching courses for which they had no real
taste, or possibly aptitude. Some of the staff were much
less Socratic than Fr Kelly had been, probably responding
to the students' own expectations. It was a great problem
staffing the college with members of the Society. Even so,
former students from that period can easily be found who
think it was still a good college then.

The Society was not afraid of modern theology. In the
journals of the Australian province, Dunstan McKee wrote
favourably about new schools of thought. He himself had a
circle of clever thoughtful Anglicans looking again at
dogma. Do we have to believe in a literal resurrection?[44]
This is the generation of *Honest to God*. Antony Snell
was a more Thomist thinker of an earlier generation; some of
his marginal notes on Fr Kelly's lectures were rather sharp.

In the 1960s, whether or not they turned to modern
theology, the brethren did examine their own Society's
purpose sharply. Some of the points made in the Australian
Report on the Aims of the Society in 1968 were candidly self-
aware.

> Theological Education
> a/ brethren live off relationships with students rather than
> with other brethren

... f/ ... obliged to specialise in non-graduate theological training ... affected the type of men from whom most novices are drawn; perhaps widened and improved it [Fr Antony Snell, the scholar]
Divine Science
...Why is it that so little serious theological and academic thinking and writing is done. . .? [Fr Thomas Brown]
Changing Circumstances
... moving towards a family fellowship and away from the military metaphor [Fr John Lewis, who had run it like a ship]
All the pi books, all the old ideas of rules of life ... are now discarded [Fr Laurence Eyers]

The move away from 'pi books' reinforced an existing tendency in the province. From its foundation, the college could never have the absolute confidence of the Anglo-Catholic party. Just like Kelham, it was visibly ecumenical towards Protestants as well as Rome, sent its students to SCM conferences, and unlike some aspects of Kelham, adopted from the outset a liturgical practice that was designed not to worry the bishops of Australia. One of the founding brethren was sent home to England because he could not cope with the low-church ways of St Michael's House: they said it was because he could not cope with the altitude, 2000 feet up.

> We hope you will like our Sunday morning service with Sermon: high mass without incense and with the propers.[45]

Much more important was losing the good opinion of ordinary conservative Anglicans. When members of the Society, and students, all in the distinctive habit, were seen in the newspapers marching against Australian involvement in Vietnam, this had a profound effect. Obviously there was something semi-official about even permitting the students there to march. The college was no longer a symbol of detached sanctity. Those who did march might look back on it with pride, but in the church of that day it was dangerous.[46]

Unlike Kelham, St Michael's House soldiered on through

the 1970s. Dunstan McKee became Director of the Society as a whole, the first non-English Director, though others came to it from working in Africa. He was under forty, and he appointed an even younger Warden of St Michael's House. Fr Thomas Brown had great promise as a theological college principal, with a good academic record and administrative skills. But it seems the college was too far gone. A decision was made to move the two final years of the course down to the city of Adelaide, where the Society had been given a parish, St John's. St Michael's House was now under-used. A room in the main house became the chapel. By 1983 the Australian Province, after bitter argument, had decided that the whole course should be in Adelaide, with far smaller numbers, and St Michael's was left more-or-less as a retreat house. This had not happened easily. There were very fierce loyalties to St Michael's House; to a number of the Society, and to even more outside, it epitomised the SSM in Australia.

There were uneasinesses between the two priories, St Michael's and St John's, and between St Michael's and the Australian Provincial. In some matters, St Michael's went its own way. Thus it came to have women associates, living in St Michael's. The same thing happened at Willen in England. When the crash came, and both big colleges, which had been the primary work of the Society, were closed, there was almost a vacuum, and the little houses that took their place, having seen so many norms go, let others go as well. There were only three women associates, not all there at the same time; they were impressive as individuals, sometimes found it difficult to get on with each other, and raised anxieties among the members of the Society. The old spartan ethos had been very male; there is also a misogynist streak in some forms of Anglo-Catholicism; though these were discreet middle-aged women, perhaps a celibacy rule is harder for most men when there are women around. After all, quite a number of professed members of the Society, after years under vows, had left to marry.

Here is something slightly unexpected. Both in England and Australia, more so in Australia, the old Mother house, or its immediate successor, custodian, sometimes almost frightened custodian, of what remained of the great tradition, found itself on the left wing of the debate over admitting women.

Since the early 1970s, there had been a priory at Canberra, the nation's planned capital, a city with some of the soullessness of the over-planned. It was in a subsidiary town centre, named Woden, and part of an ecumenical ministry. The work was successful; nevertheless, it turned out to be less innovative and more ordinarily suburban than they had hoped for in their dreams. The priory, with about four brothers, tended to be aware of its own small numbers. At St Michael's House, as at Kelham, living in community had involved an institution, with dozens of young men around in cassocks. The priory at Canberra did not feel like that sort of religious community. They lived, very sensibly, in small modern boxes, like everything else around, which could therefore easily be sold when the need arose. Even if Fr Michael Lapsley caught the eye by riding around on his motorbike in the habit with a flowery crash helmet, there was a sense that the parish saw them as ordinary clergy, one as vicar and the others as curates etc. In 1984, the bishop had no further use for them, and, to remain in the diocese, the Society volunteered to take on the small parish on the outskirts of Canberra at South Tuggeranong which was unable to pay for a clergyman, for half the going stipend. That parish, renamed St Mary's in the Valley, flourished; it went on to be one of the largest congregations in the diocese of Canberra and Goulburn. Some of the Society clearly had great pastoral gifts; it was an area where a bishop might have foreseen growth; but it is evidence of the weak standing of the Society in the eyes of the bishops that there was one just prepared to let them go.

Then there was the fire. On Ash Wednesday 1983, St Michael's House was destroyed in a bush fire. The college had always lived with the risk; it was a local fire-watching centre. The handful then in St Michael's House survived in a basement with the fire passing over them. They faced death. Ten years later travellers into Adelaide have the story of the Ash Wednesday fire as part of the general local tradition. The college library, the best theological college library in Australia, was destroyed. More books had recently come from the dispersed library at Kelham. The Society remembered with anguish a complete set of Migne's Patrology, sent out when the Kelham collection was dispersed.[47] It was that sort of library.

Before the fire the Australian Province, not without misery and a long battle, had already decided to close St Michael's House. The fire provided a symbolic close, and a large company of old students gathered in the ruins to affirm all the good that had been done. But there was no question of rebuilding it.

The Society continued with the vestiges of a theological college at St John's in Adelaide. They built a pleasant little library in the church hall, and provided one or two staff for the interdenominational Adelaide College of Divinity. Douglas Brown was in fact Dean of the first ecumenical faculty of theology in Australia. Their own students were a tiny handful who for some reason or another could not get on official lists. This normally meant women with a vocation for the Anglican ministry. The first woman to be ordained priest in the diocese of Adelaide in 1992 had been trained in the SSM college. The collective life of the college was a weekly lunch and seminar with T.V.Philip, their Indian theologian. There is a sense that the work is provisional and marginal. Good work was also done by Br Henry Arkell with young down-and-outs, first in a side room to the church hall, then in a purpose-built centre. For a time Douglas Brown was lecturing in a room with bunks for the boys alongside, a good piece of contextual theology. As the district has become gentrified over the last twenty years these neighbours roused hostility. The Adelaide house has lived with busy involvement and tension.

To provide somewhere different, a new St Michael's Priory was founded outside Melbourne, at Digger's Rest. It was purpose-built, though the buildings did not attempt to look ecclesiastical. There were several acres of land, a wonderfully twisted tree, and open views. It was a place where one might go to be quiet and unwind, perhaps a holy place. It was also, however, intentionally on the unfashionable side of Melbourne, with miles of encroaching roadworks for new cheap suburbs. The Society could afford to build because of the insurance from the old House. There was a general sense of quiet comfort in the Australian priories. It was all less spartan than Kelham. A new house was started in 1990 by Colin Griffiths and Henry Arkell at Port Augusta, in the north of South Australia, on the invitation of Bishop McColl of Willochra. It was a parish priory, with some idea of a ministry among the aborigines. Port Augusta was a large town, and the aborigines in question are not wandering the outback in dream-time, but marginalised in an urban society.

Without a theological college to run, as in England, the Australian Province had pangs of self-doubt, and little publicity. The best-known brothers found useful work as individuals no longer living in community. Thus John Lewis was bishop of North Queensland, Gilbert Sinden[48] earned an honorary doctorate devising the new Australian Prayerbook, and then found work in Jerusalem. The present (1993) Director of the whole Society is Archdeacon of Essendon, in Melbourne, and until recently lived alone in a vicarage. Throughout SSM history there are precedents for such work, and it may be that this is the way of the future. There are still novices. The Society moves its members around quite briskly, but one would normally expect to find four brothers at Digger's Rest, four at Adelaide, and two or three at Port Augusta. As well as the bishop in North Queensland, there is a brother in New Zealand. When one looks at some of the big Roman Catholic orders with closed novitiates the collapse has been somewhat less complete. The priories seem democratic and stable and friendly places. The Australian Province may well continue.

Having already recounted how the Australian province went through problems but survived them, we return to England and its period of difficulty.

Chapter 12

The Crash

POSSIBLE HINTS OF TROUBLE

For many religious orders, the 1950s were a golden age. There was something of a harvest of the good work done before, and a sense of coping with the need to modernise. SSM, under the Directorship of Paul Hume, 1952 – 1962, was prospering. In 1954 he could report that there had been ten professions in the previous year. From 63 professed brethren in 1951, the Society grew to 85 in 1961, its highest figure. This did not mean 85 available for work. Some were old men. Most numbers of the (twice-yearly) *Quarterly* carried the obituary of someone who had spent a life-time in the Society.[1] Some were on detached service. Some of the young ones did not last long. The intercession leaflet for September 1957 lists ten new novices at Kelham and four in Australia. None of these fourteen are now professed members of the Society.

Many, even half or more, of the new professions were in Australia. Kelham was still on top, but with the rise of Australia and a Director whose work had been in South Africa, SSM felt more like an international order. The provinces of England and South Africa looked speculatively at the able-bodied young recruits in Australia. The first Australian Director would be appointed in 1972.

It was a potential weakness that the image of the Society was almost completely subsumed in the theological college; these were the 'Kelham Fathers'. When Maurice Reckitt spoke of the versatility of SSM at the London meeting of 1953 he mentioned what he had learnt from

> my three personal friends in the community:- of the rela-
> tion of the faith to social order from Reginald Tribe; of
> the significant trends in contemporary culture from George

Every; .. of the far-reaching truths to which our liturgy testifies from Gabriel Hebert.[2]

But then he said, intending a compliment

none of these things . . . would be directly associated by most people with . . . 'Kelham'.[3]

So, even when SSM was publishing books, it did not, as a Society, get much intellectual credit for them. The image of the Society in the church was favourable ('Old Kelhamian spelt OK' said Maurice Reckitt) but it was for one work, running the biggest theological college in England.

In England, perhaps regrettably, apart from the little old parish priory in Nottingham, everything was at Kelham. They gave up the parish at Parson Cross in Sheffield in 1956. Richard Roseveare, who had been Prior there, went to be Provincial in South Africa, and then became Bishop of Accra. The South African work in fact encountered catastrophe in the 1950s before any other province. The high school and training college for teachers at Modderpoort closed at the end of 1955 because of the Bantu Education Act. The Society took the moral high ground – 'with such a policy we cannot cooperate' – and closed the college. This was their major work in South Africa. Nearly 1600 students, the teachers of black Africa, had passed through the schools since 1928.[4] From then on, they were hunting for a use for Modderpoort, and the South African province was unsettled.

In 1956 Richard Roseveare, provincial of South Africa, was chosen as bishop of Accra, in Ghana. Fr Roseveare was middle-class, typical bishop rather than typical SSM. [5] When he went to Ghana, he took Br Noel Welburn, a lay-brother socius to a bishop, as they used to have in East Africa. Br Noel wrote vivid descriptions for the SSM Quarterly of high Anglo-Catholic practice adapted to West Africa.

'The 1950s were Ghana's decade'.[6] The great nationalist leader, Kwame Nkrumah, who had an American degree in theology, tastelessly borrowed Christian language to glorify his revolution.

> I believe in the Convention People's Party,
> The opportune Saviour of Ghana,
> And in Kwame Nkrumah its founder and leader,
> Who is endowed with the Ghana Spirit. . .[7]

The churches objected when the Young Pioneer Movement was prescribed songs which confused what Roseveare called 'the work and example of a great man with divine acts which are unique in history'.[8] Bishop Roseveare was not alone in protesting: so did the Roman Catholic Archbishop, the Methodist President, and the Moderators of the two Presbyterian churches. But they were black, and bishop Roseveare was an expatriate.[9] So he was the one who was deported. This made him the most conspicuous bishop in SSM history. Even so he would soon be an anachronism, as the white bishop of a black diocese.[10]

Though there was little real change in the structure of command in SSM, Paul Hume's happy relaxed style felt more democratic than Fr Bedale's quarterdeck manner. In 1957 the provinces of SSM put 'consultation' on the agenda of the General Chapter.

> This arose as a result of pressure from the South African and Australian provinces, both of which were unhappy about the role of their provincial vis-a-vis the Director. Apart from the question of hierarchical roles, there was a growing feeling that some greater degree of democracy was desirable.[11]

There were changes at Kelham. Many were peripheral adjustments. For example, they fitted up the Grey House in the village in 1957 for women guests. This was run by sisters of the Community of St Laurence.

> Male visitors will of course continue to be our guests at the Mother House, but married couples and ladies [now had somewhere to stay][12]. . .

There had been another slight shift on the taboo on women, when in 1954, in the first Guest Day since before the war 'contrary to all precedent' (though the Australian St Michael's House had allowed them from the start) women were invited into 'the ground floor of the house and all the grounds'.[13] The Guest Day would only be one day in every three or four years. These are marginal changes.

Perhaps mention should be made of the impact of machines. Life at Kelham was never luxurious, but expectations changed. The students had known at home a more comfortable life-style. After years of appealing for little more than cut-down old trousers and books for the library, the *Quarterly* began to ask, rather hesitantly, for more. In September 1956 the list included requests for a car, admittedly to replace a 1937 one, an electric washing machine, a motor scythe and an Atco lawn mower, and then second-hand volumes of Punch and some Darwin tulips.

People over the years were generous. The Society gave up publishing the lists of individual subscribers in the *Quarterly*, because they were too lengthy. Instead of having the regular London preachings, when SSM members were in pulpits right across the capital, they had them round the country.[14] Both changes are understandable; both perhaps loosen the links with old friends.

After decades with almost entirely the same teaching staff, there were new young tutors[15], who had grown up in the Society, but had, as Fr Kelly had planned, gone on to degrees elsewhere after the Kelham course. They came back university-minded, and the college fostered its links with the theology department at Nottingham University, founded in 1949. As far back as 1922, the inspectors had urged upon the college 'contact in the free air of a university'. Fr Bedale, in this following Fr Kelly, did not take up the advice. But in the Fifties things were different. At the 1952 Great Chapter they discussed the possibility of a University House. The Society was interested in provincial universities. As the Kelham course included a lot of philosophy and history, these subjects should provide the natural link.

> [We] should be shy of importing trained and finished theologians who might upset the balance of our idea of theology . . . [but we] could not have too many contacts with philosophers and historians. (George Every)[16]

What actually happened was that these links scarcely materialised, and Kelham-trained theologians, coming back to their home college, were the ones to upset the balance.

Some of the distinctiveness of the Kelham course was gradually toned down. There were external changes. Students taught in the 1960s were no longer guided through the typed foolscap lecture schemes that had been the hallmark of the Kelham course. More important were the changes in the intake of students.

Ever since the 1944 Education Act, the provision of pre-theological education for working-class boys had been almost unnecessary. State education was available. In 1900 only about four or five pupils per thousand in the elementary schools were able to pass to the grammar schools; by 1960 two hundred per thousand could.[17] About half the entries to Kelham between 1920 and 1938 had been to Grammar Schools on County Major scholarships. The college thought even the weaker ones, from elementary schools or with 'matric', were better than those with 5 O-levels in the 1960s.[18] There might be some late developers; in 1954 the college re-started the pre-theological course for *men*. There were more students who had already failed to cope with examinations. There were other problems.

> In one class alone, 90% were from broken homes or other disturbed backgrounds, resulting in a large increase in psychological problems requiring pastoral help.[19]

The Cottage, training boys for the College, in 1949 had only twelve students, of whom only one in fact qualified to continue in Kelham. In the Fifties they switched to providing two streams in the Cottage, one a Sixth Form for those who had their school matric, and the other for

> those (without matric) preparing directly for the Kelham Qualifying Examination.[20]

Men without matric would have to hope to prove themselves late developers. Their academic level was below what men of their class could have hoped to achieve. In recruiting students like this, Kelham was in the same market as the two pre-theological colleges, Brasted, and the Bernard Gilpin Society. The old course at Kelham, as devised by Fr Kelly, was suited for students with the gifts, though not the income, of an ordinary undergraduate. Towards the end, though there were late developers, the college had many students who were not clever enough to cope with this. This helps explain the sort of cynical reminiscence one sometimes hears that 90% of the students were incapable of profiting from the Kellyesque Socratic method. It may also explain why the staff as a body did not fight harder to save the college.

Cleverer students from the social class that Kelham had originally drawn on increasingly had the option of going to university. People were beginning to hanker after hoods. Fr Bedale could not remember authorising the hood, 'stuff lined with maroon satin', issued by St Michael's House, the Australian SSM college.[21] Kelham did not issue one.

There would still be some who came to Kelham because it trained priests in a monastic discipline and with academic rigour. I, like many others, can remember from as late as the mid-Sixties the difference in reputation between the monastic colleges and ordinary Anglo-Catholic theological colleges. The Kelham course was known to be long and strenuous. This was not very informed knowledge. What was to be more significant was the opinion of the professionals in theological education. We turn now to the history of Church inspections of Kelham, and it is necessary to go back a little to show the perspective of these.

THE COLLEGE AND THE INSPECTORS

The college was inspected every few years by a panel from C.A.C.T.M. Each time they had the earlier report before them, and each time the Warden could answer back. In 1927 there were 103 students. 'We did not observe the untidiness there [1922] mentioned'. Obviously the regime of Fr Bedale had taken effect. They noticed there were no pictures. Other things missing in the course they accepted as part of the policy of the college.

> Students are (deliberately) not encouraged to undertake to give help in parish or mission work. Formal instruction in

> preaching is seldom given: this also is deliberate, but the
> large amount of essay-writing [compensates]. . .

In 1934 there were 90 theological students, of whom two
were graduates. 45 students were on the preliminary course,
which led to a Qualifying Examination at the end of the
5th term. If they were still under 19 they would have a
further course. The students were in two grades, A and B
by ability. The inspectors noticed that 'a large proportion
of them come from wage-earning homes'. Though the
students were sifted sternly, 'very few are sent away for
any misconduct'. They made certain suggestions: the students should be allowed to take the General Ordination
Examination in two parts, instead of all at once at the end;

> informality need not be carried to such a point that the
> lecturer should sit on his desk and swing his legs;

they disliked Kelham's non-Prayer Book canon, and the
use of the Angelus; and they felt some doubts about
making games compulsory.

Almost none of their suggestions were acted on. Fr
Bedale thought that comments on the theology implied in
Kelham's liturgy were outside their remit.

> I am not aware that CACTM has received any special
> doctrinal commission from the Church.[22]

Their canon had been cleared with the Visitor, the Bishop
of Southwell, and the inspectors need not attempt to put
pressure on him to condemn it.

In 1949 the Warden was Theodore Smith, not as confident a person as Fr Bedale, and he felt the criticisms more.
There were three inspectors, a bishop, a layman and an
academic. The academic was the young Dennis Nineham,
then an Oxford don, quite soon to be a professor. They
wanted more preaching.

> It does not appear that 'sermons' in the ordinary sense are
> ever preached in church.

An objective sacramental piety, and a distrust of students
practising at preaching, had both contributed to this. And
Kelham theology, refusing to be compartmentalised, per-

haps undercut the pietist contrast between sermons which edify and lectures which do not. Sharp things were said on liturgy: one inspector, bishop Noel Hudson, said to Fr Theodore that 'if he were the bishop he would have refused . . . we were completely deluded if we thought we were in any sense loyal to the Prayer Book'.

The inspectors thought that George Every's lectures were 'models of what lectures should be', but Nineham took the Warden aside and murmured that Fr Alfred's Old Testament lectures were not up to the mark. (Fr Alfred Kelly was then 77, and only teaching the one course). The college was nervous of Nineham, very much the academic inspector, pointing out gaps 'mainly on Form Criticism'. Fr Theodore felt Nineham was 'unpleasantly aggressive', but Fr Theodore was clearly rather touchy. The college was conscious that they no longer saw every student for every essay each week. In the library there were

> umpteen copies of Seeley's *Ecce Homo* but only three copies of Hoskyn's *Fourth Gospel*

Fr Theodore replied that the students *owned* their copies of Hoskyns, and that one could not tell from the library borrowing book which books were actually used.[23]

The inspectors' concern for the students' welfare was even more threatening. They commented on the starchy diet ('potatoes, macaroni and rice all to be found on each plate'). They thought it odd that, with all its football, the college never allowed 'away' games. There were doubts about students having no free time even to find out what was happening in the world.

> Did they have enough time to keep abreast of the news when on 'grub' [kitchen duties] every other fortnight. I [Fr Theodore] said I thought they did (yet I think there is some point in this . . .)[24]

The real threat was that the inspectors treated the students as customers rather than associate members of a religious community. They asked them, privately and individually, if they 'had any complaints'.

> I pointed out in no uncertain terms that our men were living the life of a religious community . . . we had not the slightest intention of departing from the *principles* of our training. One of these principles was that staff and students shared the same common room.[25]

Fr Theodore's reply to bishop Hudson took a long time to draft, and was full of defensive detail. It is not a narrow seminary: they have an orchestra; he lists the plays put on in the last two or three years.

> Richard II, Merchant of Venice, Murder in the Cathedral, What You Will, Arms and the Man, The Dark Lady of the Sonnets, Trial by Jury, Comus and pantomime.

Though the students are not taught preaching, they do read, he claimed, F. W. Robertson and Spurgeon, the two masters of liberal and evangelical preaching of Victorian England, and 'more sermons are to be preached in chapel'.

As time went on, the inspectors had more of the whip hand. In 1961, though they noticed the new central heating, the studies were still cold. They 'were not at all happy about the Common Room', shared by the Community and the students. There was too much bread and marmalade in the diet. The students did not seem to *own* books. Were they under pressure to go to Confession? Only three or four did not. (Someone has pencilled in the margin 'more like 10'). On the other hand they approved of the way the college spent £60 a year on periodicals. And Kelham was 'in the happy position of being able to grow its own staff', unlike other theological colleges, which had to take university leftovers.

In 1966, to the Warden's dismay, 'two of our very worst student readers were down' to read the lessons in chapel when the inspectors came. He 'resisted the temptation to change them', but the inspectors commented on the poor quality of the reading. They were defensive about the food: the inspectors wondered if the students were underfed,

> the students appeared particularly hungry at tea after either

manual labour or organised games. No student, however, made any complaint.

There was 'usually enough on each table for second help-ings'. The inspectors disliked the remaining Kelham tradi-tion of a number of private masses, but in fact all but three students were present at the main mass.

In 1970 the inspectors presented a list of recommendations, which the college set itself to fulfil. These were: that the standard of lecturing should be raised; that each student should have a year's course of instruction in preaching and in elocution; that each student should experience 'regular participation in the normal life of the local parishes'; that there should be a wider range of visiting speakers; that the college should rein back on its recently-introduced practice of group dynamics; and that the college should charge realistic fees, like other colleges. Some of these are recognis-ably matters where Kelham had been at odds with the ways of ordinary colleges for many years. Thus tradition-ally at Kelham the lectures were merely there to send them to the books; to practise preaching *alongside* learning to understand theology was seen as a dangerous waste of time; a key part of Kelham training was to live separate from ordinary life in a religious community; and the experience of living hand-to-mouth in shared poverty was one of the most valuable things about Kelham. Father Kelly or Father Bedale would have able to see off intrusive C.A.C.T.M. inspectors. By 1970 this was no longer possi-ble. In some matters the college had already moved in the 1960s, and the inspectors were urging them to go further.

Kelham was compared unfavourably with other theologi-cal colleges. There was a high wastage rate: between a quarter and a third of the students did not complete the course.[26] Kelham had a long history of people not complet-ing courses, but by then this seemed more of a failure in the original selection than it used to. In 1964 they could still cheerfully quote a bishop saying 'Kelham is justified by the number of men it turns out' (meaning sends away as unsuitable).[27] It is an odd thought that the characteristic procedures of C.A.C.T.M. (later ACCM) for selecting candidates for ordination were modelled on Kelham. Fr Bedale was a key figure in making C.A.C.T.M. what it was. But the fact that ordinands were now sifted by a centralised mechanism, instead of the whims of individual bishops, meant that a college that did any more sifting was questioning the wisdom of C.A.C.T.M.

KELHAM UNDER SIMON MEIN

Kelham was becoming more like an ordinary theological college. The press noticed this as 'Cold showers every morning are *out*'.[28] Students were now free to go out on Saturday afternoons. It was difficult to raise teams for matches. The old Kelly tradition of getting the theology right and not practising at pastoralia as amateurs had gone. There was pastoral work throughout. Each student did two weeks of social work every vacation and a sociological project. There are reports back of what it is like serving behind a bar.

Fr Theodore Smith, as Warden, had anguished over enforcing a 'no engagements' rule, to keep the students away from female attachments at Kelham and indeed as curates. He had 1000 forms printed, promising to remain single for five years, and serious-minded students sometimes left rather than make a promise they found difficult to keep. Others broke it. The new Warden in 1962, Simon Mein, changed this, allowing courtship; and whatever they liked once curates. There was still a rule:

> a man may not become engaged while he is a student. This makes possible a freer social life ... more scope for the exercise of responsibility.[29]

It no longer seemed possible to treat the students as novices.

There were also changes in the course. The more formal teaching had shifted from a stress on historical theology to one on modern biblical criticism. Simon Mein was a biblical specialist. His sub-warden, Vincent Strudwick, looking back, saw things to regret in this.

The other thing that changed (George Every fought a rearguard action, and I helped some . . .) was the crowning of Biblical studies in the course . . . George maintained that the Church History, 'doggies' [dogmatics] and philosophy were what the Kelham course was all about . . . there was some logical positivism and philosophical method but philosophy was no longer so rigorous . . . 'Doggies' became less centred in Church History and more in sociology: a reflection of contemporary insight, rather than a disciplined working through of what the Church had formulated. . . . a new lot of 'Bible boys', influenced by Alan Richardson and the university Bible schools in a way that Steve [Bedale] and Gabriel [Hebert] were not. The critical theology that they taught became pre-eminent in the Kelham course.[30]

This perhaps overdraws the picture of the old guard as being filled with the mind of Fr Kelly and the new ones as cuckoos in the nest. Some of them had degrees in history. It is difficult to see Alan Richardson, professor at Nottingham from 1953 to 1964, as being so radically different from Gabriel Hebert in his approach to the New Testament. Simon Mein was possibly more modern than Richardson. His aspersions on 'biblical theology' probably have Fr Hebert in view.

. . . many of the assured positions of 'biblical theology' are now being questioned . . . [we] cannot be content to . . . rhapsodise about the great themes that go right through the Old and New Testaments.[31]

It would be possible to show that George Every himself had a different approach to history from Fr Kelly. He was the first to set aside a Kelly scheme, and that the 'Old Man's' particular pride, the 'Church History' course. Both Theodore Smith, Warden of the College 1945–1962, and George Every became converts to Rome. They may well have represented what might be called a 'pre-Vatican II' type of orthodoxy in the Society that missed something of Fr Kelly's bolder approach.

The college was not staffed by old men. George Every was 60, but the oldest of the rest was 43 in 1970. Simon Mein, like his predecessor a bright home-bred student who had been sent away to get another degree, was warden of the college at the age of 35. The new leadership was not opposed to the past. Every number of the Society's new annual journal *Transmit*, which ran for four years from 1969, had something by Fr Kelly, such as 'How I became an Anarchist, 1917'.[32]

Much more threatening than new ways of handling the New Testament was the introduction of group dynamics. In 1967 they set up Chaplaincy Groups. Simon Mein (and others) had been on courses on 'Personal Relationships in Community', all about non-verbal communication and self-discovery, and during the 1969 Christmas holiday, there was a group dynamics course at Kelham. It is one thing learning about openness in a group of strangers whom you will never meet again. It is something else to be utterly open in a place like Kelham. With hindsight, many of those who remember the groups seem to think that for some vulnerable people they were a very shattering experience.[33] The college inspectors noticed particularly the risks 'where one person becomes the object of group attention'.[34] Some of the groups became spirit-possessed, and spoke with tongues. There is, after all, a charismatic movement within Catholicism, but it seems oddly out of place in Kelham, where there was a tradition of intellectualism and self-control. Certainly it suggests that Simon Mein was wrong when he wrote

> one feels that an undercurrent of hysteria that was often noticeable is not so apparent now.[35]

There was more to be said for the Service of Reconciliation, with which they replaced the fault chapters. Even the group dynamics can be defended, as an attempt to make relationships more natural, simple, and supportive. There had been in the past in-fighting and personal animosities cloaked as disagreements over liturgical principle. SSM since then seems kindlier than Kelham sometimes was. But at the time some of the changes were unsettling.

Simon Mein was a go-ahead young principal, with a young team, and they were largely given their head. Gregory Wilkins, as Director from 1962, who put Simon

Mein in as Warden, gambled on bringing Kelham swiftly up to date. It was not a new autocracy: Fr Mein was almost too eager to listen to his colleagues.

> At frequent intervals during the day, and sometimes the night, he came upstairs to my room to consult, confide, confess, complain – ever needing approval and support for everything he said or did.[36]

Decisions were made democratically in the Tutors' Chapter, not by the Warden's fiat. A lot of the old customs of Kelham went: the amateur theatricals guying the staff; the Principles read aloud in the refectory; curtains were installed in the showers. The changes in the college were part of a wider aggiornamento, experienced by most religious orders of the period. So SSM moved from an Office seven times a day to one four times, and from the Cowley Missal to (in the end) the ASB. Members of SSM could wear civilian clothes on occasion, and could handle money. Not everyone has dark memories of the period. Some rapid changes can be exhilarating.

THE REPORTS ON THEOLOGICAL TRAINING

The Church of England was planning centrally how clergymen should be trained. In 1963 there were 1357 men in training; by 1970 there were 834, and the numbers were still falling. There were two Reports in quick succession. Neither gave any hint of closing Kelham, but both damaged it. In 1968 the de Bunsen report gave a comparative table on cost per student,[37] and omitted Kelham, which had always prided itself on being the cheapest. This may have been a simple slip; it could scarcely have been some sort of rebuke for having unrealistically subsidised expenses, because other colleges subsidised too. (The inspectors in 1970 ordered the college to charge realistic fees).

The Report spoke of two antithetical tendencies in the study of theology in Britain, one Lancaster, the other Oxford. Lancaster University had a department of Religious Studies, founded in the 1960s, under Ninian Smart, where Christianity did not have a privileged position over other religions. The report took sides with loyally Christian Oxford against Lancaster. Its tone is one of unconsidered defensiveness, preferring the old ways. Kelham had its own old tradition of sniping at Oxford theology. What made matters worse, it now had direct links with Lancaster. The new university had SSM chaplains. The Director himself, leaving Kelham, was prior from 1965 of the new house at Quernmore, just outside Lancaster. Bright students from Kelham and from Crafers in Australia went on to do degrees in the Lancaster department. Moreover, Kelham had done a deal with St Martin's College, Lancaster, so that its students, after gaining their Nottingham B.Th. at Kelham, would go on to do a postgraduate Dip.Ed. at Quernmore. St Martin's was a Church of England college, but the Lancaster address was enough. From an Oxford-minded perspective, it looked as if SSM was deliberately siding with the forces of radical secularity.

The practical recommendations of the de Bunsen report were not very sweeping. There were far too many colleges, chasing fewer and fewer students.

> ... all colleges should be in or near a university, and actually linked with it. The only exception we have felt able to make is the special case of Kelham.[38]

This was not to guarantee a graduate ministry. There were still to be three large colleges producing non-graduate clergy. One would be Lichfield-amalgamated-with-Salisbury (120 students), the other two Oakhill and Kelham, each of these with 90 and room for expansion. Of the three, only Kelham was to be left on its current site. The other two should find a university as a neighbour. The college at Chichester should go.

In fact, circumstances got worse quickly, and the next, more drastic, Runcie report, in 1970, worked with smaller figures. The report was the work of Robert Runcie, then Bishop of St Albans, and later Archbishop of Canterbury, and Kenneth Woollcombe, then Principal of the Edinburgh Theological College, later Bishop of Oxford. It recommended that there should be 50 places at Kelham, a drop, but the same number as at Mirfield, Lincoln, and Cranmer Hall, Durham. The college at Chichester, which had survived one death sentence from de Bunsen, once again was scheduled for closure. Salisbury this time was to amalgamate with Wells.

Any inspection in a period of cuts is threatening, but Kelham was not very much threatened. After all, in 1969, it had a total of 76 students, more than any other college, though 14 of them were categorised as 'other' theological students. Even so, with 62 ACCM candidates, it still outnumbered any other college. The numbers dropped in 1970, when there were only 48 ACCM candidates, and five other colleges had more. Yet it still looked, on the face of things, secure. Neither report had proposed it for closure.

CLOSURE

The crash came quickly and unexpectedly. In September 1970 the college staff reported informally to the Director of SSM, Gregory Wilkins, that something was wrong. Diocesan Directors of Ordinands were warning men off Kelham. It still came as a complete surprise when the House of Bishops, in their recommendations to the General Synod in January 1971, following the Runcie Report, announced a change of plan.

> As St Stephen's House is to have 60 places . . . we have to choose between Kelham and Chichester for the remaining 50 places. Since the monastic colleges must bear their share of reductions . . . [we have] decided to withdraw recognition from Kelham as a theological college.[39]

What had happened between the summer of 1970 and January 1971 had partly been skilful lobbying to save Chichester, which had a new Principal and a broadened churchmanship, and partly visible troubles at Kelham. Alan Wilkinson, appointed that summer as Principal of Chichester, writes:

> He [Bishop of Chichester] said to me that if we were to argue for the retention of Chichester we had to propose

the closure of an alternative college. I said 'What about
Kelham?' or words to that effect. I told him that from
various sources, I knew that Kelham was in turmoil. Vincent Strudwick, the Sub-Warden, had left College and
SSM in July. I had heard that some students had applied to
transfer to other colleges (six or eight perhaps?) – one had
come to Chichester that autumn ... Simon Mein, the
Warden, left College and SSM in September I think ... It
was public knowledge that Kelham College was in grave
and probably terminal difficulties. To transfer from one
college to another required permission from the ACCM
Candidates Committee, and the bishops of the men concerned would have to be informed.[40]

It obviously did not help matters that both the Sub-Warden
and the Warden of the college left in the same year.
Vincent Strudwick went as unobtrusively and smoothly as
could be managed, carefully coaching his successor, and
later, as a married couple, the Strudwicks were of great use
to the Society. The parting with Simon Mein was sharper
and more painful. The Director reported later

Then the Warden divulged his personal problems to the
Director and had to be replaced by another. The news of
the ex-warden's affairs made a great stir in the gutter-press
and the church ...[41]

The Warden had come back from a trip to the United
States and told the Society that he was engaged to an
American nun. 'Father Simon to marry Nan the nun' said
the press.[42] Thousands of monks must have done something similar in that decade, but when senior men did it, it
jarred. According to the records, Fr Mein did not ask for
release, but just 'left'. At the very least, the college had to
find a new Warden halfway through a term.

The newly installed Vice-Warden, Hilary Greenwood,
was promoted to Warden, and the Director came back
from Lancaster to be Prior of the Mother House. Kelham
was bruised, but closed ranks. The decision by the House
of Bishops in January 1971 came completely as a surprise.
There was an outcry. The Society brought out a special
February issue of SSM 'which', as Margaret Dewey said,
'rightly set forth the known facts, though in a sarcastic

tone which many thought regrettable'.[43] This was rushed
round the country during a postal strike to friends and
former students, who then wrote passionate letters to the
Church Times. The Director, Gregory Wilkins, spoke
sharply to the local papers about the closure. It was all
ecclesiastical politics, and 'we are the poor mutts in the
centre'. He blamed the 'old school tie Oxbridge network',
and said

> The extreme high church don't like Kelham because they
> don't think we are high enough.[44]

Remembering that the Society's college training teachers
at Modderpoort had been closed because of South Africa's
apartheid laws, he told the Newark Advertiser that it was
'just as painful to be broken by a bishop as by a Boer'.

> You have no bishops on the bench. Other colleges have
> old students who are bishops. It is as simple as that.[45]

It fell to Fr Hugh Bishop of Mirfield, as representative of
the religious orders on the General Synod, to speak of
what it would do to the community if its principal function
were removed. One Kelham argument was that as, unlike
other theological colleges, it charged no tuition fees, there
was no economy to the Church in closing it. To teach 48
students elsewhere would cost the Church more than
£24,000. The decision was not on economic grounds.
There were so few Anglo-Catholic ordinands that if Chichester were saved, another college must go. And other
colleges did have strings to pull. Because the cuts were
carefully distributed over the parties of the Church, Kelham
at one point, with some memory of the real achievement
of Fr Kelly in being both evangelical and Catholic, but also
rather frivolously, asked if they could be reclassified as an
evangelical college. They would not have them; St John's,
Nottingham, was the local evangelical college, and Kelham
did not pass muster.

There was, however, enough of a public outcry against
the closure to persuade the authorities of the Church of
England to relent. The Archbishop of Canterbury, Michael
Ramsey, told the General Synod, on 19 February 1971,

that the House of Bishops now proposed that Kelham should have 25 places, and suggested 'a scheme for combining training for the full-time ministry with other forms of theological training'. This was 25 places all told, which meant an intake for the Kelham course of not more than seven a year. It was a grudging concession: Kelham should continue

> although it has changed character somewhat in recent years and it is not easy to single out any unique contribution to ordination training.[46]

The Society made an attempt at running a reduced college. They thought of having some students to study theology who were not going to be ordained. After all, the college in practice had always had a number who did not go forward to ordination. Some became lay brothers, others found other careers. They were not failures in the history of Kelham. (Some of them at the time undoubtedly felt they were). It might also be possible to run shorter courses.

> We could have week-ends for groups of people from a parish, a school, a college ... One chief constable has suggested that police cadets ... study together the ethical problems that a police man or woman has to face ... [It might be useful to] doctors and nurses, for instance, or to bank clerks and accountants, to shop stewards and trade union officials. Much of what William Temple College was doing might well be done in the new Kelham ... some place of learning for refresher courses [for priests] ... an expansion of the work which we always have been doing, which basically is theological education.[47]

In the event, much of this was whistling in the wind. Scruffy old Kelham was not a natural conference centre, even with new furniture. To make it a conference centre was not fair to the students.

> We are not going to run something that uses 25 students as skivvies for other people.[48]

The College was no longer viable. Though Hilary Greenwood was ingenious and persistent, there were no longer the tutors, or indeed the heart to continue.

... the young tutors came in and said they wanted a meeting. The room filled ... apart from me, the entire teaching staff felt that it had been a mistake to continue running the college when the bishops had tried to close it; none of them wanted to continue working in it; and, in any case, its continuance would be an impediment to what they hoped would be done by the priory.[49]

In any case there were not the candidates. Kelham needed large numbers to sift, and they were no longer there. As Fr Hilary Greenwood himself said:

In 1947, when I was a candidate, only 16 men were selected from 160 who were interviewed. And of that 16, only about 9 of us lasted through to the end of the course. Far from being ashamed of these figures, we gloried in them. But in 1971 there were only six candidates interviewed altogether, of whom one was an out-patient at a mental hospital and another was overtly keeping a mistress in Germany.[50]

The English Province decided by June 1972 to recommend to the Great Chapter that autumn that the college should close. It might seem that a Society with 75 professed members could surely find enough to staff a theological college. But SSM was not an order composed of scholars, and among the scholars it had, the work of running a routine theological college, as Kelham had become, was not so evidently the right way to spend their time. In a way, this is too rational a presentation of the disarray in the English Province at the time. The ending of the college was real trauma. Some friendly critics have seen this as evidence of too close a link between the Society and the college.

The fact that the closure of Kelham College had such a dramatic effect on SSM confirmed the belief that the College had never had sufficient independence from the Community and that had been bad for both.[51]

The Great Chapter, rather hesitantly, confirmed the decision. The new young Australian Director, Dunstan McKee, was confronted with a demoralised English Province. (No English name was even considered for Director in 1972). The college had already turned away any candidates for the next session, not that there were many. The last of those already enrolled completed their course in 1975. They had been living in the Red House, the retreat house in the village of Kelham, and spent the final year of their course in a hall of residence in Nottingham.

The end of the college meant the end of Kelham. There were a series of heart-rending realisations: the Great Chapel cost too much to heat; there was no need for a building the size of Kelham Hall. So, in 1974, Kelham, including the Great Chapel, was sold to Newark District Council as council offices. The deconsecrated chapel became available as a hall for hire, and there are incongruous pictures of discos and fashion parades in a building that had been an image of eternity.

Seventy years is a long time, and Kelham Hall, that amazing building, was inseparably linked with most of the memories of most members of SSM. The memory was if anything even more potent for the many priests who had trained there. The Great Chapel was a holy place. Nevertheless, Kelham Hall was an ostentatious piece, an unlikely home for a religious order, and in some ways they were well rid of it. There were members of SSM who disliked living at Kelham; some of these are still members, so this dislike was not a grumble about the religious life as such. The dispersal, into a number of little priories, described in a later chapter, was a very great change indeed.

To this day, when members of SSM of the generation which remembers Kelham get together, the wake continues. With certain misgivings, they decided to hold the centenary service for SSM in Southwell Minster, the cathedral for Kelham, though the Society has no work in that diocese. Kelham is still potent, more than memories of where they were young together. These, one should point out, were the resilient ones. At the time some brethren found they could not continue in the Society without the college. There were

> no more young men to dilute priory life . . . [Some had] coped with their emotional problems by means of young men and were unable to do so with their brethren.[52]

Many useful people thrive on the company of the young, and have not got the type of inner resources that lead them spontaneously to meditation. If the work went, then the religious life was unliveable.

It is difficult to tell the story without presenting the closure of Kelham as a catastrophe for SSM. In a later chapter we shall turn to how the Society rebuilt itself, in some ways deliberately putting behind it the Kelham tradition. The great library was dispersed, though not thereby wasted. There was more human waste. Some of the members who left might have stayed. Others who continue to this day have not had their teaching gifts properly used, especially as the Australian college went on to close as well. It is very difficult being marginal well-qualified educators.

Though the closure of Kelham was the greatest of SSM's troubles, it was not the only one, nor was SSM alone in having troubles. Almost every religious community round the world lost members in the 1960s and 70s. The purpose of any religious life was being radically questioned. The English Province of SSM was very hard hit, but so were the others. It was admittedly

> a time of upheaval and trauma in the English province, where two pro-provincials, the prior and warden of Kelham, the subwarden and two novice masters left the Society. In South Africa the provincial left while on his way to the Great Chapter of 1972.[53]

In 1970, and again in 1973, four members were released in one year. Otherwise, there was a steady drain of one or two a year, from the late 50s. Between 1962 and 1966 four members were not released but removed, the sterner parting.[54] No-one has been removed since. Members had walked out of SSM before, and the Society had not such a mystique about vows that to leave was an affront. But so many leaving, and so many of them senior members, hit the Society hard. It was, and remained, difficult to plan work ahead. On the human level, people lost their friends, whom they had expected to have around for the rest of their lives.

It is sometimes tempting for the survivors to look for

someone to blame, either the old guard who had screwed up the system too tight, so that there had to be an explosion (Stephen Bedale), or the young radicals who reformed everything in sight and then left (Simon Mein). It is difficult to say what causes a man to leave; it may sometimes be the best thing all round that he does. Circumstances, and the spirit of the age, do more damage than individuals. It was, however, a dismal period through which to live.

In the next chapter we leave Kelham and its memories, and turn to the Society beyond and after Kelham.

Chapter 13

The Day of the Priories,
And Beyond?

After the crash, and the closure of Kelham, the Society pulled itself together and carried on. Kelham was not the whole of its life, and other things had gone on alongside. These had been very low-key. Thus, when the Society re-issued *An Idea in the Working : an account of the SSM, its history and aims* in 1927, it added a supplementary chapter by Fr Tribe, the then Director, to bring it up to date. Nowhere in the book is there any reference to English priories outside Kelham. The powers-that-be were very Kelham-minded. In 1906 Fr Kelly had been startled to find that former students [Associates] 'did not know that the Society stood for anything outside South Africa and Kelham . . .'[1] but it was understandable.

In 1911 the bishop of Southwell asked the Society to take charge of St George's, Nottingham. This was the first Anglican parish ever given to a religious order in England, and was a priory of SSM until 1974.[2] Nottingham is only 12 or 13 miles from Kelham. It was a small industrial parish, in a district called the Meadows, on the wrong side of the tracks, with a munitions factory. In 1914 there was trouble with an autocratic prior. He drove himself and his two colleagues to nervous collapse. They were all 'over-worked and underslept'.[3] Fr Kelly was on the prior's side: the man had 'set himself to make the Priory a help to the church of Nottingham'[4]; but then he left to get married. The Society was tempted to leave him there as vicar and retreat, but the bishop would not have it. There was, not surprisingly, 'still an experimental feeling about the life of the priory'.[5] The next prior, to Fr Kelly's disgust, set himself to make it the 'pattern Catholic parish for the Midlands'.[6] During the 'Carleton affair', Nottingham was in trouble for being waywardly Anglo–Catholic, and had to be kept in line. The Director, Fr White, wrote:

> I want you to include in your priory rule the following: 'Each member of the Priory to spend (at least) two whole consecutive days at Kelham each month'.[7]

The Society's image of the Nottingham priory tended to be gloomy. It fell too easily into the role of the old-fashioned party Anglo–Catholic parish. [8] It is also true that rather a large number of those who had served there left the Society.[9]

Nottingham was the only English priory other than Kelham until the 1930s. Then in 1932 the Society was invited by John How, Rector of Liverpool, himself the founder of a religious community, the Oratory of the Good Shepherd, to set up a house in his parish. Basil Oddie and Paul Hume, both significant names in the later history of the Society, went to Liverpool. The priory, 'that incredibly dreadful house, dark and rat-ridden, down in the docks of Liverpool',[10] at 5 Canning Place, opposite the Customs House, was filled with hardy young curates. In what looks like revenge for his 'Babylonish exile' as rector of Averham from 1942–43, [11] Fr Bedale sent Fr Tribe, his predecessor as Director, to Liverpool in 1943. The work had shrunk: from 1940 they were no longer on the staff of the Parish Church, but they still had university students, and nuns, and two small hospitals to look after.

In 1934 the Society was invited to take over the parish of Bedminster in Bristol. The priory was much more attractive than the ones at Nottingham and Liverpool,[12] and with hindsight they felt that they had been asked because the bishop had wanted to find a use for a big house. The church was destroyed by bombing in 1941 and never replaced. The Society were there for 12 years, and as was their way in these palmy days, kept a staff of about five, which was then experienced as a small priory. For the parish it was a golden age: the organist could list from memory without prompting 10 brethren who had served there in the 12 years, with specific detail about Fr Leslie Pearse, who was the vicar, Fr Gregory Wilkins, and Fr

Denys Nightingale.[13] To a bishop this might look like over-staffing. The official SSM line was:

> ... by providing a large staff, we are trying in selected parishes to counteract the disadvantages caused by the prevalent under-manning, and establish a standard of adequate staffing for English parishes.[14]

In 1937 the Society started work in a huge overspill housing estate in the north of Sheffield, called Parson Cross. It had a population of more than 40,000 by 1940. This was Fr Roseveare's parish, and at one time (in 1941) he had six other brethren working there. Fr Roseveare had a way of getting large sums of money out of wealthy donors. Bassett's Liquorice Allsorts, the major employer of women and girls in the parish, gave a covenanted subscription of £1000 a year. [15] The Dowager Countess Ferrers built the house into which he put the Wantage Sisters.[16] One donor built the main church, St Cecilia's, Parson Cross, in 1938. The donor wanted to give the patronage to SSM in perpetuity, and when he found that this was against canon law, as the Society was not a public body, he rather grudgingly gave it to the bishop with a 'gentleman's agreement' that the bishop would appoint SSM men. The donor then safeguarded this by the 'naughty' device (his word) of leaving £5000 in the hands of SSM for the upkeep of the music at St Cecilia's.[17] There were difficulties later. In 1952 the bishop was quite prepared to appoint an SSM man, but not 'willy-nilly'. The Director wrote:

> [it is] quite obvious he does not understand anything about Religious Vocation, and I could not concede to his request to interview several of the brethren.[18]

In the event, in order to start a 'Kelham down under' in Australia, the priories at Liverpool and Bristol were closed in 1946. Later (in 1956) they withdrew from Sheffield, and the Society was back to having only one other house in England beside Kelham. There were little local regrets about this. How one assesses the work in parish priories is hard to say. Fr Bedale said of Parson Cross in 1952 'the Estate was a different place from what it might have been otherwise, and now had a greater awareness of the claims of God'. [19] Sometimes Kelham objectivity sounds immodest. A later generation of SSM might raise another question about such assessments:

> There is something contra-factual in the Christian's make-up which makes it very difficult for clergy to state what had actually happened.[20]

Certainly we are more likely to find confident verdicts on work in the 1950s than in the 1970s.

When the Society was buoyant they had toyed with the idea of making something more of one of the parish priories. Fr Bedale loved large institutions: perhaps they could have 'one large centre, eg Parson Cross, with a normal mission staff of 9 or 10', something in fact on the lines of Modderpoort.[21] He looked at the statistics of the English Province, and felt that little priories were a disaster. Of those who were released between 1919 and 1946, one was serving at the Mother House, six were in South Africa, and *nine* were in the English Province.[22] There were elements of self-fulfilling prophecy in this. Unsettled brethren, whom they could do nothing else with, were sent to small priories. This was experienced as demotion, and the community life in the priories suffered. Bedminster remembered Fr Gilks and Fr Stephens who married and got parishes elsewhere. [23] There was an ongoing debate in the Society whether parish priories were ever worthwhile. One of the problems with taking on parishes was that the people expected a vicar with curates, and did not see the monks as monks.[24]

Then came the crash. 'How well are we prepared for a future of small priories?' Douglas Brown, in asking this question in 1972,[25] rehearsed the flaws of institutionalism inherent in large mother houses. But just to copy the old pattern of small priories was not the answer.

> They seem to have been staffed by patriarchal priors who lived on in houses of their own creation, expressing their own personalities, with satellite brothers who came and went.[26]

Someone with South African experience once said that 'after six months in a priory pets need a psychiatrist'.[27]

However, the Society had to find new work. In 1965 SSM had accepted the gift of a large estate outside Lancaster. Fr Nigel Kinsella had lately been appointed the first chaplain of the new St Martin's teachers' training college, and there was the promise of the chaplaincy of the new university too. Quernmore Park[28] was a Georgian mansion, and it would have taken great resolve to refuse it. In fact it cost the Society money, because Mr Garnett, the donor, died before the dry-rot could be put straight, and the Society had no possible claim on his heirs. Perhaps it was too grand for SSM: there was disquiet about the gold leaf on the ceilings [29]. The first three brethren sent to set up the new priory left the Society, and though the Director, Gregory Wilkins, then himself moved there, he was necessarily often away. After the closure of Kelham in 1973, many of the brethren at Quernmore were elderly, and could not help but be something of a burden on the few novices. Others were busy as full-time students, or stayed in the Chaplaincy flat in Lancaster, so community life suffered.

Things settled down under Fr Laurence Eyers as Prior.[30] There were ecumenical exchanges with Spanish monks, after Hilary Greenwood spent a sabbatical year in Spain. Quite a number of SSM men, several from Australia, did degrees in the Religious Studies department at Lancaster. In 1971 two SSM men graduated with Firsts in Religious Studies. Fr Dominic Tye got a Lancaster Ph.D. There was all the student chaplaincy work, a local prison to visit and a borstal, and some parish work. But SSM had been a teaching order, with a great tradition of communicating theology, and they wanted to continue something of this. Quernmore Park became a 'Christian Institute' in 1976. They devised a programme of short courses and conferences and Saturday seminars. Hilary Greenwood and Gregory Wilkins were sparkling teachers, and some of it worked. But ill-health and poor attendances drove them to cut back.

The 'Quernmore Notes' (1976 – 9) which they published

were full of ingenious ideas, and happy turns of phrase, about doing liturgy.

> I may be weary of earth and laden with my sin, but I am not going to make a song about it. . .
> We never plough or scatter
> We're not a reaper band;
> But we make all the tractors
> that drive across the land. . .
> The cobra in the jungle
> The clothes-moth in the box,
> The virus in the blood-stain
> And the thing that gives you pox. . .
>
> [try] to celebrate the eucharist in complete silence.[31]

There was much insight in these pamphlets. Thus, for example, Fr Greenwood spoke of the

> great danger of extrovert people becoming very sentimental.. so often nowadays what happens in church or at prayer-groups is concocted by extrovert people. Some of us find the kiss of peace powerfully embarrassing; and we do not want to warm up with hand-clapping, hugging, shouting out slogans etc [32]

'Happy-clappy' religion was all too like the last night of the proms. This was not simple conservatism: there were novelties too, like a group where everyone sat huddled in their private blanket, so that they could together enjoy the retirement and the sense of withdrawal.[33] However, by 1978 *Quernmore Notes* only had 40 subscribers.[34] Even with the goodwill of the local dioceses, the hinterland was probably not populous enough to produce lay people who wanted to play with ideas in any number. The brethren could fill up their lives, 'teaching illiterates, training lay readers, lecturing on adult education schemes, working in the garden, and making things for sale',[35] but that big beautiful house was a millstone and the Society should never have accepted it. In 1981, Hilary Greenwood was moved to a new priory in Manchester (first in Moss-side then in Longsight), and Fr Edmund Wheat, replacing him, gave up trying to run the house with five brothers over 65 and one over-worked novice. They moved into a wing, filled the house with students, and brought in professional staff. The students were noisy.

The replacement, inasmuch as there was a replacement,[36] for Kelham was at Willen, set up, when Kelham closed, in 1973. It was within sight of the M1, on the boundaries of the new town of Milton Keynes. Just as at Canberra, there was a definite idea that planned new cities need a religious focus. The church at Willen, which served as the priory chapel, was a tiny gem of English Classical architecture,[37] in a mere hamlet. Over the years farming gave way to tasteful clusters of detached executive residences and public parkland. A Buddhist pagoda was built nearby. The Society constructed its priory at considerable expense [38] around the existing modern vicarage. It was all on a domestic scale, and could conceivably be split up. Alongside the church there came a hospice for the terminally ill. Willen Priory became a quiet place, which people tasted and loved. It gathered round it Associates, no longer a term for students training to be ordained. Fr Vincent Strudwick came back, a married man, and the family lived for a time on the site. They were followed by John and Linda Davis. Sir Almeric Rich, retired from governing Borstals, and an old friend of SSM, moved in. Then there were the women. Whether or not there were vows taken, Mary Hartwell, Margaret Dewey, and Liz Macey, and others alongside and before them, came to belong to that priory, living there as their home and the community their family from the 1970s. Through trial and error, the priory drew back from the SSF [Anglican Franciscan] work of offering a place to stay for tramps. Other priories watched developments at Willen with misgivings. Was this a Sixties commune? Was it a re-run of Iris Murdoch's *The Bell*?[39] On the other hand, Clement Mullenger came back on leave from Lesotho in 1977 and was delighted with Willen:

> People seem closer, more generally concerned for and attentive to one another. There seems to be order without authoritarianism, hierarchy without lordship-versus-subjugation. Most significant of all is the fact that it is no longer

a closed shop, but is open to all who feel called to share its life.[40]

The Willen way was not as tight and not as busy as Kelham. For a short time there was a house at Milton Keynes city centre. Willen Priory proved marginal, rather than a 'still centre' to the life of Milton Keynes, but there are creative possibilities in marginality.

Both at Quernmore and at Willen, the English Province found themselves spending a lot of money.

> Some brethren in South Africa and Australia seemed to think that the English brethren were sitting on a huge quantity of money which they grudgingly sent to the colonies in small doses, and themselves spent liberally on various country mansions.[41]

In fact, as Hilary Greenwood said, the English brethren were until recently accustomed to going 'to daddy for money whereas their cousins abroad had had cheque-books',[42] but there was the truth there that SSM could now take financial risks that would have ruined the Society in Fr Kelly's day. Like some other shrinking religious orders they were at least comfortably off.

With the closure of Kelham, the Society expected to have the manpower to staff a town parish relatively lavishly. They did not decide at once to close the little old priory at Nottingham. But the whole parish of dense little streets was rebuilt in this period, losing more than two-thirds of its population, and the Society wanted a fresh start,[43] so the end came in 1974. They found a new town parish in St Mark's, Sheffield, which started in 1973 with five brothers and a novice. They had slums, and student residences, and a new hospital all within the parish. Edmund Wheat and Gordon Holroyd, working in student circles, had a group talking left-wing politics and disaffection with the old ways of Anglo-Catholicism.[44] It was a very different atmosphere from St George's, Nottingham. But there are pressures on priories in cities, and by 1977 there were two brethren left, and St Mark's was more like an ordinary over-worked town parish.[45] When Fr Wheat's contract as chaplain to Sheffield University ended in 1980, they closed the Sheffield priory.

From 1972 to 1982 the Director of SSM was the young Australian Dunstan McKee. With the Canadian Ralph Martin as Provincial of the English Province, he faced a demoralised Society, often clutching at straws. The basic task was to come to terms with the new reality. The Society was not a great international order with a hierarchy of command; its houses would number handfuls of people; and no clear self-evident work would give it immediate public justification. On the other hand, the new reality had its charms.

> ... the apparatus of Director, Provincials, and Wardens, together with their associated secretaries, councils, and committees, should be allowed to fade peacefully into the background.[46]

In practice priories went their own way to a considerable extent, and it became clear that being Director was not a full-time job. Dunstan McKee drafted a new Constitution which delineated

> not how the Society should be organised in a perfect world, nor how it should be organised if it reached an as yet unattainable size; on the contrary, it simply set out how things were done at this phase in the Society's history.[47]

It was a deliberately low-key Directorship, and the Society too was encouraged just to be there, and to accept positively what came. Characteristic phrases were:

> ... listening to the truth meeting us through circumstances, through people ...our life is one of simplicity in both structures and comforts ... We have no separate life. ... Wherever people are, there we see the possibility of living and working.[48]

The Society was quiet and humble, chastened by misfortune. Members were conscious of each other's fragility. A lot of careful thought went into balancing the corporate life of each priory with finding work that was fulfilling for individuals.[49] In 1972 there was an epoch-making English provincial chapter, when the members were asked what sort of work they would like to do. They could opt for one of three smaller groups, either for academic work, or inner-city work, or for just *being* there as a focus of spiritual life. The first group would go to Lancaster, the second to Sheffield, the third to Milton Keynes. The three strands have continued. Some were shocked at being asked. One of the stories of the old encountering the new is of Fr Lewes Ward-Andrews replying 'Father, what are you asking us about? You're the Provincial'.[50] The classification has made it difficult to move individuals since.

The members of SSM also accepted, without talking about it much, that the Society, like them, was mortal, and might not last much longer. They savoured some of the darker sayings of the *Principles*:

> 'If you have given your whole life to God, why should you prefer to lose it in this way rather than that?'[51]

But there was also the activist side of Fr Kelly. In 1980 Ralph Martin and the Director were saying that the Society had been wrongly typecast as monastic. It was a missionary order, like the Jesuits, there for the work.[52] Brethren might joke about having to become contemplatives in their old age, but until then some of them were busy, and went where work offered. Gilbert Sinden, for example, was ten years Director of Studies at St George's College, Jerusalem from 1979 to 1989.[53] There was a living strand in SSM of members who would go off individually, were happy to have one of the SSM family stay with them occasionally, and came home only to go off again. The Society had an ambiguous feeling about these: 'often we felt we, too, would like to be on detached service!'[54]

With the next Director, Fr Edmund Wheat (1982–89)[55], there was a change of emphasis. The Society moved in a conservative direction, becoming more like a traditional religious order once again. The Director himself was likely to talk about 'middle-aged trendies – not always a pretty sight'.[56] First there was the question of the admission of women. There had been a time, in the memory of many of the brethren, when women were not even allowed to cross the doorstep of an SSM house. But now there were priories in England and Australia, at Willen and Crafers, where women had lived for several years within the community, with the status of Associates. The 1977 Great Chapter had opened Associateship to everybody, including married couples and non-Anglicans. Paul Hume, once Director, proposed a resolution for discussion at the 1982 Great Chapter 'That unmarried women associates who have been associates for a minimum of three years should be eligible for membership of the Society'.[57] The Great Chapter decided not to admit women to profession, but agreed to association for an indefinite period, to a province, not merely to a priory.[58] But the two provinces concerned, England and Australia, that same year voted not to implement the resolution. The women continued to belong to the community at Willen, but they were no longer called associates. After things had gone so far, a wrong was done, even if the decision was the right one for the Society. There had been, they confessed,

> deeply felt fears and worries... We acknowledged what we were and of what we are capable, with no attempt at pretence.[59]

The 1989 General Chapter confirmed the Provinces' action.

More positively, the Society tried again with young men. The Church of England had closed all its pre-theological colleges, such as Bernard Gilpin Society and Brasted. It was presumed that a well-motivated student could find qualifications, part-time if need be, enough to get into theological college, if not university. This militated against men from a working-class background, who were expected to undertake private study with nowhere to study and no support from family or peer-groups. A group in Durham called OASIS (Ordinands Assistance and Support including Study) approached the Society in 1983[60] asking them to consider setting up a small college for such students at Durham. This was opened in 1985, in an old rectory set back from Claypath, an attractive, but busy, street in the city of Durham. The Society's postulants spent the first few months crowded in an annexe on the main street, thinking thoughts of Vassall Road. The Society has since built a very beautiful octagonal chapel, with a central altar, onto the main house. By 1992 the Durham priory had twelve residents, most of them young students, living a life reminiscent of the early days of SSM. There were young men in cassocks (smarter than they were at Vassall Road); there was the possibility, lost in most small priories, of good church singing; and if they did not have the Kelham library they were in a university city with scholarship around.

There were two sides to the college's work. First, it served as a non-residential centre for the ordinands of the Durham diocese, keeping an eye on their reading, sometimes setting them essays, and indeed running some courses for them. As support[61] for those not yet ready for theological college, including some women ordinands, it worked well. The second side of the work was residential, for young men who needed a change of environment to get down to study. The residential college, as it became known, found candidates from all over the country, but failed to produce ordinands. Jonathan Ewer, the Australian prior, who had been prior at St Michael's House, reported in 1989:

> Of the thirteen people who have lived in the priory . . . four have gone into the nursing or caring industry, one had a crack at the noviciate and left, one went to Ghana to help Ralph [Ralph Martin SSM was running a theological college], three have gone on with their education elsewhere, one has gone back into the Air Force, and another is hoping to rejoin us after a year or so away to get himself together. Of one we have not heard a word since he left us!
>
> Circumstances have forced us to realise, I think, that we have been called to prepare people for *ministry*, but not necessarily for the *ordained* ministry.[62]

If this college were run by a church to breed clergy, it would be closed. The Society has no formula for breeding novices, and this would not succeed as one. But the work done is educative, and the students gain GCSEs (or more) and confidence, and quite likely something of a Christian understanding of their lives. The Society, for its part, has found a work to do, with a priory that feels like a real place, and young people around willing to share the time-table and customs of a religious community.

> So it's Mass and Offices, scapulars and silence, departments and house-lists, and endless arguments about the value (or lack of value) of these things.[63]

Around the Durham work, the Society was finding nov-ices. In 1987, after a five year gap, two new brethren were professed, and there were others coming up. They even had to delay selling the Lancaster house for a time. To the Director's covert amusement, the new generation were more traditionalist than the old.

To replace the Manchester priory, where the theologian Hilary Greenwood had lived out urban theology, the Province found another parish, this time in Middles-brough.[65] It was, significantly, a historic Anglo-Catholic parish [66] in a run-down inner city. It contrasted with the Manchester parish in being largely white. Fr Wheat himself became prior there, and drew contrasts with St Mark's, Sheffield,[67] nearly twenty years before. There now seemed to be emerging a definite underclass, that had never known employment. The parish was much more dangerous than Sheffield had been.[68] The Anglo-Catholic option of a poor parish, described over the years in tones that underlined the sacrifice involved in working there, has changed. The SSM, a large proportion of whose members came from the background of the respectable employed working class, felt the contrast.

One must not overdraw the shift to more traditional opinions and forms of work. The Society chose as its new Visitor in 1985 the famously left-wing David Jenkins, Bishop of Durham. In its publications Hilary Greenwood and others interpreted the Kelly tradition in theology in its least Thomist, least traditional way.

> . . . our theological tradition might be seen under the species
> of three characteristics of our founder: a reverent agnosti-
> cism in all things, including human morals; a tendency to
> teach and meditate with paradoxes; and (the ultimate para-
> dox) a slightly flippant attitude to human religion, eclipsed
> by a loving trust in the God of paradoxes.[69]

Since 1989 the Director has been Tom Brown in Australia.
The Provincial of England has been Br Rodney Hart, at
Willen. It is a change from the days of the Kelham Fathers
to have a lay brother as Provincial. In 1993, the centenary
year of the Society, new work was started in the parish of
St John's, Kennington, where the Society began. Raymond
Priestman-Hunt and Julian Thomas actually live on Vassall
Road, the very street where the 'mousehole' was a century
ago. This is intended to be predominantly a lay house, as
most of those who have recently joined the Society are lay.
A religious Society, such as SSM, needs a variety of types
of work, and this variety seems to be emerging. When the
English Province considered in 1992 where it should start
new work, it took account of the following principles,
drawn up by Rodney Hart:

> Respond to requests from the Church
> Work which is difficult or unattractive to others.
> Not running a Parish.
> Allow time for people / visitors.
> Urban Priority Area.
> Proximity to other Communities – to build links.
> Opportunity for courses / lectures.
> A predominantly lay house?[70]

Quite contrasted patterns are emerging. On the one hand
each priory has its own style and strength. Digger's Rest in
Australia resembles, but is different from, Willen. Durham
and perhaps Middlesbrough have kept more of the Kelham
tradition than either of these. Another strand is away from
priories as such. The phrase 'detached service' sounds as if
there is something anomalous in not living in a community
house. But much of the more conspicuous work of SSM
lately has been done by brethren who found a particular

task that needed one person to do it. Sometimes this meant a place almost became a priory. Thus when Gilbert Sinden was at Jerusalem, he very often had other SSM members staying with him. Jerusalem became part of the Society's map. The same is now true of the Anglican Centre in Rome, where Douglas Brown and Ralph Martin are both based.

In 1992, of the 42 members of SSM, 19 were then living in priories, that is in houses with at least 3 members. So what was called 'detached service' has become the norm. Admittedly some of those not living in priories are in nursing homes or retirement, linked by affection and past usefulness and prayer, but not available for work. Sometimes 'detached' has meant 'detached', a staging-post on the way out of the Society. There is a strand in SSM thinking, however, that is happy to see SSM people working alone. Thus there is a draft 'SSM New Rule for a New Century' by Ralph Martin.

> We recruit only those who will be useful in some aspect of God's mission to the world, and therefore those who have some skills to offer. . .
>
> This work can either be part of a team effort with other members, part of a team effort with non-Society members, or individual. . .
>
> Every piece of work, while a member is doing it, is a Society work. . . All programmes are of equal importance in the finances, prayers and concern of the Society.
>
> Thus every member, by exercising his own initiative, participates in working out the vision of the Society.

This is only a draft rule, but it is clearly within the SSM tradition. Contrast this willingness to be dispersed and to follow the work with Mirfield, where the community, as numbers have fallen, has drawn back to the mother house. CR was wisely more Oratorian than SSM in its early days; it is now more monastic.

After the passing of the large houses, Kelham and St Michael's House, the society had worries about how to train novices.[71] Both Durham, with numbers of young people under rule, and Willen and Digger's Rest, with a sense of a quiet place, relevant to the world, but apart from it, had something to offer here. Ralph Martin's new rule would dispense with the problem:

> The Society never undertakes to train anyone for a job. The candidate must come equipped to participate in the mission from the first day, and should not be accepted unless he has a job to go to.
>
> There is no noviciate since the person is not coming to study a sub-culture but to engage in the mission. They will be employed and participating from the first day. However the first three terms of membership can be for one year only and should probably be in a house with other members.

This is one strand in the current self-understanding of the Society. SSM, as the name implies, was founded as a missionary order, and movement is part of mission. 'An angel that stands still ceases to be an angel'.[72] It would be strange for a religious society to discover a task which is clearly the will of God, and yet which no-one else can or will do. Fr Kelly sometimes seemed to discover a task, sometimes described it as crucifixion, which can be God's will for us, and sometimes reminded his Society that finding it was impossible. The history of a Society with many fresh starts and some crucifixions seems apt enough if we presume they were trying to do God's will, but not normally sure how. To fall in with existing ecclesiastical structures or private whim was always possible, but the effort not to do so was worthwhile. For us to see what went towards the informed choice of thoughtful Christians, trying to do God's will in a particular place and period, is useful as history. Choices like Lancaster, Manchester, and Middlesbrough were not random. Nor were the individual choices that sent Hilary Greenwood to be Anglican chaplain in Prague, Robert Stretton to the Department of Mission and Evangelism of the Church in Wales, and Hector Lee to be Vicar of Burnley.

There is so much more to the history of SSM than Kelham. Twenty years after the closure of that college we can see that that particular institutional form of Fr Kelly's vision was only one form. As the Society goes back to Vassall Road in 1993, trying to recover its roots with a few young men puzzled what God wants them to do in a city, we can try to see some pattern in what has happened.

It would be silly to predict the future of SSM, but the past has its own value, one recognisable by the outsider and the historian, in part at least. But the SSM itself would wish it to contain as well a value, pointing beyond itself, which can be striven for, but is finally hidden from the chronicler's eye:

> This Society exists for the glory of God. It is for that we entered it, and for that we labour. We cannot do less or other. But God's glory is in himself, fulfilled by himself. . .
> We will try to do God's will, but our prayer is that it may be done, possibly by us, at least in us. . .
> Glory be to God for all things. Amen.[73]

NOTES

Chapter 1: Anglican Brotherhoods

1 'In the English church the Breviary has driven out the Missal'. W. Gresley: *Bernard Leslie* (1859) p71

2 Ten of the surviving orders were founded in the 1850s; foundations continued steadily through the century. He also lists more than 20 founded this century, and more than 25 in the rest of the Anglican communion. P.F.Anson: *The Call of the Cloister* (1956) Appendix 1b 591–3

3 W.S.F.Pickering: *Anglo-Catholicism: a study in religious ambiguity* 1989 131

4 The Sisters of Mercy. See Anson op.cit. 225

5 Quoted by G.W.E.Russell in his 'Life of Dr Pusey' in *Leaders of the Church* 58–9

6 'Matins was recited overnight at first, but then put back to the early morning.
   5.00 a.m. Rise
   5.20 Matins and Lauds'.
   Anson, op.cit. 233

7 Margaret Goodman: *Sisterhoods in the Church of England* 1863 6

8 'May I see the monastery?' was the enquiry. 'We have no monasteries here,' Newman replied, slamming the door in the Warden of Wadham's face. Mark Pattison: *Memoirs* 1885 190

9 The figures are based on Anson's lists. In the 1880s there was also a successful foundation in America, and a missionary order in India. P.F.Anson, op.cit. 1956: Appendices 1a, 2a, and 6a pp 590–97

10 Pickering op.cit. 1989 131

11 Statistics are difficult: Cowley refused to count, saying 'There is no constraint upon the Lord to save by many or by few'.

12 Anson op.cit. Chap.1.3 51–71

13 H.H.Kelly: *An Idea in the Working* 1967 edition 28

14 Letter of 1.12.1855 cited in C.P.S.Clarke: *The Oxford Movement and After* 1932 256

15 G.W.E.Russell: *Arthur Stanton: a Memoir* 1917 54–70

16 Anson, op.cit. 247,255

17 ibid. 305

18 A typical example is the Society of All Saints (Sisters of the Poor)

NOTES 287

at London Colney in Hertfordshire, which started in 1851 as the parish sisters for All Saints, Margaret Street, in London.

19 See the carefully compiled figures, late in the reign, from York, not a very poor city, in Seebohm Rowntree: *Poverty, a study in town life* (1900).

20 Anson, op.cit. 41

21 Denis Gwyn: *Father Dominic Barberi* (1947) 207

22 An unpublished history of the All Saints Community, cited in Anson, op.cit. 319

23 In every census between 1871 and 1921 there was evidence that 10%-12% of men never married. (Figures for single women are less clear evidence of a choice not to marry). Kenneth D. Brown, *A Social History of the Nonconformist Ministry in England and Wales 1800-1930* (1988) 171

24 Archbishop Benson in 1895 wrote of encountering 'the most comically audacious Mother in the Universe'.
A.C.Benson: *Life of Archbishop Benson* Vol.1 1899: 273

25 There is a chapter on 'Complete and austere institutions' in Michel Foucault: *Discipline and Punish* 1979

26 A.M.Allchin in *The Silent Rebellion* has two chapters on 'The Church Congresses' and 'The Convocations' filled with quotations from dignitaries advocating, in the 1860s, sisterhoods, then in the 1880s, brotherhoods.

27 By 1882 more than half the churches in London had robed choirs. Owen Chadwick: *The Victorian Church* Vol.2 318

28 P.F.Anson: op.cit. 98

29 J.H.Newman: *Loss and Gain* (first published 1848); Compton Mackenzie: *Sinister Street* (1913), and *The Altar Steps* (1922)

30 P.F.Anson: *The Benedictines of Caldey* (1940); and J.G.Lockhart: *Viscount Halifax* Vol.2 208

31 Fr William Sirr, then of the Society of the Divine Compassion, around 1902. Geoffrey Curtis: *William of Glasshampton: Friar: Monk: Solitary* (1947)

32 P.F.Anson, op.cit. (1956) 106–22

33 Bernard Aspinwall: 'Roman Catholic Orders in the 19th-Century' in W.J.Sheils: *Monks, Hermits and the Ascetic Tradition* SCH Vol.22 1985: 361

34 *Congress Report* 160

35 Peter d'A. Jones: *The Christian Socialist Revival, 1877–1914* (1968) 164

36 G.Bernard Shaw: *Plays Pleasant* (1946 edition) Preface

37 Fr Ignatius of Llanthony, quoted in Anson, op.cit. 61

38 There is abundant evidence for all this in Anson, op.cit. chapters 1.6,1.7, and 1.9.

39 In R. Mudie-Smith (ed): op.cit. 196

40 H.H.Kelly: *The History of a Religious Idea* (1898) 3

Chapter 2: Early Days

1 *Ad Fratres* (1906) in H.H.Kelly: *No Pious Person* (1960) 93 (It is 'are' in the final phrase).
2 George Every has three pages 'mainly from notes left by Father Kelly and his brother, Father Alfred' in *No Pious Person*, 19–21. 'What little 'society' there was lived on the opposite side'. 25
3 ibid. 36
4 ibid. 26–7
5 ibid. 35
6 ibid. 36
7 ibid. 37
8 His sermons as vicar of St Peter's, Eaton Square, the society church in Kensington, were widely admired, and taken down for publication by the authoress of 'Tell me the old old story'. A.J.Mason: *Memoir of George Howard Wilkinson* (1910) 214
9 H.H.Kelly: op.cit. 38
10 H.H.Kelly: Manuscript 'Autobiography', copied in *SSM Chronicle* 229
11 '. . . he was perhaps above all others my father; and so far as I can picture Jesus Christ, I picture him as not unlike the father whom I have lost'. Temple, quoted in D.L.Edwards: *Leaders of the Church of England 1828–1944* (1971) 272
12 SSM:DIR/AR/1
13 JSSM 7.10.1893
14 H.H.Kelly: op.cit. (1908) 8
15 H.H.Kelly: op.cit. (1960) 44
16 Jeffrey Cox: *The English Churches in a Secular Society, Lambeth 1870 – 1930* (1982) 42
17 SSM:Newscuttings Vol.1 [The spelling is here Korea]
18 H.H.Kelly: op.cit. (1898) 12
19 H.H.Kelly: op.cit. (1960) 44
20 H.H.Kelly: *The Missionary Brotherhood in Corea* (undated pamphlet)
21 H.H.Kelly: op.cit. (1908) 15–16
22 H.H.Kelly: op.cit. (1898) 103
23 There is a picture of the house, in the *History of a Religious Idea*. The relevant map in Charles Booth's *Life and Labour in London* (Religious Influences vol.VI Outer South London) 1902, facing 96, colours it as 'Fairly Comfortable', one step down from 'Well-to-do'.
24 *SSMQP* Michaelmas 1920
25 SSM:JCMB 6.8.1891
26 *Guardian* August 1891
27 SSM:DIR/AR/1 Director's Report 1893
28 SSM:JCMB 26 and 28 Apr. 1892
29 H.H.Kelly: op.cit. (1908) 17
30 H.H.Kelly: op.cit. (1898) 180

31 SSM:DIR/AR/1
32 eg JSSM 28.9.1892 Compline ... sermon by Father Director on
    the duties and dangers of a Festival: Huc usque auxiliatus est nobis
    Dominus.
33 JSSM Michaelmas 1892
34 A.W.Jones: *Herbert Hamilton Kelly, SSM, 1860-1950: a study in
    failure* (unpublished Nottingham Ph.D. thesis, 1971)
35 SSM:HK/Corres. 1890–91
36 SSM:HK/Corres. 1890–91, and see DIR/AR/1 Report 1891
37 P.F.Anson: *The Call of the Cloister* 424, 425
38 JSSM 28 Oct. and 12 Nov. 1892
39 Randall Davidson, Bp of Rochester 20.3.1893.: SSM:HK/ Corres.
    1892–3
40 11.7.1896, SSM/HK Corres. 1896–7
41 Letter to Fr Stephen Bedale, cited in *SSM Chronicle* 246
42 JSSM 14.11.1893
43 JSSM 21.12 1892
44 JCMB 24.8.1892 and Director's Report 1892, SSM:DIR/AR/1
45 The photograph is reproduced in H.H.Kelly, op.cit. (1898)
46 JSSM 9.5.1893
47 Cp. H.H.Kelly: op.cit. (1960) 60
48 JSSM 17.9.1893
49 JSSM 2.10.1893
50 Arthur Laws, 27.6.1895 SSM:HK/Corres. 1895
51 ibid.
52 SSM Records no.27: The bound volume of Records tabulates
    'Name. Birth. Home. Application. Entered. Novitiate. Final Profes-
    sion. Went Out. Vowed. Previous Education. Trade. Examinations.
    Diocese. Work assigned.' It is sometimes very brief.
53 HHK to Bridle, 21.7.1901 SSM:HK/C/LB/3/2
54 Director's Report 1893 SSM:DIR/AR/1
55 Director's Report 1894 SSM:DIR/AR/1
56 Director's Report 1900 (127) SSM:DIR/AR/1; and cp., for exam-
    ple, the quotation from Kelly (1911) cited by Fr R. Martin in *SSM*
    1978.
57 H.H.Kelly: op.cit. (1960) 43
58 H.H.Kelly: op.cit. (1898) 19
59 H.H.Kelly: op.cit. (1908) 28–9
60 H.H.Kelly: op.cit. (1960) 101
61 Kenneth D. Brown: *A Social History of the Nonconformist Ministry in
    England and Wales 1800–1930* (1988) 108
62 *Constitution of the Society of the Sacred Mission* 1893
63 HHK, Easter Day 1902: SSM:HK/C/LB/3/1
64 Director's Report 1892 SSM:DIR/AR/1
65 H.H.Kelly: op.cit. (1908) 41
66 H.H.Kelly: *Ad fratres* (typescript 1906)
67 ibid.

68 Director's Report 1897 (p81) SSM:DIR/AR/1
69 ibid. 1898 (p103) The tradition of SSM includes memories of 'the discipline', a too-easily-overheard whip.
70 SSM:DIR/AR/1 91
71 19.11.1901
72 HK to Fr Drake, 5.8.1903 SSM:HK/C/LB/3/1
73 Fr David Jenks: Newsletter 23.2.1911 SSM/BR/Jenks
74 SSM:DIR/AR/1&2 174
75 ibid. 198

Chapter 3: Who Joined SSM?

1   Obituary in SSMQ March 1960
2   See letter from Fr D. Jenks, 11.9.1899, SSM: BR/Jenks
3   SSM: South Africa file: S.A.History. Undated letter, c1904, probably by Fr A.D.Kelly, then Provincial of South Africa.
4   SSM:BR/ADK: Scurrilities file *Scala Coeli or the Path to Olympus* c1920
5   SSM:BR/ADK Diary 1942 [*Periit* means 'died' in Latin.]
6   See J.F.Coakley: *The Church of the East and the Church of England* 1992. He was rather accident prone.
7   'I was only kept from going to Rome by being certain that it must be wrong to go in despair and impatience'. Undated letter from Mildenhall, SSM:BR/Jenks
8   MS memories of Kelly and Jenks, by Fr Couldrey, SSM:BR/Couldrey
9   Couldrey op.cit.
10 Obituary in the *Guardian* 29.3.1935
11 SSM: D.Jenks: NL 22.10.1911
12 SSM:BR/Amor
13 SSM:BR/Neate
14 Obituary in SSMQ September 1959
15 SSM:BR/Goodey
16 Obituary in SSMQ March 1968
17 Couldrey, op.cit. 2 and 4
18 *SSM Chronicle* 251
19 ibid. 242
20 ibid. 202
21 Fr E. Wheat, Director, in funeral address March 1987, *SSM Chronicle* [*Supplement*]
22 Ledbitter, Preece, and Wyllie; Fr Hubert Hilder died naturally in 1917.
23 Obituary in May 1981 *SSM*
24 SSM:HK NL 4.7.1931
25 Hilary Greenwood, in November 1980 *SSM*
26 I owe this point to Fr Ralph Martin.

27 I owe this reference to Fr Hilary Greenwood, who shared a room with the original. There is a letter from Davies confirming this.

Chapter 4: How To Teach Theological Students

1 H.H.Kelly, op.cit. (1908) 17
2 *SSM Chronicle* 25
3 C.F.Pascoe: *Two Hundred Years of the S.P.G.* (1901) lists 6 names in the Missionary Roll for Korea to 1892. The Bishop and Fr Trollope were graduates, Fr Small had gone back to British Columbia, the other three were as listed. 8 more had been, and some had gone, by 1900. Of these 8, 3 are listed as SSM, another two, including Fr Drake (himself a graduate) were SSM, but not listed as such, and there was one Oxford man, who had gone to China after two years, one medical man (MRCS and LCRP), and a Dane, working among the Japanese in Korea, and in 1900 in fact back in Japan.
4 C.P.Williams: "Not Quite Gentlemen': an Examination of 'Middling Class' Protestant Missionaries from Britain, c1850–1900', JEH 31, no.3, July 1980 301–15
5 Eugene Stock: *History of the C.M.S.* (1899) Vol.3 703
6 C.F.Pascoe: op.cit. 780–1
7 Alan Haig: *The Victorian Clergy* 1984 191; ' . . . the list included Hooker, Pearson, Butler's *Sermons*, and Wall (on Baptism); Wilberforce's own *Addresses* were later a specially recommended item'. (footnote p210)
8 George Eliot: *Scenes from Clerical Life* (Penguin English Library 1973 53
9 Haig, op.cit. 1984 190
10 *The Times* 2.1.1864. 'Literate' was the technical term for a nongraduate ordinand.
11 See Alan Haig's chapter 'The Training of Non-Graduate Clergy', in op.cit. 116–176.
12 H.H.Kelly: *England and the Church* 1902 176
13 Baylee, Principal of St Aidan's, quoted in Brian Heeney: *A Different Kind of Gentleman* 1976 105
14 Haig, op.cit. 136. In the 1960s Tony Coxon contrasted 'normal' and 'late' recruitment; 'late', unlike 'normal', was nongraduate, and from a lower social status. A.P.M.Coxon: 'Patterns of Occupational Recruitment: the Anglican Ministry' *Sociology* vol.1 1967 73–79
15 H.H.Kelly: *Personal Thoughts Concerning Unity* 14
16 H.H.Kelly: *Training for Ordination* 1901 (privately printed, Mildenhall) 10
17 H.H.Kelly: *On the Continuation of Study* 1919 17
18 H.H.Kelly: *The Church and the Ordination Question* 1907 9
19 H.H.Kelly: *An Idea in the Working* 1908 19
20 ibid. 20

21 Quoted in A.W.Jones: 'H.H.Kelly: a study in failure' (unpublished Nottingham Ph.D. thesis) 1971 51

22 Robert Towler and A.P.M.Coxon: *The Fate of the Anglican Clergy* (1979) see these shorts as significant: 'One important feature of the total institution, according to [E.] Goffman ['The character of total institutions' in A.Etzioni: *Complex Organisations* (1961)] is a series of mortification processes... The process is typically an entirely open one, and is clearly seen in the stripping and bathing which mark admissions to prisons and mental hospitals. The new student [at Kelham], who was called a 'probationer', wore civilian clothes, while other students wore a modified monastic habit; at one time the probationer was required to wear short trousers, but even ordinary clothing served to mark the newcomer as an outsider'. (p124–5) Members of SSM were unconvinced by this analysis.

23 H.H.Kelly: op.cit. 1898: 95

24 H.H.Kelly: *Training for Ordination* 1901 (privately printed, Mildenhall) 16

25 H.H.Kelly: op.cit. 1908 44

26 H.H.Kelly: *The Church and the Ordination Question* 1907 22

27 Haig, op.cit. 156,157

28 H.H.Kelly: op.cit. 1898 144

29 George Every: 'Memoir of Father Kelly' in H.H.Kelly: *The Gospel of God* 1959 20

30 H.H.Kelly: op.cit. 1898: 145–6

31 ibid. 150

32 ibid. 155

33 John Garrett Lloyd: 'The S.S.M.: a talk with its director', from *The Treasury* May 1906 [Loose in the front of a bound volume of News Cuttings, Vol.1, in the SSM archive]

34 H.H.Kelly: *England and the Church* 1902 81

35 Typescript Church History I

36 H.H.Kelly: op.cit. 1908 75–6

37 H.H.Kelly: *SSM, A Vindication of its Principles* 1901 23

38 H.H.Kelly: 'The Universities and Training for the Clergy' *University Review* 1908, 8–9

39 George Davie, in his book *The Democratic Intellect*, argued that the old Scottish universities worked with first year students on great philosophical generalities, and that 'reformers' from England in the 19th century struggled to make the work more specialist.

40 H.H.Kelly: *Memorandum on Theological Education (The Kelham System)* 1909, 13

41 ibid.

42 Cited in H.H.Kelly: *Memorandum on Theological Education (The Kelham System)* 1909 8

43 H.H.Kelly: 'The Universities and Training for the Clergy' *University Review* 1908, 7

44 H.H.Kelly: *Memorandum on Theological Education* (*The Kelham System*) 2
45 ibid.
46 H.H.Kelly: *Ad Fratres* de fest. soc. 1906, 20
47 H.H.Kelly: *Memorandum on Theological Education* (*The Kelham System*) 1909 5

Chapter 5: Kelham Theology

1 G.Every (ed): *No Pious Person*, 1960 14
2 H.H.Kelly: *Gospel of God* 102
3 SSM/HK/NL/4.11.1908
4 H.H.Kelly: *Gospel of God* 132,133
5 H.H.Kelly: Ad Fratres 1906
6 J.R.H.Moorman: *B.K.Cunningham* 100–1
7 All this is from the SSM Quarterly Paper and Report 1901.
8 H.H.Kelly: *Personal Thoughts Concerning Unity* 1927
9 There is a complete list of his writings in Alan Jones's unpublished Nottingham thesis 'H.H.Kelly: a study in failure', 1971
10 H.H.Kelly: op.cit. 131
11 ibid. 125–6
12 ibid. 52
13 ibid. 69
14 ibid. 115
15 ibid. 54
16 ibid. 91
17 ibid. 55
18 ibid. 69
19 ibid.
20 ibid. 80–1
21 ibid. 70
22 ibid. 82
23 ibid. 104
24 ibid. 92
25 ibid. 88
26 ibid. 99
27 ibid. 101
28 ibid. 105
29 ibid. 107
30 ibid. 111
31 ibid. 119 This came from a Jesuit preacher.
32 ibid. 118
33 ibid. 120
34 ibid. 124
35 ibid. 133
36 ibid.
37 ibid. 134

38 ibid. 142
39 ibid. 141–2
40 ibid. 149. Bp Michael Ramsey, at the Kelly Centenary in 1960, recalled this passage, referring it from memory to the genealogies in Matthew and Luke. It is reminiscent of a section from Scott Holland 'As we glance down that long list of our Lord's forefathers . . . so stiff and legal, and monotonous . . . the record of the burden which the centuries had slowly built together for the Lord to carry. . .' *On Behalf of Belief* 193ff (cited in D.M.McKinnon: *Borderlands of Belief* 111–12)
41 op.cit. 5
42 *De Deo* – Historical Theology, section 11
43 F.Maurice: *Life of F.D.Maurice*, I 54
44 *Personal Thoughts Concerning Unity*, unpublished 1927.
45 F.Maurice, op.cit. II 137
46 F.D.Maurice: *Kingdom of Christ* (Everyman, vol. 1. 292)
47 Adolf von Harnack: *Expansion of Christianity* Vol. 1 294
48 H.H.Kelly: op.cit. 1927
49 F.D.Maurice: *Kingdom of Christ* (Everyman, vol.1 4)
50 Cited in Torben Christensen, *Origin and History of Christian Socialism* p306).
51 F.D.Maurice: *Kingdom of Christ* (Everyman, vol. 1 7)
52 Quoted in F.D.Maurice, op.cit. 1 13
53 F.D.Maurice: *Sacrifice* 221
54 David Newsome: *Two Classes of Men* 82–3
55 Newsome, ibid. 113
56 Torben Christensen: *The Divine Order* 158
57 F.D.Maurice, op.cit. 1 5
58 H.H.Kelly: 'On the Meaning of Church History', Christmas 1919 SSMQP
59 F.A.Iremonger: *William Temple* 532
60 H.H.Kelly: *Ad Filios*, unpublished history for students, (c.1920)
61 H.H.Kelly: *Personal Thoughts Concerning Unity*, 1927
62 H.H.Kelly: *Ad Filios*, c1920
63 H.H.Kelly: *The Use of the Old Testament*, 1913
64 H.H.Kelly: 'On the Meaning of Church History', Christmas 1919 SSMQP
65 H.H.Kelly: *History of a Religious Idea* 1898
66 Fr Stephen Bedale, writing Fr Kelly's obituary, December 1950 SSMQP
67 Letter 14.2.1934, cited in *No Pious Person*, 133
68 William Temple: *Nature, Man and God*, 318
69 S.Bedale, op.cit.
70 H.H.Kelly: *Ad Filios*, op.cit. c1920
71 S.Bedale, op.cit.
72 H.P.Liddon: *Life of Pusey* III 108
73 H.H.Kelly: typescript *Autobiography*, c1929–31

74 A letter from a Miss Wordsworth in Japan, quoted in the 30 October 1913 SSM *Newsletter*.
75 H.H.Kelly: typescript *Autobiography*, c1929–31
76 H.H.Kelly: *The Use of the Old Testament*, 1913
77 op.cit. 159 (1970 ed)
78 H.H.Kelly: *Personal Thoughts Concerning Unity*, 1927
79 F.D.Maurice: *Sacrifice* XI–II
80 *SSM Chronicle* 39
81 Cited in Iremonger's *William Temple* 86.
82 *SSM Chronicle* 36
83 B. Yogata 'Fr Kelly and the Japanese Church', SSMQP March 1960.
84 *SSM Chronicle* 53
85 ibid. 114

Chapter 6: Kelham And Ecumenism

1 Statistics from Eleanor M.Jackson: *Red Tape and the Gospel*, 20 and 32.
2 Most male students were less fiercely policed, but this aspect of it was relevant for Kelham men. 'The Rose Garden at Swanwick is no place for a Kelham student after compline' (Fr Theodore Smith, Warden of Kelham, according to Fr Ralph Martin).
3 Tissington Tatlow: *The Story of the S.C.M.* 34
4 Anon: *Fifty years Work of the YMCA 1844–1894*, 157
5 H.H.Kelly: op.cit. 1908 28–9
6 Basil Mathews: *John R. Mott: World Citizen* 144
7 H.H.Kelly: *No Pious Person* 9
8 Tatlow, op.cit. 437
9 ibid. 137
10 ibid. 137, 138
11 op.cit. 8
12 *Theology*, Oct. 1939 259–60
13 SSM:HK/SCM/'SCM Swanwick 1911–12' 1
14 ibid.
15 H.H.Kelly: *Tract on Unity* 1909 2
16 SSM:HK/SCM/Report on Swanwick, 9–16 July 1912, 237
17 SSM:HK/SCM/'Swanwick Tips' 1912
18 SSM:HK/SCM/'SCM Swanwick 1911–12' 2
19 ibid. 8
20 op.cit. 4
21 ibid. 5
22 Tatlow, op.cit. 158
23 ibid. 145
24 ibid. 393
25 ibid.
26 *The Object and Method of Conference* 1915

27 SSMQP, September 1910
28 H.H.Kelly: ibid.
29 *World Missionary Conference*, 1910, supplement to the Report of Commission V, 312
30 ibid.
31 SSM:HK/SCM/'SCM Swanwick 1911–12'
32 George Every: Memoir, in *The Gospel of God*, 25
33 H.H.Kelly: 'The Present Condition of Theological Movement in America', a paper presented to J.R.Mott in 1912.
34 H.H.Kelly, ibid., quoted in *No Pious Person*, 119–20
35 H.H.Kelly: *Personal Thoughts Concerning Unity*
36 Tatlow, op.cit. 800–1
37 F.A.Iremonger: *William Temple* 109
38 Bp Greer of Manchester, reminiscing at the Kelly centenary meeting in Manchester in 1960, SSMQ September 1960.
39 Iremonger, op.cit. 102
40 ibid. 488
41 Preface to H.H.Kelly: *Catholicity*
42 Review in *The Student Movement* 1928, cited in preface to *The Gospel of God*, p33
43 *SSM Chronicle*, 149
44 Iremonger, op.cit. 608
45 Preface to H.H.Kelly: *Catholicity*
46 op.cit. 90
47 Cited in Iremonger, op.cit. 326
48 Iremonger, op.cit. 532–3
49 Dorothy Emmet, in ibid. 535
50 ibid. 575
51 In 1942, cited in Iremonger, op.cit. 510
52 P.T.Forsyth: *The Grace of the Gospel* (1905)
53 SSM:HK/Report Swanwick 9–16 July 1912 237–8
54 Gwilym O. Griffith: *The Theology of P.T.Forsyth* 100
55 F.D.E. Schleiermacher: *On Religion* (Harper Row) 88
56 Forsyth, cited in J.S. Whale: *Victor and Victim*, 18
57 Griffith, op.cit. 27
58 P.T.Forsyth: *Holy Christian Empire* 1902
59 Griffith, op.cit. 103
60 P.T.Forsyth: *The Grace of the Gospel* (1905)
61 P.T.Forsyth: *The Work of Christ* 62

Chapter 7: Kelham And Anglo-Catholicism

1 Compton Mackenzie: *Sinister Street*
2 'I really don't see why you should be surprised at the conduct of your fathers-in-God. After all, the sign of a Bishop is a crook and of an Archbishop a double-cross'. (Attributed to Dom Gregory Dix, in Hugh Ross Williamson: *The Walled Garden*, p144) Fr Peter Clark, SSM, in later years used to say 'Never trust the bishops'.

3 SSMQP Easter 1942

4 SSM/HK/Corres., to Brown 13.9.1923

5 SSM/HK/Corres. 9.4. 1923

6 Obituary by Stephen Bedale in SSMQ June 1950

7 Bp of Chester, in Christmas 1924 SSMQ

8 SSM/BR/Couldrey MS Notes by Fr Edmund Couldrey.

9 SSM/HK/NL 31.10.1907

10 From Hilary Greenwood's obituary of him in November 1980 SSM.

11 In the whole history of SSM, there have been very few non-Kelham-trained priests join the Society.

12 SSM/HK/Corres. 14.6.1921

13 H.H.Kelly: typescript *SSM, 1929*

14 Fr Joseph White, Director of SSM, Great Chapter Minutes, 7 July 1920

15 SSM/HK/NL 3.8.1920

16 SSMQ, Easter 1925

17 SSM/HK/Corres., Stephen Bedale to HK, 13.9.1930

18 C.J.Corfe: *The Anglican Church in Corea* 1905 (Seoul) (Documents appended). Fr Drake of SSM, on detached service in Korea, wrote frequently for the SSM Quarterly. His lively letters presume Anglo-Catholic practice: one of his stories turns on his dawning recognition that the pyx in a church he was visiting was actually a silver-plated mustardpot (SSMQ Easter 1923). That they needed a pyx for reservation of the Blessed Sacrament went without saying.

19 Constance Trollope: *Mark Napier Trollope* 1936 143–4

20 'The Development of the Native Church in Worship', in E.R.Morgan (ed): *Essays Catholic and Missionary* 1928, 210 ibid.

21 SSMQ Whitsuntide 1919

22 ibid.

23 H.H.Kelly: typescript *SSM, 1929*

24 eg Bp Neville Talbot of Pretoria, SSM/HK/Corres. Letter to HK, 7.5.1921

25 SSM/HK/NL 17.1911

26 'It was you, not I, who threatened to go if GDC were elected.' Letter to Fr C.Whitworth, SSM/HK/Corres. 14.5.1922

27 SSM/BR/Rand

28 SSM/BR/Rand, 16.11.1917

29 ibid. 23.11.1917

30 ibid.

31 ibid. 23.11.1917

32 SSM/HK/Corres. 15.10.1917

33 SSM/HK/Corres. 7.12.1917

34 Hilder, op.cit.

35 SSM/HK/Corres. 13.6.1917

36 Minutes of Great Chapter 1920

37 SSM/BR/Carleton 23.1.1923

38 G.D.Carleton: *A Review of my History at SSM* – typescript 1924
39 *SSM Chronicle* 124
40 SSM/HK/NL 5.12.1920
41 H.H.Kelly: typescript *SSM 1929* 'Tarping', from the initials, is taking the ablutions at the Roman (or 'right') place.
42 H.H.Kelly: *Autobiography*
43 SSM/HK/Corres. Letter to Stephen Bedale, Michaelmas 1931
44 SSMQ Michaelmas 1915
45 SSM/HK/Corres. Letter to Stephen Bedale, January 1925
46 A.W.Jones, op.cit. 256
47 SSM/HK/Corres. 7.8.1924
48 Church Times, 20 July 1923
49 7.7.1925 Minutes of Great Chapter 1925, 75
50 SSM/HK/Corres. Fr Stephen Bedale to HHK, 29.1.1925
51 SSM/HK/NL October/November 1928
52 SSM/HK/Corres. November, 1927–8
53 SSM/HK/NL/8.12.1932
54 SSM Constitution
55 A comment from Nashdom, quoted in Colin Stephenson: *Merrily on High* 55
56 Br George Every, typescript autobiographical fragment, 87
57 SSM/HK/NL 14.12.1933
58 Fr S. Bedale at the SSM London Reunion, SSMQP Christmas 1922
59 Church Times, 11 July 1930, cited in W.S.F.Pickering: *Anglo-Catholicism: a study in religious ambiguity*, 60
60 cp. 'The Christian tradition of noblesse oblige out of which CR grew was immensely self-sacrificial in its giving, but not in its receiving'. Alan Wilkinson: *The Community of the Resurrection: a centenary history* 251
61 SSM/BR/A.D.Kelly 21.2.1918 newsletter
62 H.H.Kelly: *Review of the Position of the S.S.M.* 1909
63 SSM/HK/NL Feb. 1928
64 SSM/HK/Corres. 19.2.1929 Talbot nevertheless represented the non-spikey side of Mirfield. See Alan Wilkinson: op.cit.
65 SSM/HK/NL 9.1.1908
66 SSM/HK/Corres. 26.10.1924
67 H.H.Kelly: *Review of the Position of the S.S.M.* 1909
68 SSM/HK/NL November 1929
69 Another tradition says he was retrieving a kite.

Chapter 8: The Golden Age Of Kelham

1 H.H.Kelly: op.cit. 69
2 H.H.Kelly: *Ad Filios*, a history of SSM (undated typescript, c1920–21) 20
3 H.H.Kelly: *An Idea in the Working*, 70

4 SSM/Fr.D.Jenks (Director) NL 22.10.1911
5 SSMQ Whitsuntide 1919
6 SSM/BR/Carleton 13.7.1922
7 SSM/HK/NL September 1927
8 SSM/HK/Corres. 24.10.1947
9 SSM/HK/1937
10 op.cit. 4
11 ibid. 5
12 ibid.
13 ibid. 6
14 ibid. 9
15 SSM/HK/Corres. undated 1922–3
16 ibid.
17 SSM/BR/Jenks Newsletter 16.2.1911
18 Fr White, third Director, in SSMQ September 1921
19 Conversation with Fr Ralph Martin, January 1993
20 SSM/BR/Herold 10.8.1933
21 ibid. A later generation might have agreed with Fr Herold. 'When
   a person terminates his membership there should be a public service
   of thanksgiving for all that has been accomplished . . .' Fr Ralph
   Martin: SSM: New Rule for a New Century 1993
22 Minutes of Great Chapter 1925 90
23 SSM/HK/NL 21.11.1908
24 Minutes of Great Chapter 1925 90
25 ibid.
26 ibid. 96
27 Minutes of Mother House Chapter 17.3.1936 and 10.11.1936
28 ibid. 17.3.1936
29 Sports Captain, SSMQ Christmas 1920
30 SSMQ June 1934
31 SSMQ June 1930
32 HK writing to a Scot, T.F.Taylor. SSM/HK/Corres. 21.4.1938
33 SSMQ Christmas 1924
34 SSM/English Province Minutes, 8.5.1935
35 SSMQ June 1938
36 SSM/ Memorandum on proposed extension of Kelham 20.7.1938
   (attached to Minutes of Mother House Chapter 29.7.1938)
37 SSM/BR/Snell Diary 23.9.1946
38 SSM/Minutes of Kelham Province, 1.10.1943
39 SSM/HK/NL 12.11.1908
40 Roger Lloyd, op.cit. 192–3
41 SSMQ Christmas 1933
42 SSMQ Christmas 1927
43 Julius Rieger: 'Contacts with London', pp97–8 in W-D.Zimmer-
   mann and R.G.Smith: I Knew Dietrich Bonhoeffer
44 SSM/HK/NL October-November 1928
45 The Architect: 19.4.1929

46 *SSM Chronicle* 152
47 SSMQ Christmas 1936
48 *SSM Chronicle* 155
49 SSM/HK/NL 5.10.1927
50 Fr A.D.Kelly, in SSMQ Christmas 1933
51 SSM/Minutes of Kelham Province, 13.4.1943
52 George Every: *Modern Monasticism* (undated)
53 SSM/HK/'Excuses' to Stephen Bedale 26.9.1930
54 ibid.
55 Fr Alfred Kelly, SSMQ Easter 1932
56 Br George Every: op.cit.
57 Fr Gregory Wilkins in 1980, in *SSM Chronicle*, 138
58 T.S.Eliot at 1935 SSM London Reunion, SSMQ Christmas 1935
59 SSM/BR/Every 11.6.1944

Chapter 9: The Work Of Father Hebert

1 SSM/HK/NL 4.7.1931
2 *SSM Chronicle* 103
3 Parish Magazine, Horbury, where he was curate, September 1913
4 Obituary in *The Anglican* 25 July 1963
5 Canon J. Edwards 24.7.1963, SSM/BR/Hebert, Personal
6 SSM/BR/Hebert 22.11.1921 Letters Sent
7 SSM/BR/Hebert, Letters Sent 9.5.1922
8 SSM/BR/Hebert, Letters Sent, postscript to 31.6.1922
9 SSM/BR/Hebert, to his father 22.5.1922
10 ibid. 9.1.1924
11 ibid. 2.1.1924
12 SSM/BR/Hebert, Letters Sent 6.11.1923
13 SSMQ September 1963
14 SSM/BR/Hebert, Letters Sent 4.6.1924
15 M.Dewey: *An Idea Still Working* 1980
16 A.G.Hebert: *Liturgy and Society* 82
17 SSMQ Michaelmas 1933, cited by Hebert, op.cit. 88
18 op.cit. 98
19 A.G.Hebert: 'Belief and Authority' 1933
20 A.G.Hebert: *Liturgy and Society* 120
21 Gregory Dix, in *The Parish Communion* (edited Hebert) 1937
22 A.G.Hebert: *The Form of the Church*, 1944 88
23 *New Statesman* 13.7.1935
24 Donald Gray: *Earth and Altar* 204
25 A.G.Hebert: *Liturgy and Society* 69
26 ibid. 152
27 ibid. 157
28 ibid. 248
29 ibid. 234
30 ibid. 198

31 *Autobiography of a German Pastor*, 54–5, cited in *Form of the Church* 69

32 SSM/BR/Hebert, Parish and People 11.1.1959

33 Horton Davies: *Worship and Theology in England: the Ecumenical Century 1900–65* 39

34 See Donald Gray: *Earth and Altar*, especially Part 3, sect.1

35 C.G.Lang: *The Opportunity of the Church of England* 185

36 Hebert to R.H.Martin, 5.2.1958, in Martin Correspondence, cited in Gray, op.cit. 200

37 SSM/BR/Hebert, 31.12.1939

38 Couturier to Hebert, 30.4.1950, SSM/BR/Hebert

39 SSM/BR/Hebert Logbook, Copenhagen 6.8.1928

40 ibid. 11.8.1928

41 SSM/BR/Hebert, Sweden, letter to Hebert, 28.3.1939

42 'Thoughts of an Anglo-Catholic on the Reunion of Christendom', paper given to the Laymen's Circle at Barnet Presbyterian Church, 1931

43 SSM/BR/Hebert, Letters Sent, undated

44 SSM/BR/Hebert 1936

45 A.G.Hebert: 'On Priests' Masses'

46 Oral communication, Bengt Sundkler, 1990

47 SSM/BR/Hebert, MSS translations in Sweden file

48 Bengt Ingmar Kilström: *Högkyrkligheten i Sverige och Finland under 1900-talet* (1990) places Hebert's role in a Swedish context.

49 Hebert to H.Kühne, Jan.1939, SSM/BR/Hebert, Reviews of his Books

50 SSM/BR/Hebert, Lectures. His book *The Form of the Church* (1944) is built round the Aristotelian technical term 'form'. 'If the Spirit is necessary, so is the Form' (16), otherwise we risk saying 'there is something unspiritual in the Incarnation'. Liturgy provides 'a form requiring to be actualised in all the other actions of life' (56).

51 SSM/BR/Hebert, RC file

52 op.cit. 226

53 A.G.Hebert: 'Open Communion'

54 'Focus on Baptism' conference, May 1963, SSM/BR/Hebert Conferences

55 Bp Wand, re-reading it, was 'surprised how good and careful a book it is'. W.Wand: *Anglicanism in History and Today* 1961

56 SSM/BR/Hebert, in Reviews of His Books file, 2.2.1939

57 ibid. 28.2.1939

58 R. Newton Flew, 24.1.1933, SSM/BR/Hebert

59 30.3.1944, SSM/BR/Hebert, Reviews of his Books

60 *Modern Churchman* April 1933

61 op.cit. 119

62 A.G.Hebert: 'Theology and Theological Studies', 1955, Melbourne

63 SSM/BR/Hebert, USA

64 Gray: op.cit. 91 He was not asked back.

65 ibid. 102

66 R.H.Tribe: *Christian Social Tradition* 139

67 Fr Antony Snell, in 1981 to M.Dewey, *SSM Chronicle* 250

68 ibid. 173

69 T.S.Eliot, at the 1935 SSM Annual Reunion, *SSMQ* Christmas 1935

70 A.G.Hebert: *Liturgy and Society* 28

71 His 'Outline of Royalism' was never written. Br George Every: 'The way of rejection', in Richard March and Tambimuttu (editors) *T.S.Eliot: a Symposium* 1948

72 A.G.Hebert: *The Parish Communion* 1937, 22

73 SSM/BR/Hebert Articles etc

74 op.cit. 202

75 A.G.Hebert: *Liturgy and Society* 188

76 SSM/BR/Hebert, Lectures

77 op.cit. 230

78 ibid. 232

79 ibid. 110

80 R.H.Tribe: *Christian Social Tradition* 146

81 A.G.Hebert: 'The Christian Doctrine of Man', published by the Industrial Christian Fellowship, 1941

82 A.Wilkinson, *The Times* 18.7.1981

83 op.cit. 9

84 ibid. 205

85 A.G.Hebert: *The Authority of the Old Testament* 1947 221

86 L.B.Cross: 'The Flight from Reason in the Interpretation of the Bible', review article, *Modern Churchman* September 1949

87 ibid.

88 See his dismissal of Robert Graves, in 'Theology and Theological Study', printed lecture, Melbourne 1955.

89 Christopher Irvine, expounding Hebert: 'Hearing the Bible as Scripture', *Fairacres Chronicle*, Summer 1991

90 A.G.Hebert: *The Throne of David* (1941) 255

91 The Encyclical Letter from the bishops mentions no theologians, apart from Temple, but see, for example, 'It would, indeed be a great gain if we could cease to think and speak of "religious" as distinct from other subjects . . .' *Lambeth Conference 1948* 25

92 SSM/BR/Hebert, Corres. to Director, Easter 1954

93 SSM/BR/Hebert, Corres. 17.4.1956

94 SSM/BR/Hebert, Letters Sent 11.8.1957, to Director

95 Martin Marty, in *Christian Century*, November 1957

96 op.cit. 15

97 ibid. 71

98 ibid. 139–40

99 SSM/BR/Hebert, Letters Received, 8.7.1963, from Abbess of West Malling

100 F.D.Maurice: *Kingdom Of Christ* (SCM ed) II.163 (148 in Dent Dutton ed), cited in *God's Kingdom and Ours* (1959) 153

Chapter 10: Asia And Africa

1 In the 1890s this was the more common spelling, and the one adopted by the Anglican diocese.

2 James H. Grayson: *Korea: a religious history* (1989), chapters 10 and 11.

3 For the history of the work in Korea, I am much indebted to David Holmes: *Herbert Kelly and the Society of the Sacred Mission in Korea and Japan* (Oxford M.Litt. thesis 1990), ch.3

4 Fr Trollope refused the rank of Prior Sole, as permitted in the SSM Constitution. SSM/HK/C/LB/3/1

5 Director's Report 1893 SSM/DIR/AR/1

6 P.F.Anson: *Call of the Cloister* 390

7 Grayson op.cit. 198

8 HHK to Drake, 7.7.1898 SSM/HK/C/LB/3/1

9 *SSM Chronicle* 80

10 SSM Letterbooks Bishops, C.J.Corfe, 29.5.1901, and see HHK to Drake, 1.10.1901 SSM/HK/C/LB/3/2

11 Bridle was 'a most insufferable *snob*' HK to Drake, ibid.

12 Trollope, to Mother, Michaelmas Day 1892 (USPG X620), cited by Holmes 95

13 HHK to Trollope, 15.11.1898 SSM/HK/C/LB/3/1

14 SSM/HK/C/LB/3/2 A.F.Norton, 15.5.1904

15 H.H.Kelly: *An Idea in the Working* 88

16 D.Holmes, op.cit. 62, quoting USPG, CLRA, C.J.Corfe, 13.10.1904. On p75 he cites other letters from the bishop to SPG grumbling about SSM (CLRA, 19.3.1903, 15.12.1903).

17 HHK to Drake 18.12.1901 SSM/HK/C/LB/3/2

18 SSM/BR/ A.D.Kelly: 'Scurrilities'

19 The SPG worked in Rhodesia and Southern Africa.

20 *SSM Chronicle* p66; see MS *Autobiography*

21 Letter headed 'Retractitiones', SSM/S.Africa: Central African Province file

22 SSM/HK NL 5.7.1920

23 Fr Tribe's obituary of Fr Woodward, Michaelmas 1932 *SSMQP*

24 The bishop and his party walked 2,500 miles in 1910. *SSMQP*, Christmas 1910

25 HK NL 9.9.1908

26 *SSMQP*, Christmas 1912

27 Ibid.

28 Makins removed 1916, Carroll removed 1920, Moffatt released 1918. (Butcher, who came in 1912, was released in 1920).

29 Obituary in the Michaelmas 1934 *SSMQP*; for Archdeacon Woodward's diary of internment, see *Central Africa* XXXV 5–16

30 Fr Woodward's war diary, SSM/BR/Woodward

31 SSM/HK/Corres. Bp of Zanzibar to Archdeacon Woodward, 26.4.1921

32 SSM/HK/Corres. Statement from Archdeacon Woodward, Corpus Christi 1921

33 SSM/HK/Corres. Bp of Zanzibar to Director, 20.7.1921

34 SSM/HK/Corres. Bp of Zanzibar to Director, 21.7.1921

35 September 1921 SSMQP

36 SSM/HK/Corres. Bp of Zanzibar to Director, 8.10.1921

37 *SSM Chronicle* 119

38 H.H.Kelly: *SSM 1929*

39 SSM: Director's Chapter: Fr Tribe 12.12 1926

40 SSM/HK/Corres. Bp of Zanzibar to Fr Woodward, 20.3.1923

41 The official UMCA history says ten.

42 Michaelmas 1932 *SSMQP*

43 The circumstances of the purchase were later forgotten. 'They were bought by me – *for* the use of the Mission Brotherhood – as everyone at the time knew – and *with the money you collected for the establishment of the Society*'. Bp Twells to Canon Beckett, founder of SSA, 6.8.1884. South Africa: Modderpoort file.

44 Christmas 1925 *SSMQP*

45 C.P.Groves: *The Planting of Christianity in Africa* Vol.III 175. For a few years after the Boer war the title 'Orange Free State' was officially dropped.

46 Fr Firkins's report, May 1905 SSM/S.Africa, Provincial file

47 'David [Wells, the Provincial] said we were bedevilled by the Estate'. SSM/*Minutes of S.African Province* 3.1.1972

48 Fr Sanderson died at Modderpoort in 1925, and Fr Carmichael died there aged 95 in 1947.

49 Fr A.D.Kelly, quoted in leaflet *100 Years of Mission Work at Modderpoort* 1969

50 The work at 'T-Y' was started by Fr Millington in 1904.

51 Michael Houghton: *SSM at TY (1904–1975)* 40

52 ibid. 37

53 ibid. 28

54 Seminar at Maseru, 13.12.1973 on African Religious. SSM/S.Africa: Provincial file

55 SSM/BR/A.D.Kelly, Personal file. There is a whole album about mountains.

56 Christmas 1911 *SSMQP*

57 Cp. letter from Fr Woodward to HK, 1.5.1919 'I think more and more that if the S.Africans are right there is no place for such as myself or Fr Drake, or Fr Wrenford and others living more or less out of community life.' SSM/HK/Corres. 1919

58 Fr Frederick Rand to Director 22.10.1925. SSM/BR/Rand

59 *SSM Chronicle* 103, quoting his commission.

60 *SSMQP* Michaelmas 1919

61 *Missionary Regulations issued under the authority of the bishop* 1937 16; when Fr Wrenford was professed at Modderpoort in 1907, the service was in Sesuto. M. Houghton: *SSM at TY (1904–1975)* 23

62 Neville Talbot of Pretoria to HK, 7.5.1921 SSM/HK/Corres. 1921–22 'Can't say I took to Carleton the other day'.

63 SSM/HK/NL 4.7.1923

64 Fr Carleton to HK,18.7.1918, SSM/HK/Corres. 1917–18

65 Obituary of Fr Edwin Bradbrook by Fr A.Amor, March 1955 *SSMQ*

66 Fr Tribe, Director, *SSMQP* Christmas 1926

67 May 1985 *SSM*

68 Fr Cecil Hemsley, in May 1985 *SSM*

69 Fr Tribe, Director, *SSMQP* Michaelmas 1928

70 ibid.

71 In 1945 in the accounts of St Augustine's Priory was £39.4.6 income from Prickly Pears.

72 *SSMQ* June 1933

73 Fr Gregory Wilkins, quoting Fr Kelly, *Memorandum* 1962. SSM/ 'Theological Privileges' file.

74 SSM/S.Africa typescript, undated c1962 *The South African Province of SSM*

75 Memorandum of conversation, 14.3.1940. SSM/S.Africa/Modderpoort file

76 SSM/BR/Amor Obituary

77 Minutes of Great Chapter, 31.7.1925

78 Fr Kelly advised against a ladder of profession. 'S.Francis had no Novitiate – wouldn't have it ... I would not even give them a superior. They must all obey one another.' SSM/S.Africa/African Novitiate file.

79 The obituary of Fr Gilbert Ramahloli spoke of 'the small aristocratic figure, with the delightfully shaped hands of the Basuto'. *SSMQ* June 1934

80 Fr Patrick Maekane to Fr Tribe, 1940, quoted in *SSM Chronicle* 203

81 Minutes of Great Chapter 1952

82 June 1937 *SSMQ*

83 Fr Bedale in Lent 1946 *SSMQ*

84 SSM/HK/Corres. 1924

85 *Regulations to be observed in all Missions under the charge of the SSM in the Orange Free State* (1918) 13

86 Diocese of Bloemfontein: *Missionary Regulations issued under the authority of the Bishop* (1937) 24

87 These are 1950s statistics, but when one counts the named priests and named outstations, the pattern had not changed greatly since between the wars. (Undated typescript *South African Province of SSM* SSM/S.Africa/ S.A.History file)

88 SSM/HK/Corres. 1929–30 (undated) letter from Fr Felix Macintosh. Fr Macintosh was somewhat out of step with the rest of the province, and tended to appeal to Fr Kelly.

89 SSM/HK/NL February 1929. Bp Carey was bishop of Bloemfon-

tein. For Roland Allen, see David Paton: *Reform of the Ministry: a study of the work of Roland Allen* (1968), where there are parallels drawn with Kelly (p29). They often sounded alike: 'Well, can people be trusted?.. First: No, they cannot be trusted; and second, But you have to trust them'. (ibid. p44)

90 Fr Bedale in Lent 1946 *SSMQ*

91 Undated typescript *South African Province of SSM* (probably 1962) SSM/S.Africa/ S.A.History file

92 Fr Howard Preece in Easter 1937 *SSMQ*; there are a number of competent papers with many statistics (undated) in Fr Martin Knight's file.

93 June 1938 *SSMQ*

94 ibid.

95 Typescript undated (probably 1962) *S.A. Province of SSM*

96 Fr Paul Hume, Director, in *SSMQ* Michaelmas 1954.

97 M.Dewey: *An Idea Still Working* (1980) 40

98 'Empty rooms and silent corridors have the atmosphere of a school on perpetual but gloomy holiday'. Peter Hinchliff: *Anglican Church in South Africa* 1963 238

99 'Wrenford was our one whole-hearted pro-Roman *spike*. PH [Paul Hume] isn't.' HK to Mrs Duke, 28.8.1949. SSM/HK/Corres.1949

100 M. Houghton: op.cit. 48, thought these 'perhaps a little over drastic'. Perhaps accounts of the purge were exaggerated; some of these things were still there later.

101 Minutes of 1962 Great Chapter 186

102 There is a fine picture of the young Fr Hector Lee on horseback.

103 *Survey of Society's Work in O.F.S.* SSM/S.Africa/S.A.History file

104 Br Patrick True, paper for 1962 Great Chapter.

105 Fr Austin Masters, in Minutes of Great Chapter 1962 181

106 Ibid. 161

107 Fr Austin Masters, quoted in Minutes of 1962 Great Chapter 36

108 'The Bishop of Bloemfontein was horrified by the lack of study within the South African province of the Society' (Fr Gregory Wilkins, in Minutes of 1962 Great Chapter 78)

109 ibid. 146

110 *Mission*: SSM News from Durban no.4 Advent 1972

111 Fr Gerald Woodcock, *SSM News from the S.A.Province* no.2, October 1974

112 *SSM Chronicle* 315

113 Fr Frank Green, November 1976 *SSM*

114 Fr Clement Mullenger in May 1984 *SSM*

115 G.Every (ed): *No Pious Person* 129–30 and elsewhere

116 SSM/College Notebook 4

117 *SSM*, Kelly 1915 8

118 D.Holmes: *H. Kelly and the SSM in Korea and Japan* , unpublished Oxford M.Litt. thesis 1990 114

119 SSM/ Lectures X (vi) 85

120 SSM/HK/G 9

121 H.H.Kelly: typescript *Autobiography*

122 H.H.Kelly, American Diary, cited by George Every in introduction to *The Gospel of God* 28

123 Stephen Neill: *The Cross over India* 1948 83

124 Fr Christopher Myers, SSM: *A Vision of Catholicity for Japan in the Mid-Twentieth Century: a study of Bp Michael Hinsuke Yashiro's stand against proposals for Protestant Amalgamation 1940–1945* (unpublished M.A., A.N.U. 1991)

125 Myers, op.cit. 82. Kelly was in regular correspondence with Japan to the end.

126 An anonymous missionary, in *SSM Chronicle* 83

127 Myers op.cit. 50; Bp Nosse scrawled on his deathbed 'My dear Kelham Fathers, I am dying. I thank you very much indeed. Specially to Fr Kelly'. (Sept. 1974) SSM/ Japan file

128 Yashiro on his deathbed in 1970, quoted by Miss Leonora Lea, SPG missionary, in Alan Jones op.cit. (1971)

129 Apart from Fr Christopher Myers, who was an eager student of Japanese, the Australian brethren tended to feel exiled and useless.

130 Among other talents, Fr Moses was an accomplished amateur ballet-dancer.

131 Fr Gregory Wilkins, Director, to Chamberlain 17.2.1969, SSM/ Japan file

132 Fr Gregory Wilkins: *A Memo on the new work in Japan* 10.12.1968 SSM/ Japan file

133 SSM:HK/SSM/P2/8

134 Fr Ralph Martin, Society Newsletter November 1980

135 Alan Wilkinson, op.cit. 320

Chapter 11: SSM In Australia

1 Good general histories of Australian religion include: Ian Breward: *Australia, 'The Most Godless Place under Heaven?'* ; H.R.Jackson: *Churches and People in Australia and New Zealand 1860–1930*; Patrick O'Farrell: *The Catholic Church and Community, An Australian History*; and Edmund Campion: *Australian Catholics*

2 I am completely indebted to David Hilliard: *Godliness and Good Order: a history of the Anglican Church in South Australia*

3 This point was made to me very forcibly by Ian Breward.

4 Report of the Proceedings of Synod, in the *Yearbook of the Church of England in the diocese of Adelaide etc 1944–45* (p112)

5 ibid. p111

6 L.E.W.Renfrey: *History of St Barnabas' College, Adelaide*

7 Bp Robin to Fr Oddie, 31.10.1945 SSM/Australia/ Founding of Australian Province

8 SSM/Australia/ Founding of Australian Province file

9 SSM/Australia/ Aust. Provincial/ Report on the Province 1952–57

10 Easter 1947 *SSMQ*
11 The gift of Gwyladys O'Leary of Korralla, Mount Lofty
12 Conversation with Sr Helen Northey,OP, August 1990
13 Fr Antony Snell in *SSM Chronicle* p217
14 Conversation with Keith Chittleborough, August 1990
15 Fr Kelly almost preferred Bush Brothers to SSM. 'I never saw the SSM system being worked better or more effectively than by Halse's Bush Brotherhood'. Quoted in Fr Christopher Myers SSM: 'Revisioning a Vision' 1993
16 D.Hilliard: *Godliness and Good Order* pp82–3 and 108
17 The *Australian Church Quarterly*, the publication of the Australian Church Union, had a long article by Fr Bedale, on 'The Training of a Priest' 31.12.1946
18 Box labelled 'Miscellaneous archival material', Digger's Rest.
19 D. Hilliard: 'Popular Religion in Australia in the 1950s: a study of Adelaide and Brisbane' *Journal of Religious History* Vol. 15, no.2 1988 p228
20 ibid. p231
21 Cp. Kelham in the same period, and indeed Christianity world-wide.
22 Fr Gerald Reglar met Fr Bedale from the boat, and was told at once what he would teach. (Conversation with Fr Reglar, August 1990)
23 Conversation with Keith Chittleborough, August 1990. There was a sadder variant on the story, where he had been working enthusiastically on new material, started it, and then said 'But you know all that'.
24 Conversation with Fr Douglas Brown, December 1992
25 Fr Douglas Brown says that Fr Antony Snell, a traditionalist Anglican, got on well with the Lutherans.
26 Conversation with Davis McCaughey, August 1990
27 A.G.Hebert: Introduction to the 'Report on the Authority of the Word of God' 1960
28 *Minutes of Australian Province 1947–57* 17.11.1956
29 Douglas Davies, 'An Old Student Looks Back', June 1983 *Sacred Mission*
30 SSM/BR/AGH Corres. 18.6.1955, to Director
31 28.8.1947 Box 'Misc. Archival Material', Digger's Rest.
32 SSM/Australia/ College file
33 SSM/BR/Hebert Corres. 13.10.1960
34 Conversation with Joseph Kinsela, August 1990
35 ibid.
36 When Peter Ball set up an Anglican teaching order, the Community of the Glorious Ascension, in 1960, he and his brother spent their novitiate at Kelham.
37 Charters Towers
38 Fr Nicholas Allenby to Abp of Perth, 4.9.1959 (Perth file, Digger's Rest)

39 *Theoria to Theory* 1974 Vol. 8
40 Undated paper 'Novice Training' in Antony Snell's file. Two of the present members of SSM were novices at St John's.
41 This is based on a conversation with a now openly homosexual ex-student, who had no motive for a cover-up.
42 Fr Austin Day, of Ch.Ch. St Lawrence, Sydney, writing in 1964, of someone in the Departed and Released file at Digger's Rest.
43 Fr Jonathan Ewer to the Bp of Bendigo, May 1980. *Archives Misc. 2*, Digger's Rest
44 Conversation with Evan Burge, Master of Ormond College, Melbourne, August 1990
45 SSM/BR/Hebert Corres. to Director, 14.8.1960
46 Fr Dunstan McKee was marching against the Vietnam war. In the same period, Br Gilbert Sinden was seen expressing liberal views on homosexuality on television.
47 Conversation with Fr Francis Horner, August 1990
48 Larger than life, 'the most powerful layman in the Australian church', Gilbert Sinden had lived through a classic SSM judgement 'Oh, by the way, you're not being ordained'. Many years later, after having been principal of their college, he was.

Chapter 12: The Crash

1 For example, September 1953, Fr Bertram Lester; March 1954, Br William Hardwell and Br Hubert Ebdon; March 1955, Fr Edwin Bradbrook and Fr 'Tommy' Wrenford.
2 SSMQ March 1953
3 ibid.
4 SSMQ March 1955
5 His letters were c/o Sir Martin Roseveare, and he left a bequest to a grand-nephew at Uppingham School.
6 Opening sentence of ch.2 of Adrian Hastings: *A History of African Christianity 1950–1975*
7 John S. Pobee: *Kwame Nkrumah and the Church in Ghana 1949–1966* 109
8 Bp Roseveare's Charge of 1962
9 Pobee, op.cit. 55
10 He persuaded SSM to give £7000 to endow the church in Ghana. Later Fr Clement Mullenger was chaplain to a community of nuns in Ghana, and Fr Ralph Martin taught from 1983 to 1989 at St Nicholas College, Cape Coast, returning briefly in 1991.
11 Supplement to *Great and General Chapters, 1894–1982*, Ralph Martin and Dunstan McKee
12 SSMQ March 1957
13 SSMQ September 1954
14 SSMQ March 1958
15 eg Simon Mein (1955), Hilary Greenwood (1957), Gilbert Sinden (1957)

16 Minutes of Great Chapter 1952 156

17 Simon Mein in *SSM Magazine* March 1965, quoting the Crowther report, 11

18 SSM/Minutes of English Province 9.3.1964. But cp. Fr Stephen Bedale in 1959 saying that 'intellectually the students were better material nowadays than they were 30 years ago'. SSM/Minutes of English Province 5.1.1959. The tables of marks for three classes, 1928b, 1931c, and 1955c, show that the largest group in each case was *gamma* and *gamma minus*.

19 *SSM Chronicle*, 237

20 Vincent Strudwick, quoted in ibid. 247

21 Minutes of General Chapter 1957

22 To Bp of Manchester, 12.11.1934

23 Letter to Bp Hudson, 1951

24 Fr Theodore Smith, reporting to SSM

25 ibid.

26 In the ten years before 1964, 222 had entered the college, 73 were still there, 88 had been asked to withdraw, 21 because they had a girl-friend, 29 for serious moral reasons. The rough proportion of reasons was 25% girl-friend 25% morals 40–45% study 5–10% miscellaneous. SSM/Minutes of English Province 9.3.1964

27 *SSM*, March 1964

28 Simon Mein 'Recent Changes at Kelham', *SSM Magazine* March 1965

29 ibid.

30 Vincent Strudwick, in *SSM Chronicle*, 257

31 *SSM* Magazine, March 1966

32 *Transmit*, no.2 September 1970, p21. There is something in Fr Hilary Greenwood's barbed generalisation about being 'heavily armed with quotations from the Father Founder. Such is the method of revolutionaries.' Hilary Greenwood, MS autobiography 49

33 See Minutes of Great Chapter 1972, p58

34 Group dynamics were then widely fashionable. Prof. A. Hastings experienced them in an African Ecumenical Foundation at Mindolo, Kitwe, in 1969, with the same effects.

35 Simon Mein: 'The College at Kelham', 1967.

36 Fr Hilary Greenwood: MS autobiography

37 op.cit. 60

38 op.cit. 71

39 Bishops' Report to Synod, 26 January 1971

40 Letter from Alan Wilkinson to author, 11.4.1992

41 Report to Great Chapter 1972

42 What hurt most was that the press made up quotations: 'Father Greenwood said that theirs was a very strict order and that he was very upset'. Hilary Greenwood, op.cit.

43 *SSM Chronicle* 273

44 *Nottingham Evening Post*, 5.2.1971
45 Newark Advertiser 13.2.1971 The phrase about a bishop or a Boer occurs in the February issue of *SSM*.
46 Bp Runcie of St Albans to General Synod, 18.2.1971
47 Gregory Wilkins, in *SSM* July 1971
48 ibid. in *Newark Advertiser* 13.2.71
49 Hilary Greenwood, op.cit. 46 He went on to say: ' . . . in fact most of them left the Society soon after they had achieved their reforms of it'.
50 Hilary Greenwood, op.cit. 50
51 Letter from Alan Wilkinson to author, 11.4.1992
52 Hilary Greenwood, in Minutes of Great Chapter 1972, 43
53 Supplement to *Great and General Chapters 1894–1952* 1982 5
54 1958: Stroud, Gawn 1959: Butter 1960: Watts 1961: Mann (to OSB), Simpson 1962: Elsam, Chittleborough (Twiss and Addison removed) 1963: Castle, Fraser, Williamson (Rice removed) 1964: Munns 1965: Smith, Griffiths (Allen removed) 1966 Reynolds, Hislop (Williams removed) 1967: Clayton 1968: Watts 1969: Shaw 1970: Mein, Strudwick, Capper, Brinksworth 1971: Ambrose, Duke 1972: Stephens 1973: Every, Broadhead, Borthwick, Adkins 1974: Yogata, Jacobson 1975: Porter

Chapter 13: The Day Of The Priories, And Beyond?

1 SSM/DIR/RA/1906 201 The sentence continues 'and the former was very unpopular'.
2 The last prior, Fr Lewes Ward-Andrews, stayed on alone as vicar until retirement in 1982.
3 SSM/DIR/AR/1&2 1914–1915
4 H.H.Kelly 'Narrative' 1935 5 SSM: HK/C/1933–7
5 SSM/DIR/AR/1&2 1915–16, and 1916–17. The prior was Fr H. George.
6 H.H.Kelly op.cit. 1935 5
7 Fr Joseph White, Director, to Fr Buxcy Neate, Prior. 19.7.1922 SSM/HK/C/1922–3
8 It is fair to say that it was described as 'one of two really live centres of spiritual life in the city' in 1952. (Minutes of Great Chapter 1952 76)
9 In 1941 the Society removed Fr Christopher Richards, the Vicar, and he played the Kelly card: ' . . . the adventurous freedom in which the Society arose and lived for some years has been lost in institutionalism'. SSM/BR/Richards 17.6.40 (Edwards, explaining Fr Richards's position)
10 *SSMQ* Christmas 1938
11 Fr Tribe unexpectedly moved Fr Bedale to the local parish at Kelham, and made Fr Ranford Warden. The next year he was voted out as Director.

12 The cost of living at Bedminster was cheaper, so it was not luxury. Bedminster: £167; Liverpool: £178; Nottingham: £180; Sheffield: £192 (per person per annum in 1938). Minutes of English Province 5.5.1938

13 Letter from Mr E.A.Joyce, 17.1.1989. Fr Pearse could 'charm the parish' into accepting anything. *SSM* September 1969

14 Fr R. Tribe, Director, *SSMQ* Easter 1937

15 *SSMQ* Easter 1952

16 *SSMQ* Easter 1949. Meanwhile, Alan Ecclestone, a close friend of Hilary Greenwood, was also in Sheffield, at Darnall, preaching Christian communism.

17 SSM/ Director's Chapter: Fr Tribe 3.8.1938

18 SSM/ Director's Chapter, 13.12.1952 and 18.12.1952

19 Minutes of Great Chapter 1952 72

20 Fr Douglas Brown, Minutes of Great Chapter 1972 231

21 Minutes of General Chapter 1947 160–1

22 Fr. S. Bedale: *Statistics of Profession and Release* (1946) SSM: Soc.-Hist./Profession Some of those who left were on detached service, not in priories.

23 E.A.Joyce, op.cit. 1989. They were good priests, and remembered kindly; it was SSM that was upset.

24 'At Sheffield we were regarded largely as seculars and not as Religious'. Province of England Minute Book 14.1.1953

25 *Transmit* June 1972

26 ibid.

27 Fr David Wells at Great Chapter 1977 (Minutes 33)

28 Normally referred to as Quernmore, and pronounced 'Quorrmore' – one more on the list, as Averham was 'Air'm', Hebert was 'Heebert', and Bedale was 'B'*dale*', though they sound the 't' in Fox Covert, one of the Society houses at Willen.

29 SSM/Minutes of English Provincial Chapter 17.9.1969

30 Fr Wilkins in retirement, as his sight went, spent his time wine-making, and people had happy social memories of drinking it. (Fr Laurence Eyers, personal communication, August 1990)

31 These are from *Quernmore Notes* of 1976, April 1978, August 1978 and February 1979 respectively.

32 *Quernmore Notes* November 1982

33 op.cit. October 1982

34 Society Newsletter, April 1978

35 Fr Laurence Eyers, Minutes of General Chapter 1977 28

36 The Kelham Rood is in the garden at Willen, and the SSM archives are there. 'It's a great exciting business trying to keep up with the angels, especially when in old age you might have dreamed of retiring in quiet obscurity amid the splendours of Kelham'. (Fr Sydney Holgate, moving to Willen *SSM* Dec. 1973)

37 Built in 1680 by Robert Hooke, for whom see DNB.

38 It cost more than half the money they got for selling Kelham.

39 Minutes of General Chapter 1977 87
40 *SSM Chronicle* 322
41 Fr Hilary Greenwood, Minutes of Great Chapter 1972
42 ibid.
43 'Ecclesiastically, St George's was out of step with the rest of the Province and with considerable parts of the Church.' Minutes of Great Chapter 1972 62
44 Conversation with Rev. Clive Barrett, 18.7.1991
45 Minutes of General Chapter 1977 – English report.
46 Fr Douglas Brown: *Transmit* June 1972
47 *Supplement to Great and General Chapters 1894–1952* (1982)
48 Fr Dunstan McKee: *Society Newsletter* Aug.1974
49 See the declaration on *Deployment of Brethren* by the 1977 Great Chapter.
50 Fr Lewes Ward-Andrews was for many years in charge of the Company of the Sacred Mission, never as large as comparable groups attached to other Anglican communities.
51 Quoted in M. Dewey: *SSM: An Idea Still Working* (1980)
52 *SSM* November 1980; cp. Fr Dunstan McKee in *Society Newsletter* November 1980
53 Continuing the SSM link, Margaret Dewey, in the 1980s and 1990s, spent part of every year running the library there.
54 Fr Edmund Wheat, in July/August 1984 *Society Newsletter*
55 Instead of having a five year, almost automatically extended to ten, they settled on a seven year term in 1982.
56 *Sacred Mission* June 1986
57 See the letter from the women associates to the Director, January 1981, in *SSM Chronicle* 347–9
58 *Declaration on Women Associates* Great Chapter 1982
59 Fr Edmund Wheat, Director, *Society Newsletter* May/June 1982
60 Letters came from the Rev. Chris Armstrong, (old Kelham student) chaplain of the college of St Hild and St Bede, and then the bishop of Jarrow.
61 The acronym OASIS was dropped in 1988.
62 *SSM* May 1989
63 ibid.
64 'Departments' were groups for domestic chores at Kelham. There is a strand in SSM that dislikes scapulars etc. In Fr Ralph Martin's draft *Rule* (1993) we find 'There is no habit or uniform beyond what is necessary in the carrying out of our various jobs. In particular, medieval dress only reinforces in us and in others an image that is irrelevant and misleading'. 7
65 The Manchester priory was closed in 1988. Fr Bede Henry stayed on in Manchester as a contemplative living alone.
66 This was the church that Archbishop Temple had trouble with, where Charles Francis SSM, killed on the electricity pylon, was curate.

67 St Mark's, similarly, had been an Anglo-Catholic stronghold.
68 Fr E. Wheat, speaking at meeting of English Province, 1992.
69 *SSM* November 1992
70 SSM/ Papers for English Provincial Meeting, 1992
71 Fr Edmund Wheat in 1983 wanted more study for novices. 'I think
    we have too easily given up the attempt to make our novices
    theologically minded even in the most elementary way'. *Society
    Newsletter* September 1983
72 Ralph Martin: 'SSM. New Rule for a New Century' (1993)
73 H.H.Kelly: 'Ad Gloriam Dei in eius Voluntate' [the Society motto]
    SSMQP June 1926

BIBLIOGRAPHY

Primary Sources

The archives of the Society of the Sacred Mission are at Willen Priory, Milton Keynes. I quote from an assessment by Dr P.E.Hughes, of the Church of England Record Centre.

> ... it has a strong emphasis on the correspondence and papers of the Founder and some other well known members ... largely academic in their orientation ... ... the records of the Society generally, as well as for the development of the various Provinces. They are virtually complete as far as constitutional aspects are concerned ... The records relating to temporal administration are not nearly as extensive as I am accustomed to find ... a substantial collection of manuscript and typescript courses of lectures ... some examination statistics and lists of students ... One very unusual feature of the whole archive, other than the papers of the Founder, is that the quantity of papers retained declines most markedly over time.

As Dr Hughes began late in 1992 to put the archives in order, some of my references are to his boxes (eg SSM/DIR/AR/1&2 1914–15), and others to where documents were in the old filing cabinets (eg SSM/S.Africa/Modderpoort file). Once his work is finished, it should be easy to find everything.

The Society brought out a journal, the SSM Quarterly Paper, re-named SSM Quarterly in 1935 (SSMQ in references). Sometimes it only came out twice a year. Fr Kelly circulated a Newsletter (HK/NL in references).

Much was lost of possible Australian material in the bush fire which destroyed St Michael's House in 1983. There is a cupboard of archival material in the priory at Digger's Rest, outside Melbourne, which I have used.

Publications by the Society and its members

Hubert S. Box (editor): *Priesthood* 1937 (includes S.Bedale: 'The Training of a Priest' and A.G.Hebert: 'The Church in Relation to the World')

Margaret Dewey: *An Idea Still Working* 1980

A.G.Hebert: *Liturgy and Society* 1935

A.G.Hebert (editor): *The Parish Communion* 1937

A.G.Hebert: *The Throne of David* 1941

A.G.Hebert: *The Form of the Church* 1944

A.G.Hebert: *The Authority of the Old Testament*

A.G.Hebert: *God's Kingdom and Ours* 1959

A.G.Hebert: *The Old Testament from Within* 1962

H.H.Kelly: *The History of a Religious Idea* 1898

H.H.Kelly: *Training for Ordination* 1901

H.H.Kelly: *England and the Church* 1902

H.H.Kelly: *The Church and the Ordination Question* 1907

H.H.Kelly: *An Idea in the Working* 1908

H.H.Kelly: *Memorandum on Theological Education (The Kelham System)* 1909

H.H.Kelly: *The Use of the Old Testament* 1913

H.H.Kelly: *The Gospel of God* (1959 edition)

H.H.Kelly (edited by G. Every): *No Pious Person* 1960

Richard March and Tambimuttu (editors): *T.S.Eliot: a Symposium* 1948 (includes George Every: 'The way of rejection')

E.R.Morgan (ed): *Essays Catholic and Missionary* 1928

Antony Snell: *Understand your Faith* 1942

Reginald Tribe: *The Christian Social Tradition* 1935

Secondary Sources

Raymond W. Albright: *A History of the Protestant Episcopal Church* 1964

A.M.Allchin: *The Silent Rebellion* 1958

Josef L. Altholtz: *The Religious Press in Britain 1760–1900* Westport, Conn.

A.E.M.Anderson-Morshead and A.G.Blood: *The History of the Universities' Mission to Central Africa* 1897, 1957, 1962.

P.F.Anson: *The Call of the Cloister* 1956

P.F.Anson: *Fashions in Church Furnishing 1840–1940* 1960

F.R.Barry: *Period of My Life* 1970

Clyde Binfield: *George Williams and the Y.M.C.A.* 1973

Charles Booth: *Life and Labour of the People in London* (series 3) 1902

Ian Breward: *Australia: 'The Most Godless Place under Heaven'?* 1988 Melbourne

Kenneth D.Brown: *A Social History of the Nonconformist Ministry in England and Wales 1800–1930* 1988

Kathleen E. Burne: *The Life and Letters of Fr Andrew SDC* 1948

Edmund Campion: *Australian Catholics* 1987

W.Owen Chadwick: *The Victorian Church* Part II 1970

C.P.S.Clarke: *The Oxford Movement and After* 1932

C.J.Corfe: *The Anglican Church in Corea* 1905 Seoul

Jeffrey Cox: *The English Churches in a Secular Society, Lambeth 1870–1930* 1982

Anthony P.M. Coxon: 'Patterns of Occupational Recruitment: the Anglican Ministry', *Sociology* Vol.1 1967

Geoffrey Curtis: *William of Glasshampton, Friar, Monk, Solitary* 1947

Horton Davies: *Worship and Theology in England: the Ecumenical Century 1900–65* 1965

D.L.Edwards: *Leaders of the Church of England 1828–1944* 1971

Michel Foucault: *Discipline and Punish* 1979

W.H.T.Gairdner: *'Edinburgh 1910': an Account and Interpretation of the World Missionary Conference* 1910

Donald Gray: *Earth and Altar* 1986

James H. Grayson: *Korea: a Religious History* 1989

Gwilym O. Griffith: *The Theology of P.T.Forsyth* 1948

C.P.Groves: *The Planting of Christianity in Africa* Vols. III and IV 1955 and 1958

Alan G.L.Haig: *The Victorian Clergy* 1984

Melville Harcourt: *Tubby Clayton: a Personal Saga* 1953

Adrian Hastings: *A History of African Christianity 1950–1975* 1979

Adrian Hastings: *A History of English Christianity 1920–1985* 1986

Brian Heeney: *A Different Kind of Gentleman* 1976

David Hilliard: *Godliness and Good Order: a history of the Anglican Church in South Australia* 1986 Netley SA

David Hilliard: 'Unenglish and unmanly: Anglo-Catholicism and homosexuality', *Victorian Studies*, vol.25 no 1.

Peter Hinchliff: *Anglican Church in South Africa* 1963

Michael Houghton: *SSM at TY (1904–1975)* 1975

L.S.Hunter (editor): *Scandinavian Churches* 1965

F.A.Iremonger: *William Temple* 1948

Eleanor M. Jackson: *Red Tape and the Gospel*

Peter J. Jagger: *A History of the Parish and People Movement* 1978

Eric James: *A Life of Bishop John A.T. Robinson* 1987

P. d'A. Jones: *The Christian Socialist Revival 1877–1914* 1968 Princeton

Bengt Ingmar Kilström: *Högkyrkligheten i Sverige och Finland under 1900–talet* 1990 Delsbo

John Kent: *The Unacceptable Face: the Modern Church in the Eyes of the Historian* 1987

Cecil Lewis & G.E.Edwards: *Historical Records of the Church of the Province of South Africa* 1934

Roger Lloyd: *The Church of England in the 20th Century* 1946 and 1950

Hugh McLeod: *Class and Religion in the Late Victorian City* 1974

David B. McIlhiney: *A Gentleman in Every Slum* 1976

Basil Mathews: *John R. Mott: World Citizen*

H. Maynard-Smith: *Frank, Bishop of Zanzibar* 1926

J.R.H.Moorman: *B.K.Cunningham*

Stephen Neil: *The Cross over India* 1948

Patrick O'Farrell: *The Catholic Church and Community: an Australian History* 1985 Melbourne

Kenneth G.Packard: *Brother Edward, Priest and Evangelist* 1955

C.F.Pascoe: *Two Hundred Years of the S.P.G.* 1901

W.S.F.Pickering: *Anglo-Catholicism: a study in religious ambiguity* 1989

John S. Pobee: *Kwame Nkrumah and the Church in Ghana 1949–1966* 1988 Accra

John S. Pobee 'Church and State in Ghana 1949–1966' in J.S.Pobee (ed): *Religion in a Pluralist Society* 1976 Leiden

John S. Peart-Binns: *Maurice B. Reckitt: a Life* 1988

John H. Rodgers: *The Theology of P.T.Forsyth* 1965

Geoffrey Rowell: *The Vision Glorious* 1983

G.W.E.Russell: *Leaders of the Church*

W.J.Sheils (editor): *Monks, Hermits and the Ascetic Tradition* (Vol.22 of Studies in Church History) 1985

W.J.S.Simpson: *The History of the Anglo-Catholic Revival from 1845* 1932

C. Stephenson: *Merrily on High* 1972

Eugene Stock: *History of the C.M.S.* 1899

Tissington Tatlow: *The Story of the S.C.M.* 1933

Brian Taylor: 'Founders and Followers: Leadership in Anglican Religious Communities', in Monastic Studies 1990

T.F.Taylor: *J.Armitage Robinson* 1991

William Temple: *Some Lambeth Letters* (ed. by F.S. Temple) 1963

Robert Towler and A.P.M.Coxon: *The Fate of the Anglican Clergy* 1979

C.P.Williams: ' "Not Quite Gentleman": an Examination of the "Middling Class" Protestant Missionaries from Britain, c1850–1900', Journal of Ecclesiastical History, 31, no.3 July 1980

Alan Wilkinson: *The Community of the Resurrection: a centenary history* 1992

W-D. Zimmermann and R.G.Smith (editors): *I Knew Dietrich Bonhoeffer* 1973

Unpublished theses

David Holmes: *Herbert Kelly and the Society of the Sacred Mission in Korea and Japan* (unpublished Oxford M.Litt. thesis 1990)

A.W.Jones: *Herbert Hamilton Kelly, SSM, 1860–1950: a study in failure* (unpublished Nottingham Ph.D. thesis 1971)

Christopher Myers, SSM: *A Vision of Catholicity for Japan in the Mid-Twentieth century: a study of Bp Michael Hinsuke Yashiro's stand against proposals for Protestant Amalgamation 1940–1945* (unpublished Australian National University M.A. thesis 1991)

Index

works
  list, 69
  Gospel of God, 69–76, 109, 110
  History of a Religious Idea, 16, 69
  An Idea in the Working, 16, 69, 141, 269
  Principles, 63–4, 68, 278
  Swanwick Tips, 102–3
'Kelly-kai', 221
Kennington, St John the Divine, 17, 20, 23, 282
Keswick, 96
'Khaki Dragon', 102
Kierkegaard, 86, 89, 114
Kikuyu, 197
Kimata, Moses SSM, 222–3
Kingsley, Charles, 88
Kinsella, Nigel SSM, 273
Kirk, Bp K. E., 187
Kobe priory of SSM, 222–3
Knutsford training school, 143–4
Korean province of SSM, 29, 30, 47, 122–3, 124, 189–193
Kroonstad, 204, 213, 214
Kuching, diocese of, 236
Kuschke, Mr, inspector of native education, 208

Ladybrand, 200, 203, 210
  St. John's, 203
Lambeth Conference, 1948, 186
Lancaster (see also Quernmore), 278
  St Martin's College, 260, 273
  University, 259–60, 273
Lancing school, 193
Lang, Cosmo Gordon, archbishop of Canterbury, 118, 171
Lapsley, Michael SSM, 217, 218, 243
Latin, 21
laughter, 87–8
Law, Arthur SSM, 29
Laxton conversations, 176
lay brothers, 35, 158–9, 191, 195–6, 204, 282
Leavis, F. R. and Queenie, 157, 160
Lee, Hector SSM, 284, 306
Lebombo, bishop of, 195
Leeds University, 150
Lesotho
  (see also Basutoland), 216, 275
Lester, Bertram SSM, 38, 309
Lewis, bishop John SSM, 222, 235, 236–7, 241, 245
liberal protestantism, 68, 69, 102, 107, 112, 153, 167, 174, 178
'Life and Work' conference at Stockholm, 172
lifetimes, 39, 118
Lintott, Edgar SSM, 34, 134, 153

Little Gidding, 1
Littlemore, 3, 6
liturgical work and debates (see also under Hebert), 122, 130–1, 132–6, 138, 157, 165, 166–70, 176–7, 186, 245, 273–4
Liverpool priory, 270, 271
Livingstone, 195
Livingstone, David, 193
Llanthony, 4
Lloyd, Roger (*The C of E in the 20th Century*), 152–3
London meetings for SSM, 142, 151, 249
Longley, Andrew SSM, 218
Lovedale, 218
'low degree of inspiration', 75–6
Ludlow, J. M.F., 80
Lund, 174
Lutherans in Australia, 233–4
Lux Mundi, 10

McCaughey, Davis, 175, 234
McColl, Bp, of Willochra, 245
Macey, Liz, 275
Macintosh, Felix SSM, 38, 212
McKee, Dunstan SSM, 39, 238, 240, 242, 265, 277–8
Maekane, Patrick CSC, 209–10, 217
Magila, 194, 195, 199
Maillard, SSM student, 103
Makins, Arthur SSM, 195
Manchester
  Grammar School, 13
  Longsight priory, 274, 281
  Moss-side priory, 274
Manners, Lord John, 2
Mapo, 191
Martensen, 76
Martin, Charles SSM, 212–3
Martin, Ralph SSM, 39, 277, 278, 280, 283, 299, 309
Marty, Martin, 187
Maseru, 217–8
Masite, 209, 217
Mason, Canon A. J., 10, 14–5
Masterman, C. F.G., 4
Masters, Austin SSM, 216
Mathews, Shailer, 219
Maurice, F. D., 78–82, 85, 89–90, 158, 188, 220
Mein, Simon SSM, 180, 256–9, 262
Melanesian Brotherhood, 210
Melbourne, 244–5
Middlesbrough
  All Saints priory, 140, 281, 282
Migne's Patrology, 244
Mildenhall, 27, 78, 90, 121, 142–3, 149
Millington, Colin SSM, 31
Milton Keynes (see Willen), 273, 278